"A Rich Spot of Earth"

"A Rich Spot of Earth"

THOMAS JEFFERSON'S REVOLUTIONARY GARDEN AT MONTICELLO

PETER J. HATCH

Foreword by Alice Waters

MONTICELLO

Yale UNIVERSITY PRESS

New Haven & London

Published with assistance from the
Martin S. and Luella Davis Publications Endowment,
the Annie Burr Lewis Fund, and
the Mary Cady Tew Memorial Fund.

The Thomas Jefferson Foundation wishes
to acknowledge the generous support of Chapin
and Cynthia Nolen and an anonymous donor.

Yale University Press books may be purchased in quantity for educational, business, or promotional use. For
information, please e-mail
sales.press@yale.edu (US office)
or sales@yaleup.co.uk (UK office).

Designed by James J. Johnson.
Set in Bulmer and Shelly Script types by
BW&A Books, Inc., Durham, North Carolina.
Printed in China.

*The Library of Congress has cataloged the
hardcover edition as follows:*

Hatch, Peter J., 1949–
"A rich spot of earth" : Thomas Jefferson's
revolutionary garden at Monticello /
Peter J. Hatch ; foreword by Alice Waters.
p. cm.
Includes bibliographical references and index.
ISBN 978-0-300-17114-3 (clothbound : alk. paper)
1. Vegetable gardening—Virginia. 2. Jeffer-
son, Thomas, 1743–1826—Homes and haunts—
Virginia. 3. Monticello (Va.). I. Title. II. Title:
Thomas Jefferson's revolutionary garden at Monticello.
SB320.7.V8H38 2012
635—dc23   2011038043+
ISBN 978-0-300-20862-7 (pbk.)

A catalogue record for this book is available
from the British Library.

This paper meets the requirements of ANSI/NISO
Z39.48–1992 (Permanence of Paper).
Cloth: 10 9 8 7 6 5 4
Pbk.: 10 9 8 7 6 5 4 3 2 1

This book is a title in the Yale Agrarian Studies series:
http://yalepress.yale.edu/yupbooks/SeriesPage
.asp?Series=94

CONTENTS

FOREWORD

I first met Peter Hatch in 2009, when he took me around the grounds of Monticello on a crisp, sunny autumn day; Thomas Jefferson has long been a personal hero of mine, and I was eager to explore the garden he devoted so many years to. As Peter walked me through the rows of heirloom vegetables and herbs, I was instantly struck by his bright intellect and deep commitment to Thomas Jefferson's memory. His enthusiasm was palpable, and his knowledge of Jefferson's agrarian work limitless—as of course it would be, after nearly four decades of loving historical restoration of the sweeping Monticello landscape.

No one knows the land's story better than Peter. In *"A Rich Spot of Earth": Thomas Jefferson's Revolutionary Garden at Monticello,* he beautifully communicates the beliefs of one of our most visionary Founding Fathers: That our country is built upon the principles of our farmers, and that our relationship to the land our food comes from is one of the most fundamental relationships of all. Thomas Jefferson's garden, Peter writes, was "an Ellis Island of introductions, filled with a whole world of hardy economic plants: 330 varieties of ninety-nine species of vegetables and herbs." I am so impressed by this biodiversity, which is exactly what our country so urgently needs right now—a vegetable garden that is, as Peter frames it, "the true American garden: practical, expansive, wrought from a world of edible immigrants."

Peter has come to know the land the way that Jefferson once did, by having his hands in the soil and sensing what is right to plant in each season. This book delivers an important message at a pivotal moment for our country. Peter's vibrant and enthusiastic passion for preserving Thomas Jefferson's farming legacy at Monticello reminds us all of the time-tested continuity and historical roots of this kind of agriculture. We desperately need to reconnect ourselves to the pastoral and self-sufficient tradition that Jefferson built; nothing is more vital than returning this tradition to the very heart of American culture.

Alice Waters

PREFACE

Peter Hatch is a man of the earth. Annie Leibovitz photographed his hands when she came to Monticello. For thirty-four years, Peter has plunged those hands into the earth on the mountainside of Monticello, each year coaxing, wresting, and willing an ever more copious renaissance of Jefferson's peerless garden. Monticello is Jefferson's autobiography, his lifelong pursuit, the greatest manifestation of his genius, and the only home in the United States listed on the United Nations list of World Heritage Sites. The architecture at Monticello has long been revered, but not so Jefferson's genius with the garden. We have Peter Hatch to thank for devoting his career to the revelation of Jefferson's passion for plants and the significance of our founder's horticultural pursuit of happiness. The garden-to-table food movement sweeping this country had an early prophet in Thomas Jefferson. Among his followers are Alice Waters and Michelle Obama, both of whom have come to Monticello's garden with reverence and tasted of its bounty. We welcome nearly half a million people annually to Monticello. We hope this book is seen and shared with as many more, engaging them in the genius of Jefferson and his world-changing ideas, some of which had to do with vegetables.

Leslie Greene Bowman
President, Thomas Jefferson Foundation

ACKNOWLEDGMENTS

Good friends Chapin and Cynthia Nolen and a benefactor who prefers anonymity provided generous financial support that made this book possible. Leslie Greene Bowman, president of the Thomas Jefferson Foundation, has offered guidance, encouragement, and leadership in moving this publication forward. Sarah Allaback, Monticello's publications manager, guided the ship; photographer Robert Llewellyn steered the illustrations with buoyant good spirits; Leah Stearns came up with many pertinent images from the Monticello collection; and Eleanor Gould was my invaluable assistant in creating the final product. Other colleagues at Monticello have been kind and helpful: librarian Anna Berkes found critical citations; vegetable gardener Pat Brodowski cared for the garden and helped with the appendixes; Nini Almy offered insightful comments as she read and reread the manuscript; and Leni Sorensen, Christa Dierksheide, Mary Mason Williams, Ellen Hickman, William Beiswanger, Peggy Cornett, Sarah Leonard, Gabriele Rausse, Cinder Stanton, and Ann Lucas all helped me in many ways. My colleagues at the IT Help Desk graciously fielded my calls for assistance. I would also like to thank the editors at Yale University Press who worked on this project—Jean Thomson Black, Laura Jones Dooley, and Sara Hoover. Will Rieley, Belinda Gordon, Dean Norton, Ed Shull, David S. Wood, Sonia Brenner, and Mollie Ridout kindly provided illustrations, and Rick Britton created the maps. Librarians Heather Riser at the University of Virginia and Susan Fugate at the National Agricultural Library were especially kind in locating historical images. I appreciate Foundation Trustee Courtnay Daniels's support for the programs of the Gardens and Grounds Department, as well as the sabbatical offered by then-President Daniel P. Jordan that allowed me to put the manuscript in motion during the winters of 2007 and 2008. The Martin S. and Luella Davis Publications Endowment also contributed to the publication of this book. William W. Weaver and Wesley Greene have taught me much about the history of vegetables. My girls—Rosemary and Olivia—have been good to their Poppa, as has my lovely wife, Lou. Thanks to all.

PART I

THOMAS JEFFERSON'S REVOLUTIONARY GARDEN

1.1. "The greatest service which can be rendered any country is to add an useful plant to its culture"—Thomas Jefferson, ca. 1800

1. "A Rich Spot of Earth"

N 1811, THOMAS JEFFERSON, RETIRED FROM THE PRESIDENCY TO his lifelong home at Monticello, wrote to the Philadelphia portrait painter Charles Willson Peale a transcendent anthem to the garden:

> I have often thought that if heaven had given me choice of my position and calling, it should have been on a rich spot of earth, well watered, and near a good market for the productions of the garden. No occupation is so delightful to me as the culture of the earth, and no culture comparable to that of the garden. Such a variety of subjects, some one always coming to perfection, the failure of one thing repaired by the success of another, and instead of one harvest a continued one thro' the year. Under a total want of demand except for our family table I am still devoted to the garden. But tho' an old man, I am but a young gardener.

Jefferson's elegantly composed fantasy of an alternative career as a market gardener is well known because it resonates with gardeners from all ages (fig. 1.2). The image of repeated harvests through the season suggests the hopefulness inherent in the gardening process. Thomas Jefferson's garden during his retirement from public life at Monticello, 1809–1826, was the terraced vegetable garden, a thousand-foot-long experimental laboratory overlooking the rolling Piedmont Virginia countryside. This was the chief horticultural achievement of Thomas Jefferson's tenure at Monticello, itself described as his autobiography in the way its architecture and gardens expressed the multifaceted intellect of the author of the Declaration of Independence.[1]

Thomas Jefferson's Monticello vegetable garden was a revolutionary American garden. Many of the summer vegetables we take for granted today—tomatoes, okra, eggplant, lima beans, peanuts, peppers—were slow to appear in North American gardens around 1800. European travelers commented on the failure of Virginia gardeners to take advantage of "the fruitful warmth of the climate" because of the American reliance on "the customary products of Europe": cool-season vegetables. Jefferson's garden was unique in showcasing a medley

1.2. Thomas Jefferson by Gilbert Stuart, 1805

1.3. Costoluto Genovese tomato

of vegetable species native to hot climates, from South and Central America to Africa to the Middle East and the Mediterranean. Few places on earth combine tropical heat and humidity with temperate winters like those at Monticello. Jefferson capitalized on this by creating a south-facing terrace, a microclimate that exaggerates the summer warmth, tempers the winter cold, and captures an abundant wealth of crop-ripening sunshine. His collection of esculent talent, culled from virtually every Western culture known at the time, provided a display of warm- and cool-season vegetables unrivaled among American gardens of his day (fig. 1.3).[2]

Jefferson's Monticello garden was an Ellis Island of introduced economic plants, some 330 varieties of ninety-nine species of vegetables and herbs. Jefferson wrote that "the greatest service which can be rendered any country is to add an useful plant to it's culture," and he envisioned his garden as a means for transforming society. He distributed seeds of his latest novelty vegetable to neighbors, political allies like George Washington and James Madison, and an international community of plantsmen, with the persistence of a religious reformer, a missionary of seeds. Although it is difficult to verify that Jefferson was the first to introduce any specific vegetable into American gardens, the recitation of crops grown at Monticello is a roster of rare, unusual, and pioneering species: asparagus bean, sea kale, tomatoes, rutabaga, okra, potato pumpkins, winter melons, tree onion, peanuts, "sprout kale," serpentine cucumbers, Brussels sprouts, orach, chickpeas, gherkins, cayenne pepper, rhubarb, black salsify, sesame, eggplant. Jefferson summed up his experimental proclivities in a letter to Samuel Vaughan Jr. in 1790: "I have always thought that if in the experiments to introduce or to communicate new plants, one species in an hundred is found useful and succeeds, the ninety nine found otherwise are more than paid for" (fig. 1.4).[3]

The vegetable garden in itself is the true American garden: practical, expansive, wrought from a world of edible immigrants. The Monticello garden is distinctly American in its scale and scope. More than two hundred thousand cubic feet of Piedmont red clay was moved with a mule and cart by a crew of enslaved men Jefferson hired from a Fredericksburg, Virginia, farmer. Over three years they created the garden terrace, which was retained by five thousand tons of rock laid as high as twelve feet and extending the length of the garden. Jefferson's four-hundred-tree south orchard, surrounding two vineyards, extended below the wall and vegetable terrace, and the entire complex was enclosed by a ten-foot-high paling fence

1.4. Jefferson planted an abundance of greens suited for fresh salads

1.5. Jefferson's garden was uniquely American in the way that it served as an experimental laboratory for an Ellis Island of garden vegetables from around the world that ran for more than half a mile. Looking east from the garden plateau today, one is struck by the "ocean view" and, to the southwest, by the pleasing pattern of rows of vegetables against the background of Montalto, Jefferson's "high mountain." Atop the massive stone wall, Jefferson designed a classically inspired temple or pavilion, described appropriately as an "observatory" by some Monticello visitors. The pavilion is a deliberately designed perch upon which to gaze into the Virginia landscape, and the terraced garden was a stage from which to look down at what Jefferson referred to as "the workhouse of nature . . . clouds, hail, snow, rain, thunder, all fabricated at our feet" (fig. 1.5).[4]

Thomas Jefferson liked to eat vegetables, and the Monticello kitchen expressed a blend of new culinary traditions based on these recent garden introductions. In 1819 he wrote Dr. Vine Utley of his recipe for healthy living, "I have lived temperately, eating little animal food, and that . . . as a condiment for the vegetables which constitute my principal diet." A recipe for okra soup, or gumbo, long attributed to Jefferson's daughter Martha Jefferson Randolph, is an apt metaphor for the Monticello garden. The Jefferson family gumbo is a rich blend of "native" vegetables like lima beans and Cymlings, or Pattypan squash, that were grown by American Indians on the arrival of the first Europeans. It also included new vegetables found by Spanish explorers like potatoes, an Andean discovery adopted by northern Europeans, as well as tomatoes, collected in Central America and embraced by Mediterranean cultures as early as the seventeenth century. Binding the soup was an African plant, okra, grown and "creolized" by both the French and enslaved blacks in the West Indies. The dish was ultimately prepared by African American chefs trained in the fine arts of French cuisine in the kitchen at Monticello. Jefferson, according to culinary historian Karen Hess, was "our most illustrious epicure," our only epicurean president, and his devotion to fresh produce, whether in the President's House at a state dinner, or

at Monticello for the large numbers of guests who crowded the retired president's table, remains a key contribution of his gardening career.[5]

In the same way that Jefferson's Declaration of Independence defined a legacy of democracy and liberty, the Monticello garden broke with European tradition. The Old World kitchen garden, complex and labor-intensive, was geared to overcome the cool, cloudy northern European climate by bringing fruits and vegetables to maturity out of season, using hotbeds of fermenting manure to harvest asparagus in December or melons in April. The dynamics of this bustling European kitchen garden—its functional architecture of greenhouses, fruit walls, and frame yards, the tools and forcing paraphernalia, and the gardeners themselves—represent the very essence of the art and craft of horticulture (fig. 1.6). Jefferson had observed these gardens during his service as minister to France and in his travels through English gardens in 1786, but he was unimpressed by the inordinate amount of labor required to harvest common vegetables that could be grown so easily at home.[6]

The Monticello library was stocked with conventional horticultural wisdom by English kitchen garden writers like Philip Miller, curator of London's Chelsea Physic Garden, and American imitators such as Philadelphia's Bernard McMahon, Jefferson's practical gardening mentor. This Old World horticultural tradition was alive in Virginia and in the young Republic, but not at Monticello. Plantation owners such as George Washington and John Tayloe, two of the wealthiest men in Virginia in 1800, hired professional gardeners to care for old-style kitchen gardens with hotbeds, greenhouses, and, mostly, cool-weather European vegetables. One visitor described the Mount Vernon garden as "well cultivated, perfectly kept, and . . . quite in English style" (fig. 1.7). As work reports of the gardeners at such plantations indicate, their role often seemed superficial, focused on grooming and tidying—weeding, mowing, rolling gravel walks, picking weeds from the lawn—fussy jobs probably never at-

1.6. Frontispiece to John Abercrombie's
Every Man His Own Gardener, 1776, displaying a
democratic version (that is, everyman) of the
traditional British kitchen garden

tempted at Monticello. "The Englishman prepares his borders while the American digs his holes," wrote one nineteenth-century Virginia horticulturist. The Monticello vegetable garden was much less refined than the English kitchen garden, but Jefferson could grow more vegetables with significantly less skill or labor because the garden's microclimate suited the new, warm-season vegetables and extended the growing season. In addition, Jefferson's garden was all about planting and harvesting, and rarely did he record how crops were cared for. Not only were the horticultural activities—soil preparation, fertilization, staking—more casual at Monticello, but the terraced garden was, in many ways, one big hotbed. Jefferson's vegetable garden was a uniquely pragmatic, and American, experiment in growing vegetables.[7]

Few Jefferson biographers have omitted a discussion of the source of Jefferson's intellectual experimentation. According to Dumas Malone, he was a child of the Enlightenment, holding "an abiding conviction that human intelligence can unlock not only the treasure house of the past but also the secrets of the universe, thus leading mankind onward to a richer and better life." This embrace of the scientific method, of observation and definition, "launched itself on a limitless career of intellectual conquest." In a variety of fields, from astronomy to meteorology, from agriculture to paleontology, Jefferson's mind is unveiled as painstakingly precise with an innate passion for measuring, counting, and recording. Eighteenth-century American garden writers such as Williamsburg's Joseph Prentis advocated planting by the phases of the moon, and Colonel Francis Taylor, a planter from nearby Orange County, set out his cabbage plants in the middle of the night by a full moon, a practice Jefferson would have shunned as superstitious.[8]

Jefferson's garden diary, or Garden Book, is an enduring expression of Enlightenment thought. Begun at his boyhood home, Shadwell, on March 30, 1766, with the notation "Purple hyacinth be-

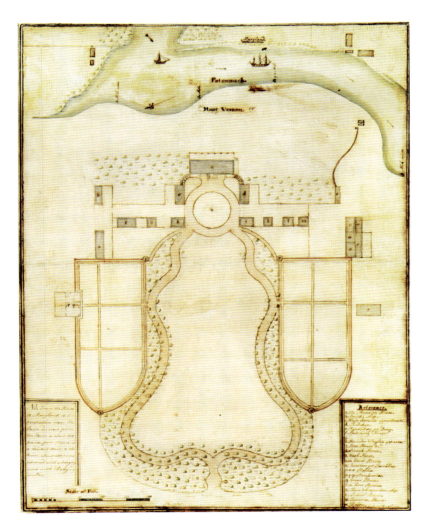

1.7. Samuel Vaughan's plan for George Washington's Mount Vernon, 1787, shows the bullet-shaped north and south gardens. One visitor remarked that "after seeing his house and his gardens one would say that he had the most beautiful examples in England of this style."

gins to bloom," the Garden Book concluded on September 15, 1824, with the completion of his vegetable garden Kalendar and the planting of Winter spinach and Brown Dutch lettuce (fig. 1.8). Sixty-six pages long, bound in leather, and residing today at the Massachusetts Historical Society, this diary reveals Jefferson as a garden scientist. He records how many lima beans would fill a quart jar, which in turn would plant so many feet of row in square VII of the garden, or he observes that six slaves could fill so many wheelbarrows in an hour, daily create 127 yards of a roundabout road, and thereby complete the road in so many months. Jefferson's organizational scheme for the vegetable garden in 1812, dividing the long terrace into "Fruits, Roots, and Leaves," was a reflection of the Enlightenment ideal to neatly categorize the natural world (fig. 1.9). Jefferson's Garden Book is a unique legacy that provides a model of the scientific method at work, written at a time when American horticulture was in its infancy. Fortunately, in 1944, Edwin Morris Betts, a professor of biology at the University of Virginia, assembled Jefferson's gardening diary, relevant letters, and other valuable memoranda into a single volume, *Thomas Jefferson's Garden Book*.[9]

As the Garden Book and his letters show, Jefferson used plants and gardens as a means of relating to friends, family, neighbors, and even political allies. The spring pea competition between Jefferson and his Charlottesville neighbors is a poignant expression of how Jefferson used plants as a vehicle for social intercourse. The Jefferson family tradition held that whoever harvested the first spring pea hosted a community dinner that included a feast on the winning sample of fresh peas. A thread of garden gossip weaves its way through his published correspondence, as Jefferson prefaced letters on the future of the American republic with a discussion of how his gardens fared at Monticello. Vegetable seeds, from the mysterious "sprout kale," which he boasted "no body in the U. S. has," to the rutabaga, a legitimate candidate as a Jefferson American introduction,

1.8. Jefferson began his garden diary, or Garden Book,
in 1766 at Shadwell, his boyhood home

were tangible tokens of friendship. This was Jefferson's personal garden, but it was also a family garden where he sowed cabbage seed with his daughter Martha; a community garden where he shared harvests and vegetable curiosities with neighbors; a national garden of seeds from the Jefferson-sponsored Lewis and Clark expedition, the Spanish Southwest, and America's finest plantsmen; and an international garden of vegetables from around the globe.[10]

Jefferson's horticultural experiments displayed an innocent sense of adventure. He reveled in the promiscuous cross-fertilization resulting from planting Cucurbit varieties and species alongside each other to form new types of squash, cucumbers, and melons. He delighted in odd-colored vegetables, many-headed cabbages, and other curiosities of the vegetable world. Jefferson mixed his planting beds, or "squares," by combining tomatoes with okra, carrots with sesame—culinary companions but lively juxtapositions of plant textures. Flowering beans were trained to climb an arbor along the long walk of the garden as an ornamental flourish. The superlatives he used to describe his favorites attest to this peculiarly unabashed enthusiasm. Whether praising the "long haricot" bean as the "best kind he [Jefferson] has ever seen in this country," the sesame as "among the most valuable acqui-

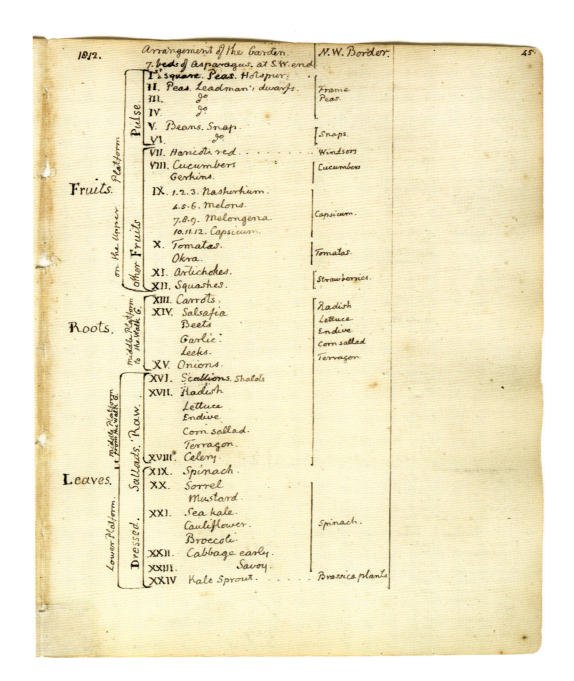

1.9. "Arrangement of the Garden," 1812, from Garden Book

1.10. Restored Monticello garden, 1998

sitions our country has ever made," or the Cymling squash as "one of our most finest, and most innocent vegetables," this garden was fun, and Jefferson's Garden Book documents one man's wonder at the natural world. Thomas Jefferson was crazy about vegetables.[11]

In 1801, Jefferson confessed to his Parisian friend Madame de Tessé that he had "rarely ever planted a flower in my life," and it is doubtful that he toiled manually in the soil planting grape vines or setting out ornamental trees. Nonetheless, Jefferson worked in the vegetable garden with his hands. Jefferson's Garden Book notes about the spacing of seed and the amount allotted to each row suggests, at the least, that he was in the garden. Isaac (Granger) Jefferson, an enslaved blacksmith and tinsmith, recalled in 1847 that "for amusement he [Jefferson] would work sometimes in the garden for half an hour at a time in right good earnest in the cool of the evening." Margaret Bayard Smith, a friend and chronicler of Washington society, suggested that seeds were sown by Jefferson himself when describing a portable seed rack used at Monticello, "a frame, or stand, consisting of two upright pieces of about two inches thickness, in which were neat little truss hooks. On these were suspended phials of all sizes, tightly corked, and neatly labeled, containing garden seeds, of the smaller kind; those of the larger were in tin canisters. When in his garden this stand could be carried about and placed near him, and if I remember, there must have near a hundred kinds. It is well worthy the adoption of all gentlemen and lady gardeners." Although he is often portrayed as among the more cerebral figures in American history, Jefferson was good with his hands. He not only sowed seeds in the garden, harvested fruit with his grandchildren, and staked out garden beds with a transit and chain, but, according to Isaac, "was neat a hand as ever you see to make keys and locks and small chains, iron and brass."[12]

Jefferson never regarded himself as a skilled and polished horticulturist. Even at sixty-eight, he was still a "young gardener" or, as he had written the French botanist André Thöuin, "a zealous Amateur." Jefferson was a student of gardening as much as he was an accomplished practitioner, and the word *amateur*, deriving from the Latin *amo*, "I love," captures the spirit of Jefferson's enthusiasms, whether expressed by his grandiose, and at times impractical, vision for the thousand-foot-long terrace or his puppy love for peas. Jefferson's innate curiosity was expressed when he wrote to his daughter Martha, "There is not a sprig of grass that shoots uninteresting to me."[13]

Nicholas King, mapmaker for the Lewis and Clark expedition, forwarded kitchen garden seed to Jefferson in 1806, writing that "no person has been more zealous to enrich the United States by the introduction of new and useful vegetables." Nor had any person created a garden so uniquely American in its scale, diversity, composition, and experimental character. Jefferson's vegetable garden, with its scenic panorama, uniquely contrived microclimate, breakthrough collection of vegetables, and pioneering blend of culinary traditions, was something new and revolutionary (fig. 1.10). Ever the garden scientist, Jefferson documented his triumphs and failures over fifty-eight years in his Garden Book, a horticultural diary without parallel in early American garden history. This rich record of one man's horticultural dance with the elements has made possible one of the most accurate garden restorations in America. Today the visitor to Monticello can enter the garden pavilion to look across the rolling Piedmont Virginia countryside or walk through Jefferson's revolutionary garden—down the rows of his favorite Marrowfat peas, tree onions, and Brown Dutch lettuce. The Monticello vegetable garden is a living expression of the genius of Thomas Jefferson and one of the great success stories of his life.[14]

2.1. "I know nothing so charming as our own country. The learned say it is a new creation . . .
Europe is a first idea, a crude production, before the maker knew his trade, or had made up his mind as to
what he wanted"—Thomas Jefferson to Angelica Church, 1788

2. Building the Garden

I N 1767 THOMAS JEFFERSON was a twenty-three-year-old lawyer still living at his boyhood home, Shadwell, almost two miles down the "little mountain" and across the Rivanna River from Monticello. There, on February 20, Jefferson began his lifetime romance with the garden pea by sowing "a bed of forwardest and a bed of middling peas," the adjectives describing the seasons of ripening. From this early date, Jefferson's Garden Book illustrates his dedication to measurement minutia, the facts and figures regarding the details of the horticultural world: "500. of these peas weighed 3 oz.—18 dwt. about 2500 fill a pint" (fig. 2.2). What was this studious young man—beginning a legal career that involved sixty-eight cases that year, managing the tobacco farm at Shadwell, caring for his mother and four brothers and sisters, envisioning the building of a home and plantation across the river, falling in love in Williamsburg, reading the Greeks and Romans—doing counting the number of peas that would fill a pint jar? Such rational record keeping, a product of the Enlightenment, was perennially seductive to Thomas Jefferson and defined the pages of the Garden Book for the next fifty-eight years.[1]

Jefferson's Garden Book entries at Shadwell in 1767 and 1768 suggest fun and fairly productive seasons in the garden of a young man, with favorite crops sowed in early spring, including lettuce, celery, onions, and asparagus. In 1769, he planted fruit trees in what would become the south orchard and first recorded the word "Monticello" in his Garden Book. A conscientious student of all things, Jefferson noted the horticultural wisdom of Albemarle County neighbors Nicholas Meriwether and Nicholas Lewis regarding the quantities of garden space that should be devoted to watermelons and cucumbers to provide for a "middling family." Although he had not yet moved to his mountaintop, excavation for the south pavilion had been begun, bricks were fired, and a well was dug. After his marriage to Martha Wayles Skelton on January 1, 1772, Jefferson settled into his new home during the spring planting season, alluding to the "patches" of peas and the harvesting of cucumbers and potatoes. He also records sowing

2.2. Page 2 of the Garden Book, counting peas and gardening at Shadwell

a "patch of peas for the Fall" in July. From this early date, the planting of a fall garden would become a consistent feature of Jefferson's horticultural practice (fig. 2.3).[2]

The year 1774 marked a flurry of gardening, as Jefferson recorded some sixty-nine entries for vegetable sowings and plantings and inaugurated a labeling system of numbered sticks at the head of planted rows. On March 31 he described a large new garden just below the plantation road, Mulberry Row, on the southeastern slope of the mountain. Here he "laid off ground to be leveled for a future garden. The upper side 44.f. below the upper edge of the Round-about [Mulberry Row] and parallel thereto. It is 668. feet long, 80 f. wide, and at each end forms a triangle, rectangular & isosceles, of which the legs are 80. f. & the hypothenuse 113. feet." Although the two ends are symmetrical and regular, this layout is an odd shape, perhaps owing to the way earth was excavated and moved. As his calculations indicate, Jefferson's knowledge of surveying and mathematics enhanced his Enlightenment zeal to organize the natural world. His father, Peter Jefferson, was a professional surveyor who taught his son the necessary technical skills so competently that Thomas Jefferson himself was appointed surveyor of Albemarle County, a post he never assumed. Jefferson avidly surveyed his Monti-

2.3. Summer vegetables continue bearing late into the Monticello autumn, when Jefferson would often sow greens and other hardy vegetables for harvests into the winter

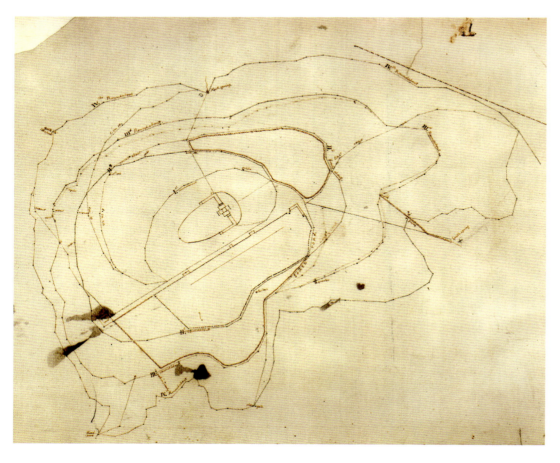

2.4. Jefferson's drawing of the road system and "roundabouts" on Monticello Mountain, 1809

cello properties, including fields, fence lines, roads, and other natural features (fig. 2.4). His various odometers calculated mileage to Philadelphia, Washington, and his plantation near Lynchburg, Poplar Forest, and he made scores of maps of his numerous landholdings. Jefferson owned a theodolite, a type of transit that measures both horizontal and vertical angles, and a thirty-three-foot, or two-pole, chain with which to precisely lay out and stake, then later revise, his garden terrace. In 1785 Jefferson composed the Northwest Ordinance, approved and implemented by Congress in 1787, which imposed a mathematical grid upon the western territories, essentially the American Midwest. Airline travelers view Jefferson's geometric legacy today as they fly across the country and observe the squares that define the landscape.[3]

Although extreme weather—a fruit-killing frost and a snowy, river-freezing winter—dominated the few Garden Book notations of the late 1770s, Jefferson provides hints that the 1774 garden layout had been partially installed. Peas were planted in a "square" on April 1, 1777, suggesting a minimal structure to the garden. A surviving scaled drawing, perhaps composed as late as the early 1780s, shows a one-thousand-by-eighty-foot-long garden divided into nine one-hundred-by-fifty-foot rectangular beds,

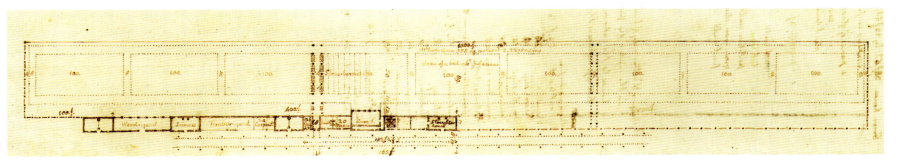

2.5. Jefferson's earliest scaled plan for buildings along Mulberry Row and the vegetable garden,
drawn around 1780, showing regular one-hundred-foot-wide squares divided by walkways

or "squares" (fig. 2.5). A rock wall along the southeast edge of the garden probably supported a mildly graded terrace, but it may have served as an enclosure to define the garden's limits. Though never fully executed, this garden plan is similar to a scaled drawing Jefferson prepared in 1806 that anticipates the garden of his retirement years.[4]

Vegetable gardening requires more vigilance and on-site monitoring than fruit growing. Between 1778 and 1782, beginning his career as a public figure and serving as governor in both Williamsburg and Richmond, Jefferson limited his horticultural activities to establishing trees in the south orchard. In fact, 1778 was the last year Jefferson recorded vegetable garden plantings at Monticello until the 1790s. As governor, Jefferson became involved with the British and German prisoners of war who took up winter quarters at the barracks in western Albemarle County. He was concerned with their comfort but reassured himself that "their own gardens will furnish them a great abundance of vegetables through the year." Distracted from gardening by the death of his wife in 1782 and his election to Congress in 1783, Jefferson left for Paris in the late spring of 1784 to serve as minister plenipotentiary to France.[5]

During his stay in Paris, Jefferson's correspondence and journals indicated an indefatigable interest in European agriculture, particularly grape growing, and in gardening of all kinds. He initiated the importation of American trees and shrubs in order to share with his French friends the prosperous natural productions of the New World. His obsession with economic plants as a vehicle for social change became readily evident in his zeal to import olive trees, "manna from heaven." Jefferson played the part of a seed missionary, when, under the threat of a death penalty, he smuggled out of Italy seeds of upland rice by hiding them in his coat pockets. Jefferson believed that this treasured rice variety, able to thrive in dry mountain soils, might serve as an alternative crop for Lowcountry South Carolina planters. He hoped that the unique rice could spur the move of plantation owners away from their malaria-ridden swamps to the healthier climate of the rolling Piedmont. Although noble in conception, Jefferson's vision for a new agriculture based on this dry land species never materialized.[6]

Jefferson observed highly crafted kitchen gardens throughout his European travels. In Paris he visited the Jardin des Plantes, where he met its director, André Thöuin, an internationally renowned plantsman (fig. 2.6). The friendship that evolved between Thöuin and Jefferson resulted in an annual shipment of seeds to Monticello from 1808 until at least 1822, some years including as many as seven hundred species. Jefferson also toured the Jardin du Roi in Paris, curated by the Count George-Louis Buffon, the scientist who argued in *Histoire naturelle* that the humid climate in eastern North American caused an inherent degeneracy among American botanical, zoological, and human species. Jefferson visited landscaped gardens constructed on a scale beyond anything he had experienced: the enor-

2.6. André Thöuin portrait by Jules Boilly,
engraved by Nargeol

mous and geometric Versailles; Chaville, the "charming gardens" of his intimate friend Madame de Tessé; and Bagatelle, a *jardin anglais* where he walked with both John Adams and his close friend Maria Cosway (fig. 2.7).[7]

In the spring of 1786, Jefferson, accompanied by Adams, toured some sixteen English landscape gardens and kept a casual diary of his impressions. He wrote an old Virginia friend, John Page, that "the gardening in that country [England] is the article in which it surpasses all the earth. I mean their pleasure gardening." Jefferson's European garden tourism profoundly influenced the ornamental landscape at Monticello. His vision for a *ferme ornée*, or ornamental farm for the larger landscape, the serpentine flower walk along the west lawn, and the conception of "the grove," or ornamental forest on Monticello's northern slopes, were inspired by his journey to England and stay in Paris. In contrast, the art and craft of Old World kitchen gardening—the formal edging of geometric beds, the tidiness of immaculate rows, and the use of garden structures like frames and hotbeds—had surprisingly little effect on gardening at Monticello. Jefferson was unimpressed by the lavish attention to common garden vegetables that could be grown with such ease and in such large quantities at home. He wrote Ferdinand Grand, a French banking official and acquaintance, from Paris in 1786 and asserted the superiority of American vegetables: "The only garden vegetable I find here better than ours, is the turnep." William Cobbett, English émigré and author of *The American Gardener* (1821), blamed this horticultural nonchalance on the sheer expanse of the United States, "where land is abundant, attachment and even attention to *small spots*, wear away."[8]

Historians consistently describe Jefferson's European interlude—its "vaunted scene" of architecture, art, and political discourse—as an experience that transformed his intellectual and aesthetic sensibilities. Jefferson's immersion in French food was just as transformative. According to culinary historian Damon L. Fowler, "the cuisine of Paris represented an 'international culinary language' that communicated style and substance." Before his trip to Europe, Jefferson had enjoyed meals prepared by French chefs at the colonial capitol in Williamsburg and in Annapolis while sharing a residence with James Monroe. He was so impressed by French cooking that he brought the enslaved James Hemings from Monticello to learn the art of continental cuisine in Paris. Once he returned, Jefferson's taste for rich and flavorful French food was tempered by the adoption of his "native vittles." His culinary experience in France is reflected in subsequent family documents describing the cooking of vegetables at Monticello—with ample butter, herbs, and cream—as well as in his outfitting of the kitchen with the latest accoutrements of French food preparation. As president, Jefferson would hire a French chef for the President's House, emulating the "style and substance" he had experienced at the former capitol and abroad. The influence of Jefferson's European travels is also apparent in the character and culinary function of many of the plants selected for the vegetable garden, including artichokes, parsley, sorrel, garlic, haricot and fava beans, and endive.[9]

Jefferson's Parisian residence, the Hôtel de Langeac, included a parklike landscape with a luxuriant plantation of ornamental trees. Here, Jefferson employed a gardener who cared for a rectangular kitchen garden bed, or *potagère*, that contained vines on trellises, seeds of "Indian corn," and an experimental foraging herb, sulla. He also purchased gardening tools and in 1787 wrote to Nicholas Lewis, a friend who was overseeing Monticello in his absence, to send him seeds of a "drying corn from Cherokee country," "best" watermelon, "fine cantaloupe melon," and sweet potato. The watermelons, corn, and sweet potatoes, like the native trees and shrubs Jefferson was repeatedly ordering from home, were tangible examples of American natural bounty that he aspired to share with the European community of gardeners and natural scientists.[10]

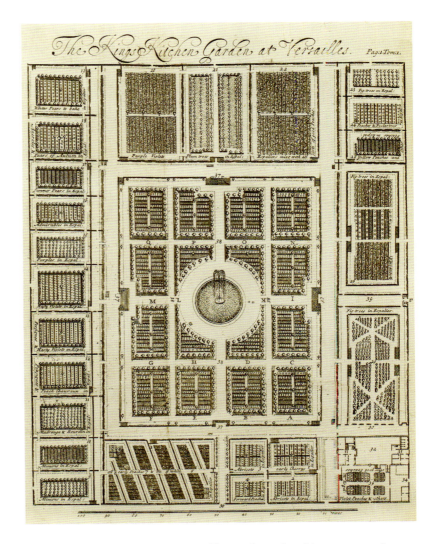

2.7. The kitchen garden at Versailles, perhaps the ultimate expression of the Old World kitchen garden, was seen by Thomas Jefferson in Paris. From Jean de La Quintinie, *The Compleat Gard'ner*, 1693.

The Monticello vegetable garden appears to have been abandoned until Jefferson's return from Europe in December 1789. Soon after landing in Norfolk, Virginia, Jefferson learned of his appointment by President Washington as secretary of state, to be served first in New York, then later in Philadelphia. Before departing, Jefferson stayed at Monticello to preside over the marriage of his eldest daughter, Martha, to Thomas Mann Randolph Jr., a savvy farmer eager to please his increasingly famous father-in-law (fig. 2.8). Longing for the tranquillity offered by his family and garden, Jefferson wrote home regularly between 1790 and 1794 complaining of the burdens of political life. Vegetable gardening occasionally occupied the attentions of Martha (known as Patsy) and her sister, Maria (known as Polly), Jefferson's youngest daughter, who later married John Wayles Eppes. Family correspondence during this time reveals a doting father ever chiding his children on to unwelcome horticultural challenges. Jefferson implored Martha in 1791, "You will be out in time to begin your garden, and that will tempt you to be out a great deal, than which nothing will tend more to give you health and strength." Maria's silence on horticultural matters caused him to complain, "I find I have counted too much on you as a Botanical and Zoological correspondent, for I undertook to affirm here that the fruit was not killed in Virginia, because I had a young daughter there who I was sure would have mentioned it." Whatever the wisdom of Jefferson's paternal voice, his insistence on the recreational and social value of vegetable gardening is clear.[11]

Under the direction of Thomas Mann Randolph, with the participation of the two daughters and through the labors of enslaved gardeners Tom Shackleford, George Granger Sr., and John (often known as "Gardener John"), vegetable gardening continued at Monticello without Jefferson. Randolph assured him that his daughters "had become quite enthusiastic in gardening," and Martha proclaimed herself "a much better gardener." Jefferson had forwarded his daughters garden seeds, and based on the number of people involved and Jefferson's exhortations, one can assume that typical vegetables—peas, lettuce, radishes, cabbage—were planted in the garden. Nonetheless, Martha confessed the tragic-comic fate of the 1792 garden: "What I told you of my garden is really true indeed if you see it at a distance it looks very green but it does not bear close examination, the weeds having taken possession of much the greater part of it. Old George is so slow that by the time he has got to the end of his labour he has it all to do over again . . . Dear papa the heat is incredible here." In Martha's defense, Virginia gardeners, no matter how competent or committed, commonly give up in July.[12]

2.8. Jefferson's daughter Martha Jefferson Randolph, by Thomas Sully, 1836

2.9. "Objects for the garden this year," 1794,
from page 28 of Jefferson's Garden Book

Mistakenly assuming that his resignation from the role of secretary of state meant a life of retirement, Jefferson returned to Monticello on January 16, 1794. He worked passionately and joyously to renew his plantation: remodeling his house, substituting a mixed, wheat-based agriculture for tobacco, and reorganizing his fields. This chapter of Jefferson's tenure could be titled "agricultural reformation" because of his energetic devotions to transforming Monticello's farms by adapting the latest writings of progressive agriculturists. Notations about gardening—sowing and harvesting of peas, lettuce, and asparagus—began anew in the Garden Book. Jefferson hired a professional Scottish gardener, Robert Bailey, paying him fifteen pounds a year and an annual distribution of five hundred pounds of pork "with bread for his family." Jefferson also inaugurated an expansive list of intended plantings in the 1794 Garden Book, entitled "Objects for the garden this year" (fig. 2.9). He listed more than fifty species and varieties of vegetables, including many unusual delicacies for an eighteenth-century garden of the western Virginia Piedmont, such as "peendars," or peanuts, potato pumpkins likely obtained from Monticello slaves, and a variety of melons.[13]

Early the next year Robert Bailey composed his own list of the seeds of forty-

2.10. The garden in 1794 was dominated by such traditional European vegetables
as cabbage, beets, and carrots

two vegetable varieties harvested from the previous year's growing season. According to this document, garden activity was significantly more intense in 1794 than Jefferson's Garden Book indicated. Seed saving was essential at Monticello in order to preserve the sophisticated array of vegetables. Jefferson later wrote to Philadelphia nurseryman Bernard McMahon about his experimental process to "avoid degeneracy" caused by mixing too many garden varieties of the same species and about his goal to preserve only the best bean or finest lettuce. Although Bailey's list included Virginia watermelons and American bean varieties, the dominance of Old World crops—cold hardy roots, leafy salad items, and cabbage family members—suggests that his influence resulted in a more traditional British kitchen garden, not Jefferson's international repository of vegetable immigrants (fig. 2.10).[14]

Jefferson departed Monticello for Philadelphia and the office of vice president in February 1797. While stationed there, and later in Washington, Jefferson spent long periods at Monticello, sometimes as much as six months of the year. Monticello was often occupied by the Randolph and Eppes families, particularly when Jefferson was home, and vegetable gardening continued despite the departure of Robert Bailey, who moved to Washington in 1797 to start his own commercial nursery. Enslaved gardeners such as John and Goliah were instructed to assist Martha or her husband in the planting of the garden. Monticello was full of people, and the garden needed to provide for them. For example, while president, Jefferson sent home garden seed of "the very best kind" for his overseer, John Freeman, to sow so that its produce could be harvested during Jefferson's summer visit. Jefferson added, "The sowings should be large as our daily consumption of such things is great." Even when she lived at the neighboring farm of Edgehill, Martha would write to her father about enjoying produce from Monticello.[15]

Except for a small bed of endive supplied by Jefferson's former gardener Robert Bailey, no vegetable garden is documented at the President's House during the Jefferson tenure, perhaps due to the availability of produce in the local farmers' markets. Deprived of his own garden, Jefferson created a detailed chart delineating the first and last appearance of thirty-seven vegetables in the local market between 1801 and 1809. This chart of the vegetable markets in Washington, DC, is among the most revelatory documents in the history of American cuisine. Jefferson's passion for new types of vegetables became so well known that Margaret Bayard Smith recalled how foreign embassies "vied with each other" to provide him with seeds of the rarest kinds. Jefferson personally distributed the seeds to nearby market gardeners and instructed his maître d'hôtel, Etienne Lemaire, to pay the highest prices for the season's earliest produce. Lemaire, in turn, kept a record of produce purchases from this market in 1806 that suggests the cornucopia of vegetables served at the table of the President's House. Lemaire's accounts indicate the purchase of thirty-nine vegetables, fifteen fruits, and occasional herbs. Lettuce was the most commonly mentioned vegetable with ninety-eight purchases, followed by parsley (eighty-four) and cabbage (fifty-seven) (fig. 2.11).[16]

Beginning in 1804, following the death on April 17 of his daughter Maria due to childbirth, Jefferson found solace in preparations for a retirement garden. Six weeks after her death, he first introduced the central concept of terracing the Monticello vegetable garden in a letter from Washington to John Wayles Eppes, his son-in-law, who was overseeing certain branches of the Monticello plantation. Sometime before September 4, 1804, Jefferson composed a memorandum titled "General ideas for the improvement of Monticello," which described the terracing and wall building that would take place over the next four years. Jefferson also discussed the idea of constructing four "temples" in alcoves along the edge of the future garden terrace: "1. a specimen of Gothic, 2. model of the Pantheon, 3. model of cubic architecture, and 4. a specimen of Chinese." On second thought, he concluded that "after all, the kitchen garden is not the place for orna-

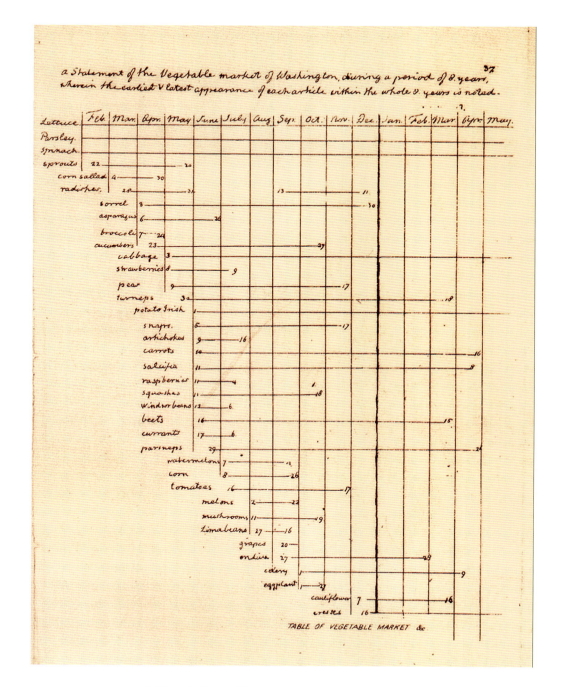

2.11. Jefferson's chart of the first and last appearance of produce
from the Washington markets, 1801–9

ments of this kind. Bowers and trellises suit that better, these temples will be better disposed in the pleasure grounds." He ultimately changed his mind again and eventually constructed a "cubic" garden pavilion at the midpoint of the terraced garden. Jefferson's "Memorandum," written during the dreariest years of his service in Washington, expresses his visionary design for Monticello and a gardening retirement.[17]

While mourning for his daughter, Jefferson followed the progress of the Lewis and Clark "Corps of Discovery," which had reached St. Louis by May 1804. A key goal of this Jefferson-sponsored expedition was botanical exploration, and Jefferson would eventually receive some of the edible bounties collected from Northern Plains

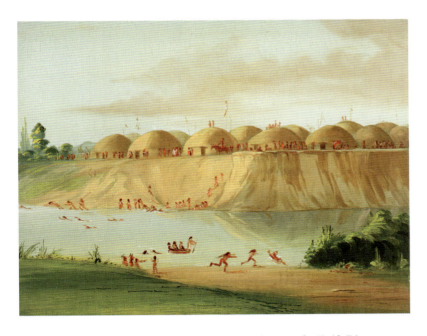

2.12. *Hidatsa Village, Earth-Covered Lodges, on the Knife River,* by George Catlin, 1832. The gardens of the Hidatsa and Mandan Indians were along the bottomlands of rivers.

Indian tribes. As the corps traveled north along the Missouri River in the fall of 1804, in their fifty-five-foot-long keelboat and two rowboats called pirogues, the Mandan, Arikara, and Hidatsa tribes were among the first Native Americans encountered (fig. 2.12). Northern Plains Indian horticulture, based on the cultivation of bean, corn, and squash varieties that could thrive in the severe climate of what are now the Dakotas, was perhaps the most evolved of all North American Indian tribes. Seeds of promising practical plants were brought to President Jefferson on Meriwether Lewis's return in 1807. Although he reserved a few species for planting at Monticello, including a number of Native American bean and corn varieties, Jefferson, "in too indifferent a situation to take the care of them which they merit," forwarded the rest of the seeds to more skilled horticulturists like McMahon and William Hamilton, the noted Philadelphia plant collector. Jefferson sowed the Arikara bean at Monticello in 1809. He noted that it "is one of the most excellent we have had" but concluded, "I have one kind only superior to them, but being very sensibly so, I shall abandon the Ricaras." Such was the nature of Jefferson's experimental laboratory at Monticello; Jefferson focused on the usefulness of plants and left the collecting of species to the scientific community (fig. 2.13).[18]

In February 1806 Jefferson shipped home four thousand hawthorn plants purchased from the Washington nurseryman Thomas Main, from whom Jefferson often bought ornamental trees for Monticello. These "thorns" were planted as a living fence around the south and north orchards. The idea of organic fencing became an obsession for Jefferson. Later that year, another shipment of plants included a crude map of the top of Monticello showing where "everything is to be planted." This instructive sketch, conceived to document the course of the hedge, clearly identifies the location of the "garden" in relation to other features like the south orchard and the Monticello grove. The overseer John Freeman proved to be incompetent and was soon replaced by Edmund Bacon, whose extended tenure at Monticello

2.13. The spring garden in 2010 and the paling fence that surrounded it and the south orchard below

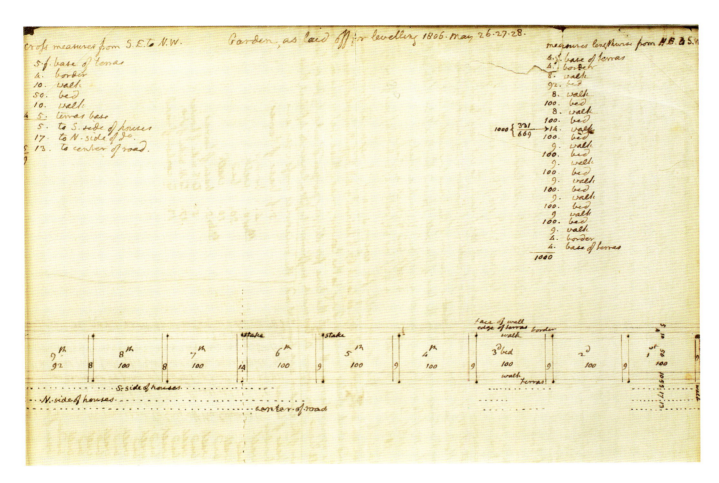

2.14. Jefferson's scaled drawing of "Garden, as laid off for leveling 1806"

during Jefferson's retirement is a testament to his worthiness. This landmark horticultural year also marked the documented appearance of the enslaved Wormley Hughes as the chief Monticello gardener. Until his death in 1856, Hughes was endeared for his optimistic persona and sixty years of faithful service to the Jefferson family.[19]

The creation of the one-thousand-foot-long vegetable garden was the fulfillment of Thomas Jefferson's retirement yearnings, and he finally began to direct the actual work during a late spring 1806 visit to Monticello. Jefferson prepared a scaled drawing of the proposed "Garden, as laid off for leveling 1806, May 26, 27, 28" (fig. 2.14). This 1806 plan was similar to the earlier circa 1780 plan in its organization of the garden into nine beds, or squares, each one hundred by fifty feet. The ninth bed (the easternmost) of the 1806 plan is only ninety-two feet long. Two ten-foot-wide walkways run the length of the garden, and the squares were divided by nine-foot-wide crosswalks. A long border bed follows the outer, or southeastern, edge of the terrace just above the supporting wall of stone. The survey notes that accompanied Jefferson's 1806 plan suggest a picture of him in the field, perhaps at sixty-three a bit bent with age, likely assisted by Hughes, with his theodolite, or transit, compass, measuring chains, and other surveying instruments. The 1806 plan would undergo alterations between 1808 and 1814 to adapt to the practical realities of the enormous task of earthmoving, as well as the shifting requirements of adapting the right crop to the proper place.[20]

Jefferson hoped finally to begin terracing the garden in 1807 after hiring a crew of seven to nine slaves from a Fredericksburg farmer, Lewis Dangerfield, to perform the labor. He had written Edmund Bacon on December 28, 1806, "I pray you to arrange your work so as to spare your whole force to be at work in leveling the garden from the 10th of March to the last of April while I shall be at home" (fig. 2.15). More pressing economic needs, however, required attention before the crew of Dangerfield slaves could be delegated to moving earth. These included repairing the toll mill along the river and its accompanying dam, both of which were perennially damaged by periodic flooding. Fence building, corn planting, and the sawing of 180 cords of wood for charcoal also delayed this long-awaited leveling.[21]

Earthmoving in the garden began anew during the winter of 1807–1808, interrupted by another flooding of the mill, but continuing at a decent enough pace so that 220 feet of terracing had been completed by January 29, 1808. Beginning at the southwestern end, the earth was moved by excavating the high side of the future garden, manually loading a mule-driven cart, and moving the soil to the low side, where a rock wall, in some places twelve feet high and ten feet deep, was constructed to retain the unloaded earth. It was backbreaking work, and one can imagine, particularly in wet winter weather, the heavy, raw, red clay, slippery to even stand on, being chiseled out

2.15. Edmund Bacon, Monticello's overseer from 1806 until 1822, supervised the terracing of the garden

of the earth one spade at a time. Bacon, who was instructed to write Jefferson when every hundred-foot section was completed, expressed frustration at having to dig so deep to create a perfectly flat garden and suggested that the terracing could be completed if it were not for this requirement (fig. 2.16). Bacon's challenge was not only to cut and fill across the eighty-foot terrace but to ensure that the earth flattening continued lengthwise, southwest to northeast. Jefferson's stipulation required the earth to be moved longer distances. Bacon also complained about the delays caused by his need to divert labor to cut wood for charcoal and to repair the Rivanna River canal.[22]

2.16. The garden was terraced into three subtle platforms, running lengthwise from southwest to northeast. This photograph from the 1940s shows the middle (foreground) and upper (background) platforms and the mild slope that divided them.

2.17. Thomas Mann Randolph by
an unidentified copyist, 1919

Finally, in a letter to Bacon on February 23, 1808, Jefferson reconsidered his original design and made significant changes to speed the work. He decided to adapt to the varying land contours and shorten the distances required to create the southwest to northeast plateau by creating four 250-foot level terraces running the length of the garden; the garden would be subdivided into two- to four-foot-high "platforms." Jefferson commissioned Thomas Mann Randolph to survey and lay out this new plan, writing that "should we go on in the same level we assumed at first, the labour will be enormous on account of the prodigious mass of earth we have to dig & the great distance to carry it" (fig. 2.17). He instructed Randolph to estimate

the locations of these new platforms and to use a rafter level to stake the dividing line between "the part to be dug from that to be filled." Under the tutelage of Randolph, Bacon and his crew had completed almost five hundred feet by April 15, when the overseer alerted Jefferson of the need to go back to begin blasting unmovable rock from the garden subsoil.[23]

Spring planting of cash crops again diverted men from the garden, and Jefferson was compelled to direct Bacon to work on additional tasks, such as monitoring the water in the mill canal and constructing a stable along Mulberry Row. By early June, however, Jefferson returned to the garden with renewed energy, urging Bacon to "consider the garden as your main business, and push it with all your might when the interruptions permit." Ten days later, Bacon responded that the new "level" was "nearly as high as the one done," and announced, "I am Going on fast as possople with the Garden." On June 30 Bacon had "nearly done 3 thirty foot troughs in the garden . . . since you Left heare [on June 8] but my gang being so interrupted I can not go on as fast I would wish." The interruptions continued through the growing season of 1808, and by October Jefferson also seemed frustrated. He wrote from Washington, "I think it will be better to employ the rest [of the slave labor force] on the garden & let us have that off of our hands." Bacon and the crew persevered, and on December 1 the Monticello overseer proudly proclaimed, "We have this day finished the second Levil [or "platform"] of the garden[.] I think it looks beautiful," but then he added, "I don't think we shall be able to get it done by that time [he had promised in late December] as the work is very heavy." The terracing was now completed all the way to what was then called the stone house, now known as the weaver's cottage.[24]

Work on the final platform (expedience had reduced them from four to three) continued that winter with the goal of completing the entire thousand feet before Jefferson's final return from the presidency in March 1809. Jefferson urged Bacon on, stating how "very inconvenient" it would be to have to complete the earthmoving after the construction of the "enclosure," or paling fence, that would ultimately surround the entire seven-acre fruit and vegetable complex. Jefferson had assigned this to a separate crew headed by the newly hired carpenter, Elisha Watkins, who supervised the enslaved carpenters, including Davy, Abram, and his son Shepherd. This monumental barrier, more than half a mile long, was recalled by Jefferson's slave Isaac (Granger) Jefferson: "My Old Master's garden was monstrous large: two rows of palings, all 'round ten feet high." [25]

Another parallel assignment, carried out by "head gardener" Wormley Hughes, was the manuring of the garden. This project involved hauling sixty to seventy wagonloads of manure from Milton, the river port on the Rivanna River, a lengthy, hilly journey of four miles along a road in need of substantial repairs. Meanwhile, Bacon had completed the terracing of another 195 feet by mid-January, again complaining about the struggle to haul the dirt, likely mud in midwinter, to fill the spaces behind the garden wall. The wall was now nearly twelve feet high in order to accommodate the fill and create a flat terrace. An 887-foot terrace was completed by late January, when Jefferson, surely balancing his financial anxieties with the goal of completing the terracing by March, ordered Bacon "to quit the garden" in order to prepare for corn planting. [26]

Jefferson wrote to Samuel Dupont de Nemours a week before leaving the President's House, "Never did [a] prisoner, released from his chains, feel such relief as I shall on shaking off the shackles of power." He returned to Monticello from Washington on March 17, 1809, finally retired, after a "very fatiguing" journey due to bad roads, snow, and general spring slop. He began planting his garden with Frame peas six days later, along one hundred feet of the northwest border. Despite the "remarkably backward" (cold) season the garden was apparently in a state of general completion, a miraculous

feat considering the haste in which work had proceeded over the previous winter. The main part of the terrace was organized into eighteen squares, and they were designated by Roman numerals, beginning at the southwestern end and running east. An inner or northwest border, the "warm beds," extended the length of the garden, and a grass walk, described by Margaret Bayard Smith in her visit during the summer, ran along the outer or southeastern side. At this time, Jefferson inaugurated a new feature of his Garden Book, a "Kalendar" that documented plantings in neat columns, each describing the seasonal process by which a vegetable was grown: "what," "where," "sowed," "transplanted," "come to table," "gone," "seed gathered," and "observations." [27]

Jefferson's retirement year was the most active and prolific vegetable gardening year in his lifetime, with the Kalendar including nearly one hundred different plantings. These spilled exuberantly from the terrace—to the asparagus squares, nursery, orchard, and vineyards below the garden. Countless new, and what were to become favorite, vegetable varieties were documented at Monticello for the first time, including novelties like sea kale, tomatoes, okra, and eggplant; Leadman's Dwarf and Blue Prussian (Prussian Blue to Jefferson) peas; Tennis-ball, Brown Dutch, Marseilles, and Ice lettuce; Early York cabbage; and Jerusalem artichokes. Many of the seeds—at least thirty of the new vegetable varieties—were purchased from Washington seedsman Theophilus Holt a month before Jefferson left Washington (fig. 2.18). Bernard McMahon provided Early York and Sugarloaf cabbages, George Divers contributed tomatoes, black-eyed peas, and parsnips, and General Thomas Sumpter of Georgia sent the unusual asparagus bean. Jefferson described his retirement to Etienne Lemaire on April 25 in the flush of spring: "I am constantly in my garden or farms, as exclusively employed out of doors as I was within doors when at Washington, and I find myself infinitely happier in my new mode of life." [28]

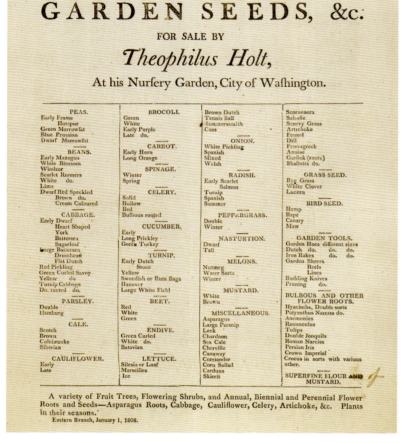

A CATALOGUE OF
GARDEN SEEDS, &c.

FOR SALE BY
Theophilus Holt,
At his Nursery Garden, City of Washington.

PEAS.	BROCOLI.	Brown Dutch	Scorzenera
Early Frame	Green	Tennis Ball	Salsafie
Hotspur	White	Hammersmith	Scurvy Grass
Green Marrowfat	Early Purple	Coss	Artichoke
Blue Prussian	Late do.		Fennel
Dwarf Marrowfat		ONION.	Dill
	CARROT.	White Pickling	Fennugreek
BEANS.	Early Horn	Spanish	Annise
Early Mazagan	Long Orange	Mixed	Garlick (roots)
White Blossom		Welsh	Shallotis do.
Windsor	SPINAGE.		
Scarlet Runners	Winter	RADISH.	GRASS SEED.
White do.	Spring	Early Scarlet	Rye Grass
Lima		Salmon	White Clover
Dwarf Red Speckled	CELERY.	Turnip	Lucern
Brown do.	Solid	Spanish	
Cream Coloured	Hollow	Summer	BIRD SEED.
	Red		Hemp
CABBAGE.	Bulbous rooted	PEPPERGRASS.	Rape
Early Dwarf		Double	Canary
Heart Shaped	CUCUMBER.	Winter	Maw
York	Early		
Battersea	Long Prickley	NASTURTION.	GARDEN TOOLS.
Sugarloaf	Green Turkey	Dwarf	Garden Hoes different sizes
Large Battersea		Tall	Dutch do. do.
Drumhead	TURNIP.		Iron Rakes do. do.
Flat Dutch	Early Dutch	MELONS.	Garden Sheers
Red Pickling	Stone	Nutmeg	Reels
Green Curled Savoy	Yellow	Water Sorts	Lines
Yellow do.	Sweedish or Ruta Baga	Winter	Budding Knives
Turnip Cabbage	Hanover		Pruning do.
Do. rooted do.	Large White Field	MUSTARD.	
		White	BULBOUS AND OTHER
PARSLEY.	BEET.	Brown	FLOWER ROOTS.
Double	Red		Hyacinths, Double sorts
Hamburg	White	MISCELLANEOUS.	Polyanthus Narciss do.
	Green	Asparagus	Anemonies
CALE.		Large Parsnip	Ranunculus
Scotch	ENDIVE.	Leek	Tulips
Brown	Green Curled	Chardoon	Double Jonquils
Colebrooke	White do.	Sea Cale	Roman Narciss
Siberian	Batavian	Cherville	Persian Iris
		Canaway	Crown Imperial
CAULIFLOWER.	LETTUCE.	Corriander	Crocus in sorts with various
Early	Silesia or Loaf	Corn Salad	other.
Late	Marseilles	Carduus	
	Ice	Skirrit	SUPERFINE FLOUR AND
			MUSTARD.

A variety of Fruit Trees, Flowering Shrubs, and Annual, Biennial and Perennial Flower Roots and Seeds—Asparagus Roots, Cabbage, Cauliflower, Celery, Artichoke, &c. Plants in their seasons.'
Eastern Branch, January 1, 1808.

2.18. Many of the vegetable seeds planted in 1809 were purchased from Washington seed dealer Theophilus Holt

The 1809 Garden Book Kalendar illuminates one of the most organized years of Jefferson's record keeping. Garden squares were generally relegated to specific crops, particularly peas and beans. Square IX, however, was ordered into thirteen numbered rows filled with diverse crops that were replanted as many as two more times later in the season. Peas, lettuce, endive, beans, spinach, radishes, cucumbers, and corn salad were planted successfully, providing "continued harvests throughout the year." A produce shortfall, however, inspired a letter of November 28 to neighbor Mary Walker Lewis, nicknamed "Captain Molly" for her severe but good-humored disposition. Jefferson composed a list of the quantities of six root vegetables he felt would be sufficient for the Monticello family table. Subsequently, he realized that he had underestimated his usage by more than 50 percent and asked Lewis to provide the difference. The letter is another example of Jefferson's effort to account for every detail.[29]

The 1809 Kalendar also reveals another theme of the Jefferson horticultural experience: "The failure of one thing is repaired by the success of another" (fig. 2.19). The word "failed" is recorded twenty times under the column titled "tranplantd." Few gardeners recorded their failures as often as Thomas Jefferson, and his unrelenting effort to overcome one catastrophe after another is a reflection of his experimental, scientific, and Enlightenment aesthetic. Crop failures were caused by a double blow of cold ("rarely one growing day without two or three cold ones following") and drought. Virtually no rain fell during a chilly April and May, and the dryness—only two inches of precipitation when fourteen was normal—continued from July until well into the autumn. Jefferson wrote that the Monticello farms and gardens had experienced "the most calamitous year ever since 1775." Certainly bad luck ruled Jefferson's retirement to the garden and reinforced his pithy lament to James Monroe that "in the lotteries of human life . . . farming is but gambling." In addition, it seems doubtful that even the sixty wagonloads of soil-conditioning manure

	where	sowed	transplant	come to table	gone	seed gather	observations
frame peas	bord. I–IV	Mar. 23		May 23	June 8		2 quarts sow 140... 40 f. gave 1 quart of seed. 3 pints sow 140 @ 2 i. distance
Hotspurs	square I	Mar. 27		June 5			
Cabbage early york	bord V	mar. 25	failed nearly				
Lettuce Marseilles	stonehouse	Mar. 25	2 as. May 19	May 15			
Radishes	do	Mar. 25					
Spinach prickly	bord VI	Mar. 29		May 20	June 5		
Parsley double	bord VI	mar. 29		July 1			
Ledman's dwarf pea	square III	Apr. 10					less than 2.9 = 440 f
alpine strawb. seed from Marzei	lower bl. ... earthen trough	Apr. 10					
Seakale	4th aspar. bd	Apr. 10					
Terragon	bord. VII	12	failed				
cucumbers	bord. VII	12					
Cabbage Early York	bord. V	12	failed nearly	2 plants			2 plants transplanted July 10 to W. side sq. VI
Windsor beans	square II	13	killed by bug				
cucumbers early	nursery	20	failed				54 plants of these transp. June 30. sq. XI. of which some however were of May 3
Cauliflower early	S.W. end bed	20	failed				
Roman Broccoli	do N.E. end	20	failed nearly				
Ice lettuce	do artichoke bed	20					
radishes. E. scar		20	failed				
lettuce tennisball	sq. IX. 12.13	20					of these seed bulbs, 911 fill a pint.
radish E. scarlet		20	failed				to plant a square of 40. f include
Lettuce Marseilles	S. asp. bed NE	21	failed				12.9 apart & 4.9 in the drill
radish E. scarlet	do SW	21	failed				will take 5½ gallons. Lay
tree onion	5 & 6 do	21	failed				3 pecks.
carrots. orange	7th do	21	failed				
beets scarlet		21		July 3			
Snaps E. dwarf	V. SW s rows	21		July 1			
Ricara	do NE 5 do	21					
Spinach. summ	IX. 1	22					
Parsley	2	do	failed				
Sorrel	3	do	failed				
Okra	4. 5	do	failed				
Eggplant	6	do	2 plants				
Chinese melon	7	do					
Spanish onion	nursery	24. 24					
squash. warted		24					
parsneps	do	24					
giant Cabbage	do	25	failed				
Early cucumbers	do	26		Aug. 19			
Lima beans	sq. VIII	28					
celery solid	low ground	May. 1	failed				
do red	bord VIII	May 3	June 30.XI				
Broccoli Roman							
Ice lettuce	bord. IX	do					
radishes E. s.		do					
Spinach. smooth	do	do					
parsley common	N.E. wing I.	4	failed				
Lettuce tennis	2. 2 drills						
Radish. E. s.	do		Aug. 18. 2½ rows W.				
Kale. Malta	do 4th		3 middle				
Scotch	do 5th		3 E. rows				
Delaware	6						
Cabbage Early York							
Peas Hotspur	SW sq. IV		5	July 10			
do Pruss blue	NE						
Roman Watermelon. 1. terras							
Salsafia	1. N. Vineyard 2. 3. 4 do	9					
frame peas	4th do	10					
Potato pumpkin	E. appendix	13		July 26			
Peas. Ravensworth	orchard	16		Aug. 21			from the 7th of Apr. to this day, excessive drougt & cold. now a good rain.
Jerusalem cow Topinambours	E. below R's walk	19					

2.19. Garden Book Kalendar, 1809. Few gardeners failed, or confessed to failure, as often as Thomas Jefferson.

would significantly improve the damaged tilth and structure of the wet, sticky, transplanted soil. Margaret Bayard Smith visited in July and was hardly impressed.

> Mr. Jefferson first led us to a garden, which he is laying out on the south side of the mountain, where it commands a most noble view. Little is yet done; a terrace of seven hundred feet, and about forty wide, is already made, and in cultivation. Against the wall which supports it, are raised fine figs; on the outer side is a grass walk; and the interval is laid out in beds for various culinary vegetables. The terrace is to be doubled in length and another made below it. It is still in a rough unfinished state, and I rather think Mr. Jefferson will find, in chusing a southern aspect, and in laying out his garden so as to expose it to the greatest degree of heat, that in our climate, he will have not only more than sufficient, but a degree, which will prove destructive to vegetation. He has, all his life, been so exclusively engaged in public affairs, that he has little practical knowledge of rural or domestic management.

Nevertheless, Jefferson's sunny outlook remained indefatigable. As he wrote to architect Benjamin Latrobe at the end of the growing season, "what nature has done for us is sublime, beautiful and unique."[30]

During 1810, Jefferson continued tinkering with the garden's layout, essentially finalizing the plan for his retirement garden. Squares XIII through XVIII were laid out, thirty-seven and one-half feet wide (except for square XIV, which was twenty-five and one-half feet wide) and divided by two-foot-wide "alleys" and nine- or ten-foot-wide "walks." The western squares and allies of the garden were also realigned, "making them all exactly 36. [and] 24. & 2. feet," except for some minor variations. The sloping bank, what Jefferson called a "terras," on the northwest or Mulberry Row side of the garden, was sodded in the last week of February with turf dug from below the wall. Jefferson also plotted the location of six shade-producing cherry

2.21. The reconstructed Garden Pavilion

trees, a welcome addition, "along the brow of the garden wall" adjacent to the outer walkway running the garden's length (fig. 2.20).[31]

Jefferson's notes from an 1810 document reveal plans to design a light and airy brick structure, thirteen and one-half feet square, with arches on all four sides enclosed with sashes similar to those used in the Monticello south piazza or greenhouse (fig. 2.21). The structure was to have a pyramidal roof surrounded by a Chinese lattice railing. A reference to the twenty-eight-dollar expense of "laying 7000.

(opposite) 2.20. In 1812 Jefferson laid out narrower beds four to five feet wide, here planted in chives, nasturtiums, and young basil plants

bricks in temple" in 1812 suggests this was the year of its construction. Henry Gilpin visited Monticello soon after Jefferson's death and described the garden pavilion: "We walked into the gardens, to see the places where the best views presented themselves, & which Mr. Jefferson had fixed on as favourite spots for walking, reading or reflection . . . On a point of the mountain . . . there is an eminence where Mr. Jefferson had erected a little Grecian temple & which was a favourite spot with him to read & sit in—we stood on the spot, but a violent storm some years since blew down the temple & no vestiges are left." Archaeological excavations in 1958 and 1980 confirmed the brick foundations of what is today referred to as the pavilion, but it was also discovered that the foundation was one foot smaller than specified. Jefferson's amended notes show that he contracted the width and height to preserve a simple cube form. The pavilion's unfortunate demise, in what Gilpin described as "a violent storm," was understandable because of the foundation's perch atop the unstable fill behind the garden wall.[32]

Although plantings slowed in 1810—a year when Jefferson spent April at Poplar Forest, became distracted by a passionate promotion of merino sheep, and suffered the consequences of another "extreme" early summer drought—work in the garden intensified in 1811 with some seventy-eight sowings noted in the Kalendar. The lowest platform at the northeastern end of the garden had still not yet been planted, as gardening extended only to square XVIII, just below the weaver's cottage. Harvests of asparagus and artichokes were the earliest recorded—on April 3 and May 28, respectively. The "Submural" beds at the base of the garden wall were first mentioned as planting sites in order to take advantage of the warming microclimate created by the stonework. Notable harvests included perennially dependable peas, lettuce, and asparagus and, impressively, two months of artichoke. The fall garden continued to be dutifully sowed in mid- to late summer, and Jefferson recorded testing the sowing dates of his late-season Winter spinach to ascertain when the latest fall planting would produce an edible harvest. New introductions included sea kale from McMahon; the rare "esculent" rhubarb, unfortunately planted in the hottest place at Monticello, the submural beds; and "tomatas Span." from an undisclosed source.[33]

Jefferson returned to the vegetable garden in 1812 with the heightened energy and passion he displayed in the 1809 Kalendar. He composed "Arrangement of the Garden," an enduring document in the Garden Book organizing the garden into twenty-four squares that were further compartmentalized into "Fruits," "Roots," and "Leaves" (see fig. 1.9), roughly following the division of the terrace into three platforms. The "warm beds" were now labeled "N.W. Border," the "Leaves" were additionally divided into species eaten "Dressed" for "Sallads," or "Raw," while the "Fruits" were technically separated by whether they were "Pulse," beans or peas, or "other Fruits" like tomatoes and okra. Jefferson kept not only the traditional Kalendar detailing ninety-eight discrete plantings from February 15 to September 1 but also a "Calendar for this year," which summarized all the activity, including cultural tasks like pruning and fertilizing, through the long growing season. An edited version of this document, "A General Gardening Calendar," was published in the *American Farmer*, a Baltimore periodical, in 1824 (fig. 2.22).[34]

The diversity of planting sites in 1812, specified in the column titled "where," suggests that Jefferson was seeking a variety of microclimates in his garden—borders, boxes, hogsheads used as planters, the newly installed circular beds, the nursery, "terras" slopes, and submural beds—to suit the cultural needs of particular vegetables. In March Jefferson "laid off anew, & differently, the middle platform of the garden" to accommodate his need for varied quantities of root crops: the carrot and salsify squares were thirty-six and twenty-four feet wide, respectively, while garlic (four feet) and leek (five feet) beds were considerably narrower, the space allocated based on the needs of the Monticello kitchen. He lavished unusual attention upon his "tomatas," planting them in "boxes" on February 22, two months before the usual frost date, and documented their first-ever recorded Monticello harvest on August 14. Three varieties of "Melongena," or eggplant—White, Purple, and "Prickly"—were another novelty vegetable that complemented the "many head" cabbage, sea kale, sesame, Lewis and Clark salsify, sprout kale, and asparagus bean grown to feed and entertain Monticello visitors. Varietal collections of broccoli (Purple, White, "green"), carrot ("early," "large," "orange"), cabbage (eleven sorts), cucumber (Early White, gherkins, Early Green), and leek ("flag," "common") were also planted in rows, side by side, so Jefferson could carefully compare their different qualities. One senses Jefferson was growing more horticulturally confident, not only in the decisive way he planted the 1812 garden or wrote his modest "Calendar for this year," but also in his correspondence. He dispensed advice on growing sprout kale to the national authority, Bernard McMahon; he instructed his Poplar Forest overseer on how to sow lettuce; and he recommended the proper means of cultivating and preparing salsify to the Rev. Charles Clay, his Poplar Forest neighbor.[35]

The spring of 1813 began with intensive organization and plantings—the dry winter made for ideal soil preparation and seed sowing—but activity waned as the season progressed. No planting was recorded between May 24 and July 24, when Monticello was "laboring under the most extreme drought ever remembered at this season." Jefferson also confessed to declining mobility—"I am weakening very sensibly. I can walk no further than my garden"—and spent parts of the planting and harvest seasons at Poplar Forest. Nonetheless, he persevered through a challenging growing season, harvesting his favorite asparagus, artichokes, tomatoes, peas, and beans. Dr. Samuel Brown, living then in Natchez, Mississippi, and the source of the rare Texas bird pepper (fig. 2.23), complimented Jefferson on May 25: "But how blest is that Country where those who have spent their youth in

A GENERAL GARDENING CALENDAR,
Being a copy of one in use by an Illustrious Philosopher and cultivator of literature and the peaceful arts, not far from Charlottesville in Virginia.

Feb. 1. *Hophills*—manure and dress them.
    Asparagus—dress and replant.
  15. Sow *Frame-Peas,* the first open weather.
    Sow *Lettuce* and *Radishes.*
    Spinage—sow.
    Celery } Sow—also *Malta* & *Sprout*
    Cabbages } *Kale.*
March 1. *Frame-Peas,* } Sow all these, and they
    Hotspurs, } will come in succession
    Ledman's, } of a fortnight's interval.
    Potatoes, early—plant.
  15. *Nasturtium, Tomatos, Carrots, Beets, Garlic, Leeks, Onions, Chives, Shalots, Scallions,* and forward *Turnips*—sow, plant, and transplant.
April 1. *Ledman's Peas, Snaps, Capsicums, Salsifis, Long Haricots, Lima Beans, Forward Corn.*
  15. *Ledman's Peas, Snaps, Cucumbers, Gerkins, Melons, Eggplant, Okra, Squashes, Sorrel.*
May 1. *Red Haricots, Snaps, Honey Beans, Swedish Turnips.* N. B. A thimbleful of *Lettuce* should be sowed every Monday morning, from Feb. 1st to Sept. 1. *Spinach* should be sowed 2 or 3 times in the spring, at intervals of a fortnight, and again weekly from August 15, to Sept. 1, for winter and spring use.
November, } Litter *Asparagus,* Cover *Lettuce,*
     | *Spinach,* and tender plants. Plant
December, } and trim *Trees, Vines, Raspberries,*
     | *Gooseberries, Currants.* Trench
January, } beds, bring in manure, and turf.

2.22. "A General Gardening Calendar" by an "Illustrious Philosopher" from Charlottesville, *American Farmer,* May 21, 1824

2.23. Seeds of Texas bird pepper were sent to Jefferson by
Dr. Samuel Brown, who had obtained them from San Antonio

the dangerous toils of Planting the Tree of liberty can, in despite of the Tyrants of the earth[,] devote the evening of their lives to the pleasing amusements of Horticulture!!!"[36]

After 1814 Jefferson no longer mentioned plantings in the fruit garden, and the documentary record for the flower beds and borders and for ornamental landscaping at Monticello—the planting of trees and shrubs—also became dormant. The Kalendar was the sole feature in the Garden Book until its closing entry in the fall of 1824. Vegetable gardening continued to be an adventure for Jefferson, and 1814, the wettest year in his record with more than sixty inches of rain, was a bountiful season. A Garden Book entry from November 25 records the harvest of eighteen bushels of carrots and eleven of salsify. Even on his retreats to Poplar Forest, Jefferson longed for his Monticello garden, writing in June that "I have not seen a pea since I left Albemarle, and have no vegetables but spinach and scrubby lettuce." The Kalendar suggests that virtually the entire terrace was planted with traditional favorites, and Jefferson still stubbornly followed a modified

version of the "fruits, roots, and leaves" scheme. Jefferson thanked Samuel Brown for chick peas and more bird pepper seeds and wrote, "Planting is one of my great amusements, and even of those things which can only be for posterity, for a Septuagenary has no right to count on any thing beyond annuals."[37]

The Kalendar from 1815 to 1824 reflects the efficiency of a mature garden and the wisdom of a mature gardener. The garden was now a cultivated display of Jefferson's favorite vegetables, specific varieties he had winnowed out during a lifetime of experimentation. Four pea varieties stand out for their "simple pleasures": Frame peas because of their earliness; Leadman's Dwarf for their midseason harvest; Hotspurs, also for their frantic growth; and Marrowfats, less delicately flavored than the spring varieties but treasured for their late ripening season and storage capability. Lima beans were ideal for the microclimate of the garden, but Jefferson also had chosen the "very delicious" "long haricot," a pole bean from Georgia's General Thomas Sumpter, and a bush bean, the "grey" snap he described as "the best kind of Snap." Jefferson continued to rely on both summer and winter spinach. Four favorite lettuce varieties—White Loaf, Brown Dutch, Tennis-ball, and "Ice"—dominate the Kalendar pages. Endive and the unusual cold-hardy orach were essential greens for salads of lettuce and spinach, while beets, carrots, the "delicate" salsify, and radishes ruled the tribe of "roots." Tomatoes and okra became culinary trophies, but also necessities for the Monticello table. Sea kale was finally established in the 1821 garden, and Jefferson was endlessly fascinated with the sprout kale he received from André Thöuin. He described it as "the finest winter vegetable we have." Savoy was established as the cabbage variety of choice, turnips were sowed yearly for the winter garden, and both parsley and celery, which Jefferson decided could be more successfully grown in the moist "low grounds," became Monticello staples. Jefferson described his health as "good" but "feeble," and farm management had been passed to his grandson,

Thomas Jefferson Randolph. The landscape of Poplar Forest, which he visited four times that year, and the building of the University of Virginia, dominated Jefferson's creative energies.[38]

Gardening was Jefferson's defiance of age, but the size of the garden was gradually reduced to accommodate his increasing debility. The average number of annual plantings from 1817 to 1824 was thirty-eight, though Kalendar columns on planting sites and harvest dates were mostly blank. Throughout these years, Jefferson continued to exchange plants and seeds with friends and neighbors, but time was catching up with him. He turned eighty-one on April 13, 1824, and wrote the following March that he was "worn down by time in bodily strength, unable to walk even into my garden without too much fatigue." At eighty-two, Jefferson's irrepressible enthusiasm for experimenting with the latest horticultural curiosity was temporarily rekindled. On November 29, 1825, he wrote Thomas Worthington, a former Ohio governor, and asked if he would "spare a few seeds to a beggar" of a "mammoth" cucumber described in a Cleveland newspaper. Jefferson's echoing statement, "Tho' an old man I am but a young gardener," never seemed so apt a summary of one man's late-life passion for the powers of the earth.[39]

3.1. "How sublime to look down into the workhouse of nature, to see her clouds, hail, snow, rain, thunder, all fabricated at our feet"—Thomas Jefferson to Maria Cosway, October 12, 1786

3. The Garden and Its People

THE SITE OF THE MONTICELLO VEGETABLE GARDEN was chosen not only because of its southeast exposure but also for the dramatic, forty-mile view to the south and east, an expansive panorama over the rolling Virginia Piedmont broken by the picturesque uplift of Montalto, the "high mountain" to the southwest. George Tucker, a professor at the University of Virginia, described this "sea view" in 1837: "a vast extent of wooded champaign which . . . has that appearance . . . where it approaches the horizon, its uniform gray tint is nearly the same as a distant view of the ocean." Margaret Bayard Smith recalled how "the interval between MONTICELLO and the Alleghany mountains (from sixty to eighty miles) was covered with a thick fog or vapor which had the appearance of an ocean, and was unbroken, except where wood-crowned hills rose from the plains and looked like verdant islands." This was an evolving scene during the time Jefferson lived at Monticello (fig. 3.2). The forested landscape of 1770 gradually gave way to a checkerboard of forest and field, and as tobacco culture declined and wheat growing increased, larger expanses of cultivated land became more dominant during the last twenty years of Jefferson's life.[1]

Most eighteenth-century Virginia plantation homes were on elevated sites, generally along the James, Rappahannock, and Potomac Rivers, and many Virginia gentlemen created artificial terraces that descended from the prominence of their homes to the river. Terraced or "falling" gardens were common along what the Marquis de Chastellux described as "the garden of Virginia," the James River. Belvidere, William Byrd III's seat on the falls above Richmond, William Byrd I's Westover, and David Meade's Maycox possessed commanding sites and elegant terraces leading to the James River. Nearby Carter's Grove was organized in a series of turfed terraces that culminated in an enclosed kitchen garden laid out in a symmetrical, geometric plan (fig. 3.3). Landon Carter's Sabine Hall (fig. 3.4), built on the north side of the Rappahannock River, had six deep terraces, the highest cultivated with ornamentals and vegetables, and John Tayloe's Mount Airy included a terraced kitchen garden, greenhouses, and a

3.2. Margaret Bayard Smith wrote in 1809 that the garden "commands a most noble view"

bowling green. Of course, not all American vegetable gardens around 1800 were terraced. Colonel Francis Taylor owned and oversaw the farming activities at Midland Plantation, within walking distance of the Orange, Virginia, courthouse. Taylor's diary, kept between 1787 and 1799, shows how his garden sprawled from the main house in a series of squares, beds, and patches, resembling an agricultural truck garden more than a formally laid-out terraced kitchen garden. Joseph Hornsby identified vegetable plantings in his diary of 1798 at the "bottom" of his Kentucky garden, suggesting a significant topographical variation. On the other hand, George Mason's Gunston Hall on the Potomac and Mount Clare in Baltimore, the home of Charles Carroll Barrister, were additional examples of elevated houses with descending terraces. After a visit to Mount Clare, John Adams wrote, "There is a descent not far from the house; you have a fine garden, then you descend a few steps and have another fine garden; you go down a few more have another." Many of these "falls" were planted with turfgrass, some had elegant grass ramps or ornamental plantings of herbaceous flowers or even fruit orchards, but others were cultivated in kitchen vegetables (fig. 3.5).[2]

The Monticello garden's terrace, so deeply gouged from the hillside, as well

3.3. The garden at Carter's Grove Plantation, built and developed by Robert "King" Carter for his grandson Robert Burwell in 1755, was laid out in a series of turfed terraces that led to an enclosed kitchen garden. It was re-created after archaeological excavations in the 1970s.

3.4. The upper terrace at Landon Carter's Sabine Hall along the Rappahannock River was planted in ornamentals until Carter, depressed by ill health in 1777, plowed up his flower beds to plant turnips

3.5. Re-created terraced garden at the Governor's Palace, Colonial Williamsburg

3.6. The vegetable garden runs parallel to what was once the bustling "plantation street" called Mulberry Row (right)

as the ten-foot-high paling fence above, compounded the effect of the garden's southern exposure by creating a warm man-made micro-climate, sheltered from cooling winds and general air movement (fig. 3.6). Entering the Monticello garden on a hot, humid July afternoon, then hoeing crabgrass or harvesting okra, is a torturous visit into the muggy furnace of the underworld; however, visiting on a cold, sunny January morning is one of life's trips to a sun-washed paradise. The advantages of a southern exposure are obvious: the earth warms and planting begins earlier in the spring, the growing season is extended into the early winter, and vegetables can be harvested every month of the year. Jefferson's success with tender perennial crops like artichokes, his ability to harvest cold-hardy vegetables like spinach, lettuce, endive, and cabbage in winter, and his opportunity to plant peas, cucumbers, and even tomatoes much earlier than his neighbors were all due to the garden's southeastern exposure. In addition, the Monticello vegetable garden is elevated sufficiently, 865 feet, to take advantage of a natural air inversion whereby warmer air lifts while cold air settles, particularly in the critical period around dawn. Frosts that lay waste to lowland gardens and orchards are often avoided at Monticello. Overseer Edmund Bacon recalled, "I have never seen such a place for fruit. It was so high that it never failed."[3]

Although impressively massive for today's visitors, the size of the garden—two acres of kitchen vegetables and another four or five of fruit—was typical for a Virginia plantation owner. Examples of similar-sized kitchen gardens include George Washington's garden at Mount Vernon, Landon Carter's Sabine Hall, John Tayloe's Mount Airy, and the archaeologically revealed gardens at Kings Mill, Carter's Grove, and Bacon's Castle, south of the James River in Surry County. Bernard McMahon vaguely recommended gardens of one quarter to six acres; Philip Miller suggested three to four acres; and William Cobbett thought an acre sufficient. The garden needed to be large enough to accommodate Jefferson's zeal for experimenting and to provide vegetables for the crowd of family, friends, and tourists who visited Monticello.

Thomas Jefferson, First in Food

Jefferson once labeled his philosophy of life "Epicurean" in his conviction that general happiness was the goal of one's mortal days. Jefferson's lifelong fascination with food and wine has elevated him to a lofty place in the popular history of American cuisine. His statements about wine, "No nation is drunken where wine is cheap," and "Wine . . . [is] an indispensable to my health," endear him to modern wine lovers. His adoption of French culinary traditions, the testimonials of those who ate at Monticello and the President's House, "in good taste and abundance," and the exaggerated claims about his introduction of ice cream, pasta, and tomatoes have reinforced his reputation as a singular public figure who loved good food.[4]

Jefferson himself recorded only ten recipes, and our knowledge of what and how food was prepared at Monticello is based on a series of sources, including the "family" recipes composed by Jefferson's granddaughters Septimia Meikleham and Virginia Randolph Trist and reputedly taken from their mother, Martha Jefferson Randolph. Many of these were similar, and even identical, to some fifty recipes in Mary Randolph's *Virginia House-wife*, first published in 1824 and considered by food historian Karen Hess the "most influential" cookbook of the nineteenth century (fig. 3.7). Randolph was Jefferson's second cousin and operated a boarding house in Richmond. Jefferson's personal copy of her book includes a recipe for mashed potatoes in his own hand. A window into the vegetable cuisine at Monticello, Mary Randolph's cookbook has seventeen recipes involving "tomatas," an extraordinary promotion of a little-known vegetable that was shunned for centuries in the English-speaking world. The recipes of President Jefferson's French chef Honoré Julien, some of

3.7. Mary Randolph, author of *The Virginia House-wife*,
1824, by Charles Ferret de Saint-Mémin

which were adapted in *The Virginia House-wife,* provide insight into what and how vegetables were prepared. Jefferson compiled a "master plan" of presidential meals, probably dictated from written or oral reports by Julien or Lemaire, which reveals a decidedly French influence between 1801 and 1809. The Jefferson family also supplemented its vegetable choices with purchases from enslaved men and women, who cultivated their own gardens and maintained an independent economy based on the production and sale of produce. Tabulating these purchases, as well as surveying the contents of the family recipes, provides another key to understanding Jefferson's vegetable world.[5]

According to his granddaughter Ellen Randolph Coolidge, Jefferson "lived principally on vegetables, and friends of a vegetarian system might almost claim him as one of themselves. The little meat he took seemed merely as a seasoning for his vegetables." Jefferson was hardly a true vegetarian. During Jefferson's presidency, Etienne Lemaire purchased massive quantities of beef, lamb, pork, and mutton for President's House dinners. Jefferson enjoyed guinea fowl, lamb, mutton, and his favored boiled beef "Bouilli." Cornelia Jefferson Randolph recalled years after her grandfather's death, "I have no doubt that his Bouilli and his vegetables and his silver fork were all looked upon with good humoured indulgence by his friends and perhaps considered by his enemies as so many proofs of his being under French influence and conspiracy with Bonaparte." Nevertheless, Jefferson's preference for vegetables justified the singular importance of the Monticello garden, and its exaggerated size was necessary to feed the large family that resided at Monticello, even during his absences, and the "streams of visitors" that came to Monticello after his retirement (fig. 3.8). Nineteenth-century plantation protocol held that no visitor was turned away, and Martha Randolph affirmed the record number of overnight guests at fifty. Dinner guests came from far and wide, "from all the States of the Union," to pay homage to the sage of Monticello.[6]

The Jefferson family recipes, including those passed to and conceived by Mary Randolph, present a savory tableau that exploits the rich flavors provided by the vegetable realm. Surprisingly involved preparations include the elaborate stuffed cabbage puddings and Monticello "chartreuse," an artfully arranged display of root crops, "for a ceremonious dinner." President Jefferson served French fries at the President's House, perhaps a first, and Mary Randolph provided what may have been the first American recipe for potato chips, both influenced by French chefs. The internationalism of the Monticello kitchen is expressed by the family recipes for Mexican black bean soup and the Spanish dish *olla*. Eggplant can be traced through a maze of cultures and was first prepared for Jefferson by his enslaved cook, Peter Hemings, from a recipe recommended by a French neighbor, Peter Derieux. Northern Europeans were scared of tomatoes, yet Jefferson planted them every year, and family recipes abound for the strange and sexy "love apple." Indian corn was as much, and perhaps more, of a staple of the early nineteenth-century table—across the entire social spectrum—as it is today. Finally, the centrality of black-eyed peas, turnip greens, and sprouts prepared with ham in the "Virginia style," tomatoes and okra, lima beans, cymlins, sweet potatoes, and West Indian gherkins reflect the vernacular Virginian and, at times, the African American, influence on the vegetable cuisine at Monticello (fig. 3.9).[7]

Gardening with the Neighbors

Although regarded as among the foremost cerebral figures in American history, Jefferson was so immersed in public life and a staggering world of outside interests that his cultivation of personal friendships is a surprising facet of his personality. He sought "rational society" which "informs the mind, sweetens the temper, cheers our spirits, and promotes health." This desire for companionship was expressed early in Jefferson's youth by his close friendships with boyhood pals John Page, William Fleming, and

3.8. The restored Monticello kitchen

3.9. Monticello harvest

Robert Skipwith. As a student in Williamsburg, Jefferson's search for a rational society based on a warm and open intellectual commerce was shown by his association with George Wythe, Governor Francis Fauquier, and William Small. Jefferson elevated conversation to one of the fine arts in the salons of Paris, in dinner parties at the President's House in Washington, and in retirement at Monticello. When he established the University of Virginia, Jefferson drew another group of like-minded friends into his companionable social orbit. "Rational society" was expressed by the free and easy flow of conversation at the dinner table and over wine after the meal. He wrote, "From dinner to dark I give to society & recreation with my neighbors & friends."[8]

The spring pea competitions Jefferson held with his neighbors enhanced the union of gardening and sociability. George Divers, a wealthy merchant and owner of Farmington, was the traditional winner of the contest. The story passed down through the family by Jefferson's grandson, Thomas Jefferson Randolph, suggests that the one year Jefferson won the pea competition, he refused to divulge the victory to Divers for fear of rocking the pride of his closest friend outside the world of politics. Jefferson was reputed to have stated, "No, say nothing about it, it will be more agreeable to our friend to think that he never fails." Jefferson's reluctance to claim the first spring pea, his competitive wariness, was affirmed by his granddaughter Ellen Randolph Coolidge: "He had less the spirit of rivalry than any one I ever knew, and took the most genuine pleasure in the success of others, heartily enjoying the triumph of his friends where they were more fortunate than himself in the cultivation of their grounds."[9]

Divers not only named his stillborn, and only, child after the sage of Monticello but also served informally as Jefferson's personal nurseryman. His gardens at Farmington, three miles west of Charlottesville, functioned as a seed bank for some of the special plants received and planted by Jefferson that perished at Monticello (fig. 3.10). In 1809 Divers sent Jefferson the "early black eye pea which

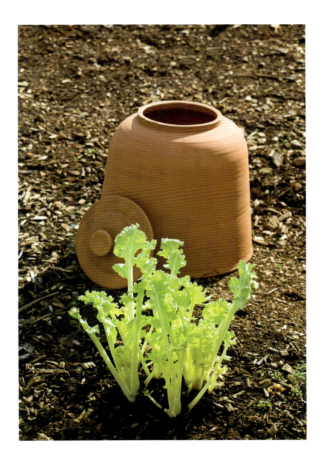

3.10. Sea kale plants were among George Divers's horticultural gifts to Jefferson

you brought from France," perhaps twenty years earlier and presumably lost at Monticello. Seeds of Jefferson's sea kale, obtained from Philadelphia nurseryman Bernard McMahon, never germinated in Monticello plantings in 1809, 1811, 1812, and 1819, but in 1820 Divers forwarded four hundred plants to Jefferson, who finally enjoyed har-

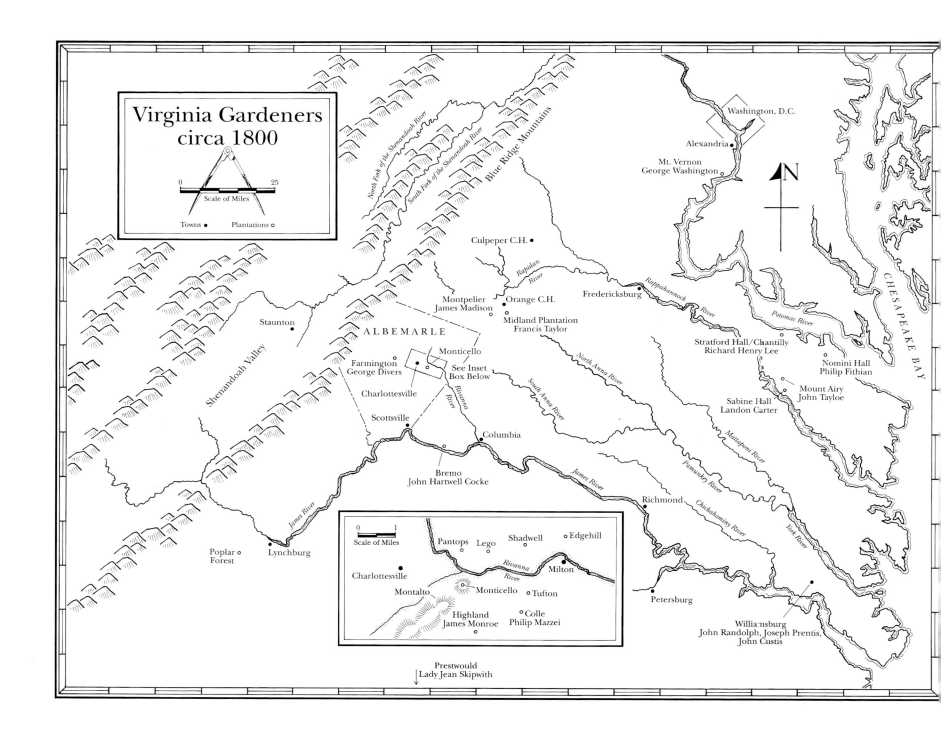

Virginia Gardeners
circa 1800

0   25
Scale of Miles

Towns ●   Plantations ○

North Fork of the Shenandoah River

South Fork of the Shenandoah River

Blue Ridge Mountains

Washington, D.C.

Alexandria

Mt. Vernon
George Washington

Culpeper C.H. ●

Rapidan River

Orange C.H. ●

Montpelier
James Madison

Fredericksburg

Rappahannock River

Potomac River

Staunton ●

ALBEMARLE

Midland Plantation
Francis Taylor

Stratford Hall/Chantilly
Richard Henry Lee

North Anna River

Nomini Hall
Philip Fithian

Monticello

Farmington
George Divers

See Inset
Box Below

Mount Airy
John Tayloe

Shenandoah Valley

Charlottesville

Rivanna River

South Anna River

Sabine Hall
Landon Carter

Scottsville

Columbia

CHESAPEAKE BAY

James River

Mattaponi River

Bremo
John Hartwell Cocke

James River

Richmond

Pamunkey River

Chickahominy River

York River

Poplar ○
Forest

Lynchburg ●

0   1
Scale of Miles

Pantops ○   Lego ○   Shadwell ○   Edgehill ○

Charlottesville ●

Rivanna River

Milton

Montalto

Monticello

Tufton ○

Petersburg ●

Highland
James Monroe

Colle ○
Philip Mazzei

Williamsburg
John Randolph, Joseph Prentis,
John Custis

Prestwould
Lady Jean Skipwith

vests annually between 1822 and 1825. It must have been comforting for Jefferson to have the skillful Divers backing up his experimental efforts at Monticello.[10]

According to George Divers's niece, the belle Judith Page Walker Rives, who was married at the age of seventeen at Farmington, "Everything about it [Farmington] was fat except its owner . . . The gardens, of which he had three equally well nurtured, produced every fruit and flower that a temperate climate can bestow in rare perfection, and high brick walls fostered many that might have perished in a less genial situation." Jefferson copied Divers's growing directions for various vegetables in the Garden Book. The first documented mention of tomatoes in the Monticello vegetable garden was the result of a Divers gift in 1809. One of Jefferson's favorite dessert apples, Esopus Spitzenburg, for many the finest table apple of all time, as well as novelty vegetables like crowder peas, Brussels sprouts, and lima beans, came from Divers. Although Jefferson reputedly backed off claims of his pea contest victory, one senses some playful banter in an 1807 letter to Divers: "We had strawberries yesterday—when had you them?" The dinner table at Farmington rivaled Monticello in the scope of fresh fruits and vegetables and, according to Rives, was an alternative to the "rational society" Jefferson aspired to create at Monticello. She wrote, "Whenever Mr. Jefferson had any distinguished visitors of the bon vivant order, he always had them invited to Farmington, as furnishing rather a higher specimen of Virginia good cheer than they found at Monticello."[11]

One neighbor who certainly contributed to the "rational society" of gardeners and had a profound effect on the gardens of Monticello was Philip Mazzei, a physician, merchant, and horticulturist from Poggio a Caiano, near Florence (fig. 3.11). Jefferson and Mazzei were merely friends through correspondence until 1774, when Mazzei appeared on Jefferson's doorstep with a band of Italian farmers and vinedressers on their way to the Shenandoah Valley. Mazzei had set

3.11. Philip Mazzei by Jacques-Louis David, 1790

out for the colonies in 1773 with grandiose visions of a Mediterranean paradise and the promise of land from the Virginia legislature, but he was later frustrated to learn that the property was divided into separate parcels. Intrigued by Mazzei's ambitious agricultural schemes, Jefferson offered Mazzei 193 acres adjacent to the south side of Monticello. By 1778, Mazzei had purchased 700 additional acres and established a property he called Colle, "hill" in Italian, perhaps in reference to the "little mountain" next door. Mazzei's philosophical allegiance to the ideals of the Revolution brought him into the fold of political life,

3.12. Upper Bremo was John Hartwell Cocke's architectural masterpiece. Painting by an unidentified artist, ca. 1830s.

ble varieties planted in 1774 in Jefferson's garden came from Mazzei and were commonly identified with their place of origin—Pisa, Tuscany, Paris, Provence—others came from Virginia gardeners and, in the spirit of Mazzei's presence, were described in Italian. Most were new to the gardening Jefferson, such as garlic from Tuscany and sorrel from Pisa, and some were exotic novelties like the white pumpkin ("Zucche Bianche") and Neapolitan watermelon ("Cocomere di seme Neapolitane"). Jefferson's exuberant Garden Book compilation of these novelties reflects both his friendship with Mazzei and an enthusiasm for Italian culture that would persist throughout his lifetime. Following Mazzei's return to Europe, two of his skilled workmen, Anthony Giannini and Giovannini da Prato, stayed behind as occasional gardeners in the gardens and orchards of Monticello.[13]

John Hartwell Cocke, another friend of Jefferson's, developed his 3,184-acre estate, Bremo, into a model agricultural and architectural village along the James River forty miles southeast of Monticello (fig. 3.12). Cocke was a general in the War of 1812, an abolitionist, a progressive agriculturist, the first president of the American Temperance Society, and, with Jefferson, one of the founders and designers of the University of Virginia. He possessed both a superb command of the practical arts—in farming and architecture—and a quirky and energetic genius. In 1816, Jefferson sent Cocke paper mulberry trees, Marseilles figs, aspens, prickly locusts, and snowberry bushes—some of the greatest hits of the Monticello collection—in return for Cocke's scuppernong wine, which Jefferson described as "singular." Cocke kept a garden diary similar to Jefferson's Garden Book. Just as Jefferson jotted down George Divers's recommendations for the number of carrot rows sufficient for a family's consumption, Cocke recited Jefferson's plant histories: how the weeping willow and Lombardy poplar were introduced into America, or how the first red cedar known in Albemarle County was planted by Jefferson's brother-in-law at Shadwell in 1755. The dinner tradition honoring the arrival of the

and he eventually helped form a local militia and inspired Jefferson's efforts at a Virginia constitution. He went to Europe as an envoy of the young republic in 1779 and became a vocal advocate of the patriots' cause.[12]

Even if the loquacious Mazzei at times tried Jefferson's patience (Jefferson wrote that Mazzei's arrival would result in a "double quotidian head-ach"), no neighbor had a greater influence on the Monticello garden. Inevitably, Mazzei's enthusiasm for grape growing and wine making captivated Jefferson. Although Mazzei's experiments in the field were generally inconclusive, his Tuscan farmers planted the first vineyards at Monticello, described in painstaking detail by Jefferson in the Garden Book. While many of the vegeta-

first spring pea was carried on by the Cocke family, and Cocke, like Divers, was a source for Jefferson's treasured sea kale. The gardens at Monticello were nourished generously by a society of local gardeners.[14]

Other Monticello friends and neighbors also provided for Jefferson's garden. As noted earlier, Philip Mazzei's French son-in-law, Peter Derieux, introduced Jefferson to eggplants, and Mary Walker Lewis helped with the winter's supply of root crops. James Madison was an integral figure in this rational circle of neighborhood gardeners. Although at thirty miles' distance Montpelier is nearly a day's horseback ride from Monticello, Madison often stayed with the Jefferson family and was invited by Divers to the pea contest dinners. Jefferson and Madison shared cuttings and seeds, but Madison was not as avid a plantsman as Jefferson. Their correspondence focused more on agricultural matters, such as a shared ambition to distribute Merino sheep to every Virginia county. Jefferson's letters indicate that his exchanges with other talented gardeners displayed a pragmatic selflessness when it came to potentially valuable economic plants. He wrote to agriculturist John Taylor in 1816 and, thanking him for turnip seed, noted that he would plant a sample at Monticello, but also "commit it to the depository of the neighborhood, generally found to be the best precaution against losing a good thing." Although the Monticello garden was a national garden, it also served as a type of community garden.[15]

The diaries of contemporary gardeners, such as Colonel Francis Taylor, William Faris of Annapolis, and Joseph Hornsby of Kentucky describe local networks of enthusiastic vegetable gardeners. Taylor's diary includes detailed notes on planting and caring for a vegetable garden that provided abundant harvests, plants, and seeds shared with numerous relatives and neighbors. Vegetable varieties were often named for their nearby source ("Major Morris' overseers' Indian peas"), and cabbage seedlings, as many as two hundred

3.13. Watermelons invite mirthful companionship

at a time, were sent from Taylor's Midland Plantation to neighboring farms. A neighbor's white asparagus graced the dinner table at Midland while Taylor was a certain source for prized vegetable seeds and plants, such as onions, "Indian peas," and carrots that were sent weekly to neighbors throughout the growing season. Eating watermelons is inevitably a social occasion; they are too large to eat alone, and the fruit's playful sensuality—the dripping red juice, awkwardly disposed seeds, and profound bulk—invite mirthful companionship (fig. 3.13). In 1787 Taylor recorded the lineup of neighbors and friends who paraded to his farm in Orange for watermelon eating: "Aug. 25, J. Colonel Francis Taylor came after and had some Watermelons; Aug. 27. C.T. family . . . came with us to eat Watermelons; Aug. 28, Hubd. Taylor called to eat Watermelon." The gardening process provided a welcoming forum for sharing not just plants and seeds but the aspirations and follies of everyday life.[16]

Labor

Documentary and archaeological evidence generally fails to reveal the quality of the horticulture at Monticello two hundred years ago: the smoothness of the turf, the vigor of garden plants, or the abundance of weeds and other pests. Such statements as "It was messier back then" or "They had fewer bugs in Jefferson's time" reflect our modern aesthetic sensibility more than the realities of early nineteenth-century landscape gardening. A properly cared for kitchen garden, according to Bernard McMahon, required one gardener per acre. Jefferson intended to provide professional care for the gardens at Monticello and wrote as early as 1771 to a friend in Scotland, Alex McCaul, requesting he "send me a gardener from 10 to 15 [pounds] a year, indentured for five years." With the exception of Robert Bailey's short tenure between 1794 and 1797, the hiring of a professional gardener was an investment Jefferson never completely made. Martha Jefferson Randolph's observation that "at a distance it [the garden] looks very green but it does not bear close examination the weeds having taken possession of much the greater part of it" captures the reality of the horticulture quality of Jefferson's garden, as maintenance at Monticello appears to have been sporadic and sometimes haphazard.[17]

The mature flower gardens at Monticello—the winding walk and oval beds installed in 1807 and 1808—were cared for by Jefferson's granddaughters, especially his oldest, Anne Cary Randolph, and by enslaved African American Wormley Hughes (fig. 3.14). According to granddaughter Ellen Randolph Coolidge, Jefferson himself "directed" the work, spaced bulbs, and labeled the varieties with inscribed wooden stakes. Hughes was "armed with spade and hoe," preparing the beds for Jefferson's daughter Martha and her two daughters, Anne and Ellen, to do the actual planting. The Monticello fruit garden and vineyards, on the other hand, were cared for, at least at times, by European professional gardeners. Anthony Giannini, who arrived with the Philip Mazzei party in 1773, was later hired by Jefferson as a Monticello gardener, as was Giovannini da Prato, another remnant of the Italian workers who settled initially at the nearby farm of Colle.[18]

William Cobbett wrote that "the best security against the effects of this foible of human nature is, for the owner of the garden to be *head gardener himself.*" Jefferson's detailed recording of the Kalendar from 1809 to 1824 is convincing evidence that, at least, he was counting the bean seeds that were sowed in regularly spaced rows. Isaac (Granger) Jefferson's recollections of Jefferson working "in right hard earnest" reinforce the assumption that he actively participated, as does Margaret Bayard Smith's reminiscence of her visit in 1809, when she implied that he sowed the vegetable seeds himself (fig. 3.15). But others performed most of the basic and necessary garden duties, transporting the portable seed rack from site to site, hoeing weeds, digging the soil, hauling manure, harvesting produce, and even sowing lettuce seed when Jefferson was at Poplar Forest. A series of enslaved Monticello gardeners—Tom Shackleford, John, George Granger Sr., and Goliah—sometimes aided by the "veteran aids," "senile corps," or "old people," were mentioned as gardeners in the 1790s and early 1800s. During this time, Jefferson was immersed in political life and gardening was managed by overseers, Jefferson's daughters, and Thomas Mann Randolph. Most of the enslaved gardeners were dead or dispersed by the time Jefferson returned from the presidency. Despite the dearth of documentary evidence placing Wormley Hughes in the vegetable garden, the 1809 directive that he drop sixty to seventy loads of manure along the recently terraced plateau makes him a likely candidate. When Jefferson looked into his seed supply to provide his brother Randolph vegetables in 1813, he wrote, "I find on examination that my gardener has made a very scanty provision." "My gardener" was surely Hughes.[19]

3.14. View of the west front of Monticello by Jane Braddick Peticolas, 1825

According to Jefferson, Wormley Hughes was "one of the most trusty servants I have." Born at Monticello in 1781, the grandson of Elizabeth (Betty) Hemings Hughes, Wormley had many responsibilities aside from gardening. He worked in the nailery from 1794 to about 1809 and was considered the "least wasteful" of the youthful nail makers. He dug the "ha-ha" ditch around the mountaintop along the first Roundabout, blasted rock for the construction of the Shadwell canal, and succeeded Jupiter as hostler in the Monticello stables. Hughes was delegated many skilled horticultural tasks, including the sowing of precious seeds in the Monticello nurseries and collecting and packaging seeds and plants for shipment to Jefferson's gardening friends. Jefferson's horticultural directives were often written from afar to his overseer, Edmund Bacon, or else to Anne or Ellen. Instructions sometimes included the assurance that "Wormley will do it," or "Wormley knows where" to find that plant. Hughes's propagating skills were expressed in the varied species of seeds he sowed in the nursery. After serving Jefferson for more than thirty years, Hughes dug his master's grave in July 1826.[20]

Hughes was informally freed by Jefferson's daughter Martha but continued to live with, and care for, members of the Jefferson family until his death in 1858. Known as "Uncle Wormley," he nursed Jefferson's grandson James Madison Randolph, whose sister-in-law, Jane Hollins Randolph, recalled, "I never saw such a servant as he is. He keeps his room like a picture. Harriet [Hemings] goes in to make his bed twice a day and Hughes does everything else and there is never a spot on the paint or hearth." As a trusted confidant, Wormley inspired family members with his optimistic nature. Jefferson's grandson George Wythe Randolph recalled his sunny refrain, "I am in no wise discouraged," when circumstances became particularly bleak during the Civil War. Wormley Hughes's son, Robert Hughes, was founding minister of Union Run Baptist Church at nearby Shadwell,

3.15. Isaac (Granger) Jefferson, 1847. An enslaved blacksmith at Monticello, Jefferson later moved as a free man to Petersburg.

and Fountain Hughes, his great-grandson, furthered the family legacy as a professional gardener as late as 1949.[21]

Other enslaved vegetable gardeners preceded Hughes. In 1792 Jefferson wrote to Martha from Philadelphia, "I suppose you are busy in your garden. Shackleford promised me on his honor to cover it with manure. Has he done it?" Martha responded affirmatively that "Tom [Shackleford] has been a man of honour with respect to the manure." Although enslaved wagoner Tom Shackleford's gardening career was secondary to other roles, George Granger Sr., a larger-than-life figure at Monticello, worked primarily in the orchards and vineyards while Jefferson was in Paris and was among the handful of slaves not leased to neighboring farmers. A skilled blacksmith, Granger helped Martha Jefferson Randolph in the vegetable garden during the 1790s, and although she complained that "Old George is so slow," he soon rose to the role of overseer. In 1796 George was charged with the oversight of fifty men and responsibility for the cash crop of tobacco. The 1797 harvest was a failure, but the 1798 crop was, according to Jefferson, "so extraordinary that I may safely say if there ever was a better hogshead of tobacco brought or sold in New York I may give it [the Monticello tobacco] to the purchaser."[22]

John, or John Gardener, the appellation differentiating him from enslaved Monticello joiner John Hemmings, followed Granger in the vegetable garden from 1798 to 1800. Trained as a carpenter, John may have been tutored in gardening by the professional European gardeners at Monticello, Robert Bailey and Anthony Giannini. Jefferson himself asked his daughter Martha to train John by using "my little calendar," probably an early draft of the one eventually published in the 1824 *American Farmer.* Gardening may have been the job of last resort for John, who was rejected as a "guard" at Monticello because he "sleepwalked" and was dismissed as cider maker because of his weakness for strong drink. Nevertheless, he propagated cher-

3.16. Grapes in the northeast vineyard at Monticello were "espaliered" by the enslaved gardener John

ished seeds of horse chestnut and pecan in the Monticello nurseries and "espaliered" vines in the vineyards, a task requiring skill with the pruning knife (fig. 3.16). In 1799 John was needed to repair the canal, but, according to Jefferson, "the old people can do all that will be necessary in the garden with some direction from him." Goliah followed John in the garden. From the President's House in Washington, Jefferson announced to his daughter Maria, "Goliah is our gardener, and with his veteran aids will be directed to make what preparations he can for you." Goliah, like John and George Granger Sr., was assigned assistants who were also referred to as the "senile corps." The garden was a likely refuge for elderly enslaved laborers no longer fit for toiling over a cash crop of tobacco or wheat.[23]

Jefferson transferred his devotion to the ideals of classical antiquity, at least in his imagination, to a deep respect for the well-rounded citizens of late eighteenth-century Italy. This sparked an idealistic plan to import Italian workmen who could also form an orchestra. Jefferson wrote Giovanni Fabbroni in 1778 with a description of his clever "twofer":

> The bounds of an American fortune will not admit the indulgence of a domestic band of musicians. yet I have thought a passion for music might be reconciled with that oeconomy which we are obliged to observe. I retain for instance among my domestic servants a gardener . . . weaver . . . a cabinet maker . . . and a stone cutter to which I would add a Vigneron. In a country, where like yours, music is cultivated and practiced by every class of men I suppose there might be found persons of those trades who could perform on the French horn, clarinet or hautboy and bassoon, so one might have a band of two French horns, two clarinets, and hautboys and a bassoon, without enlarging their domest[ic] expenses.

Unfortunately, Jefferson's naive aspiration to find a gardener who could also play the clarinet was never realized.[24]

At this time Jefferson was employing Mazzei's Italian gardener Anthony Giannini. His work became more sporadic on Jefferson's return from Paris in 1791, and his ultimate fate may have been troubled. Jefferson observed in a letter that, despite thriving as an Albemarle County farmer, Giannini "has become embarrassed and little esteemed." The other Italian workman who gardened at Monticello, Giovannini da Prato, earned wages in 1781 and 1782 that amounted to as much as six hundred pounds of pork and $291. Jefferson described him then as "sober, industrious, and honest." In 1799, Prato was said to be "sickly and miserably poor," but thirteen years later, his condition had evidently improved and Jefferson was still paying him for work in the vineyards.[25]

Although Jefferson wrote to Thomas Mann Randolph in September 1793, "I shall find it necessary to have a gardener constantly

3.17. The re-created kitchen garden at Mount Vernon suggests the horticultural polish probably not found in the garden at Monticello

at his business, and think to teach a negro at once," he hired Scotsman Robert Bailey only three months later. Bailey's list of the seeds of forty-two vegetable varieties he saved from the growing season of 1794 suggests professionalism and success in the Monticello vegetable garden. After Bailey moved to Washington around 1797 to establish his own commercial nursery, he became a regular supplier of woody plants that Jefferson shipped to his friend, Madame de Tessé, in Paris. Jefferson's patronage, however, wasn't enough to sustain Bailey, who died of "bilious fever" in 1804. The impoverished fate of the three European gardeners at Monticello and, with the exception of Wormley Hughes, the sporadic role of the slave gardeners suggest that horticultural maintenance may never have fulfilled Jefferson's idealized vision.[26]

The gardens at Mount Vernon and Mount Airy were cared for by professional gardeners and likely exhibited a horticultural pol-

3.18. "Abram's Garden" was plotted by Jefferson in this general area at Tufton, one of Jefferson's satellite farms. Jefferson's "little mountain" is in the distance.

ish nonexistent at Monticello (fig. 3.17). George Washington tinkered in his "Botanic Garden," a nursery of exotics, but his kitchen gardens were maintained by a succession of European indentured servants, assisted by one or more enslaved African Americans. Unlike Jefferson, Washington appears the diligent taskmaster, as expressed in a description of his ideal head gardener: "I do not desire any of your fine fellows who will content themselves with Planning of work. I want a man that will labour hard." The high turnover in the position likely reflected troubled labor relations. Washington's plantation manager and distant cousin, Lund Washington, wrote the president in 1783, "Indulge him [Mr. Bateman, the gardener] but in getting drunk now and then, and he will be happy. He is the best kitchen gardener to be met with." The most common tasks documented in the weekly work reports of the Mount Vernon gardeners were "wheeling manure," "hoeing," and, repeatedly, "cleaning and sweeping," "cleaning and digging," and "cleaning and working." Similarly, the 1805 "Gardener's Work" of Mount Airy's European gardener was focused on creating a tidy appearance: "Rolled the grass & Gravel & Cleaned Walks," "Mowed [the bowling green and garden slopes], watered [greenhouse plants], and we[e]d the garden." It seems unlikely that George Washington or John Tayloe toiled in their kitchen gardens.[27]

The chief laboring tasks in the vegetable garden of Francis Taylor at Midland Plantation—planting and digging potatoes, harvesting beets, burning fresh garden sites—were performed by slaves. Taylor regularly used the verb *had* to express orders, as in "had old Peter plant sugar beans." More refined, less physically demanding gardening jobs such as harvesting seed or sowing spring vegetables were performed by the master. Taylor maintained a "rough barter" labor- and plant-sharing agreement with his slaves, who traded their sweet potato plants, cabbage seedlings, and onion sets for both whiskey and cash and weeded both their own and Taylor's potato patches on the same day. Many Virginia gentlemen enjoyed working recre-

ationally with their hands. According to his wife, John Hartwell Cocke planted apple trees at Bremo "by a mathematical rule" to commemorate the treaty ending the War of 1812 and probably labored casually in his earliest kitchen garden. Like both Jefferson and Washington, Cocke had trouble keeping a trained European gardener. Archibald Blair, who arrived with newly purchased garden tools and scores of commercial vegetable seeds in 1817, lasted only one year in Cocke's employ. Around 1800 William Faris, an Annapolis craftsman, and Joseph Hornsby, a wealthy Kentucky plantation owner, both kept garden diaries and worked in the garden in a manner similar to Jefferson: performing planting and seed-saving chores themselves but relegating more laborious tasks like digging potatoes or building water ditches to enslaved gardeners.[28]

3.19. Slave gardens provided everyday staples like cabbage and beets for the Jefferson family table

African American Gardens at Monticello

Thomas Jefferson's terraced garden was not the only vegetable garden at Monticello. Jefferson's Memorandum Books, which detailed virtually every financial transaction that he engaged in from 1767 to 1826, as well as the accounts ledger kept by his wife, Martha, and granddaughter Anne Cary Randolph between 1805 and 1808, document hundreds of transactions involving the purchase of produce from Monticello slaves. Another ledger, known as the Randolph Household Account Book, was compiled by Martha Jefferson Randolph and her daughter Mary from 1822 to 1827. These documentary records of the purchase of twenty-three species of fruits and vegetables, bought from as many as fifty-three different individuals, suggest the gardening vitality and entrepreneurial spirit of the Monticello slave community. These transactions confirm the existence of slave gardens, probably cultivated on Sundays and in the early morning or late evening, that were near quarter farm settlements or dwellings on Jefferson's five-thousand-acre plantation. Jefferson himself identified only one site on the plantation as a slave garden; his 1794 map of Tufton Farm identifies an area as "Abram's garden" (fig. 3.18). According to Monticello historian Lucia Stanton, the choice location of this garden, on flat land close to the center of Tufton's agricultural world of barns and sheds, suggests that this may have been a community garden supporting individuals living on the satellite farm.[29]

If Monticello's thousand-foot-long garden provided such a legendary variety of vegetables, why did the Jefferson family require outside sources to provide for the table? Most of the surviving documented transactions—in the account books of Thomas Jefferson and his daughter and granddaughters—occurred during the relatively dormant periods of the Monticello garden, before 1774 and after 1820, or between 1805 and 1808, when Jefferson was in Washington. Produce

3.20. Subfloor pits in Monticello slave dwellings likely served as storage bins to preserve harvested produce

harvested from slave gardens at Monticello consisted of everyday garden staples, such as cucumbers, cabbages, and potatoes, rather than such new gourmet novelties as eggplants and sea kale found in the Jefferson garden (fig. 3.19). Also, no matter the size of a garden, chefs inevitably confront shortfalls when a sizeable number of guests are imminent, or when large-scale preserving projects are scheduled. The one hundred cabbages Jefferson purchased from Critta Hemings in 1825, or the five dozen cucumbers Anne Cary Randolph bought from Caesar, a farm laborer and gardener, in 1806, were surely intended to be processed into pickles or some sort of cabbage-based slaw. Finally, occasional produce purchases were out of season. Potatoes were sold in December and February, hominy beans and apples in early spring, and cucumbers in December and January. Archaeological excavations of slave dwellings at Monticello indicate the widespread

3.21. Re-created slave garden at Great Hopes Plantation, Williamsburg

presence of subfloor pits, which served not only as "private storage" for precious items but also as repositories for root crops and other vegetables amenable to cool, dark storage (fig. 3.20). Conversely, inventories of the Monticello cellars fail to mention garden produce and are dominated by fancy, imported delicacies like capers, olive oil, and parmesan cheese.[30]

Slave gardens were not unique to Monticello. Similar cash transactions between George Washington and enslaved African Americans took place at Mount Vernon, and numerous eighteenth-century Virginian travelers documented slave gardens. William Hugh Grove in 1732 mentioned "little Platts for potatoes peas and cymlins, which they do on Sundays or at night," and in 1734 Edward Kimber, an early English traveler in Virginia, described the "little plots" that slaves were allowed to cultivate "at vacant times" (fig. 3.21). John Custis of Williamsburg noted how in 1737 one of his slaves grew "a multitude of melons," and Philip Fithian, tutor for the Carter family at Nomini Hall, observed slaves "digging up their small Lots of ground allw'd by their Masters for Potatoes, peas, etc. All such work for themselves they constantly do on Sundays, as they are otherwise employed every other Day." Francis Taylor developed a labor arrangement with his slaves, giving them time off to plant their own potato patches after planting his. In 1799 he recorded how the "Negroes finished digging Irish potatoes in morning, and went about Digging their own—and finished them next day."[31]

Gardens allowed enslaved people to reserve a degree of autonomy from Jefferson's purview. On their own time, slaves cultivated produce to feed their own families or sell to the Jefferson household. Enslaved men and women then used the proceeds to buy imported goods from local merchants—tea, coffee, colorful cloth, fine ceramics, and other tablewares. At Monticello, when Anne Cary Randolph was between the age of fourteen and seventeen, she purchased vegetables from more than forty slaves (fig. 3.22). One can only speculate about the bartering process. At this meeting of white and black worlds, with Anne hoping to pass the rites of adulthood and elderly slaves like Squire aspiring for some marginal self-sufficiency, one wonders which party had the advantage. Who drove the hard bargain?[32]

A debate waged among Southern plantation owners about the desirability of these gardens. Some argued that they encouraged domestic tranquillity and tied slaves more securely to the land. Others felt that the gardens, and the independence they encouraged, led to discontent and distracted slaves from their labor in the fields. Questions inevitably arose about what crops were whose, master's or slave's? Anthony Giannini wrote Jefferson in Paris and complained of slaves stealing Monticello grapes before they ripened. At Poplar Forest, the enslaved carpenter John Hemmings reported that a disgruntled slave, Nace, had stolen cabbages and other greens from the vegetable garden: "The very moment your back is turned from thee place Nace takes every thing out of the garden and carries them to his cabin and burys them in the ground and says that they are for the use of the house. I don't set up Myself for the things that made for your table." Jefferson wrote his son-in-law Thomas Mann Randolph in 1792 and thanked him for banning the cultivation of tobacco around slave

3.22. Anne Cary Randolph by
James Westfall Ford, 1823

dwellings. He wrote, "I have ever found it necessary to confine them [slaves] to such articles as are not raised on the farm, there is no other way of drawing a line between what is theirs & mine." Both Landon Carter and Francis Taylor complained of vegetable thievery among their enslaved African Americans.[33]

Jefferson, Martha Randolph, and Anne Cary Randolph specified the person from whom they purchased vegetables and fruit; however, the person involved in the sale might not have been the one gardening. Approximately thirty-seven males, averaging about thirty-seven years of age, and sixteen females, averaging about age thirty-five, were involved in the transactions. Since many of the sellers were older than fifty or younger than twenty—Eston Hemings,

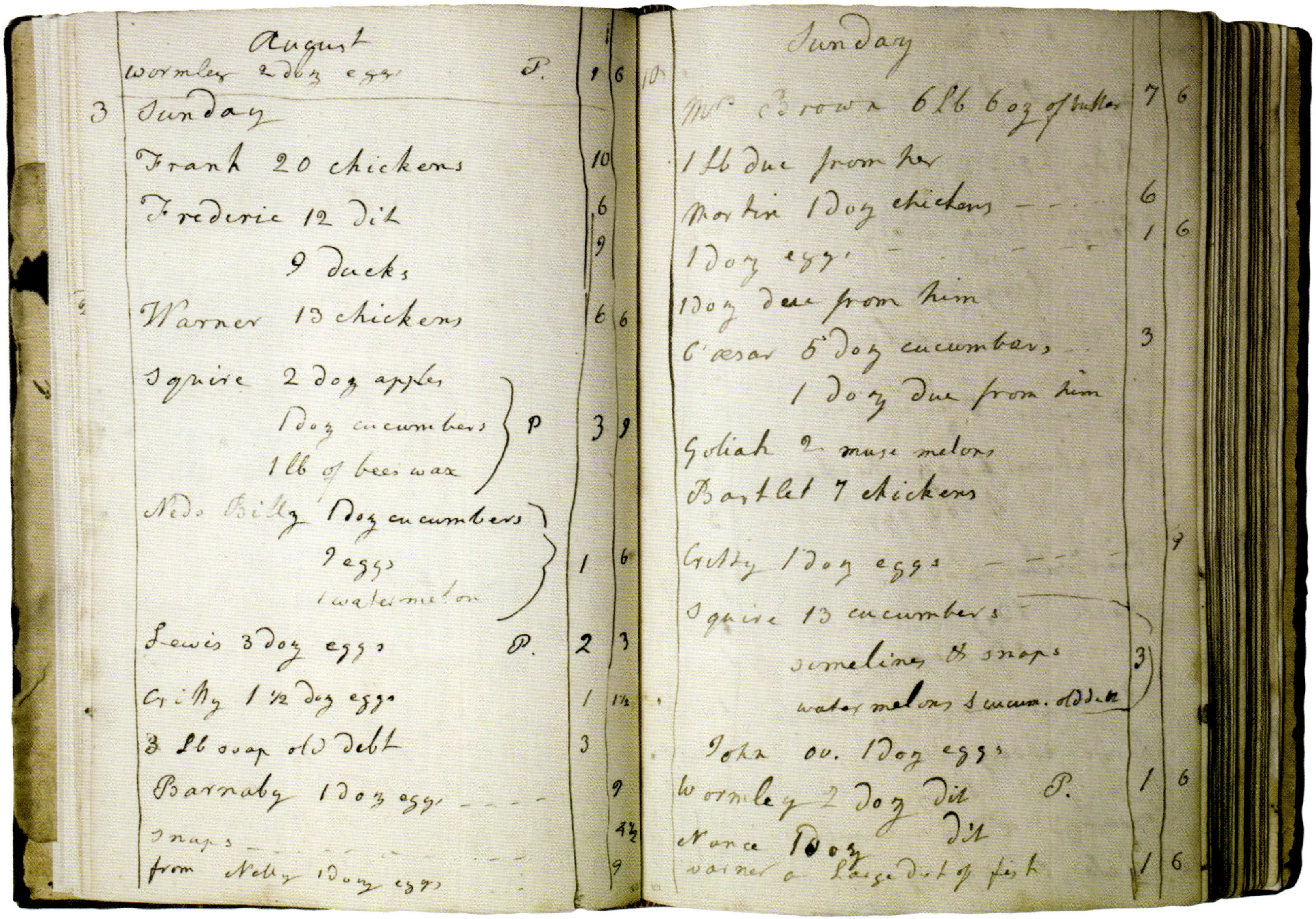

August

Wormley 2 doz eggs   P. | 1 | 6

3   Sunday

Frank   20 chickens | 10 |

Frederic 12 Dit | 6 |
          9 ducks | 9 |

Warner   13 chickens | 6 | 6

Squire   2 doz apples
         1 doz cucumbers   } P | 3 | 9
         1 lb of bees wax   }

Ned. Billy 1 doz cucumbers   }
            9 eggs   } | 1 | 6
            1 watermelon   }

Lewis   3 doz eggs   P. | 2 | 3

Gilly   1½ doz eggs | 1 | 1½

3 lb soap old debt | 3 |

Barnaby 1 doz eggs - - - - - - - - - - | 9 |

snaps - - - - - - - - - - - - - - - - - | 4½ |

from Nelly 1 doz eggs - - - - - - - - | 9 |

Sunday

Mrs. Brown 6 lb 6 oz of butter | 7 | 6
1 lb due from her
Martin 1 doz chickens - - - - | | 6
1 doz eggs - - - - - - - - - - | 1 | 6
1 doz due from him
Cæsar 5 doz cucumbers - - | 3 |
       1 doz due from him
Goliah 2 muse melons
Bartlet 7 chickens
Gilly 1 doz eggs - - - - | | 9
Squire 13 cucumbers
        snaplines & snaps   } | 3 |
        watermelons & cucum. old debt }
John ov. 1 doz eggs
Wormley 2 doz Dit   P. | 1 | 6
Nance 1 doz Dit | 1 | 6
Warner a Large dish of fish

son of Sally Hemings, was seventeen in 1824 and Billy seven years old when selling ten quarts of strawberries in 1806—they may have been representing the family garden as the most able, or appealing, salesperson. Wormley Hughes, Goliah, and John, at one time or another, cared for the Jefferson garden and so were experienced growers; however, Squire, a former Peter Jefferson slave leased by Thomas Jefferson from his mother, cultivated the most sophisticated garden. He sold thirteen different commodities, including Cymlings, wild greens, watermelons, apples, and muskmelons (fig. 3.23). On January 12, 1773, Squire sold a cucumber to Jefferson, suggesting that the fruit was pickled or preserved in dry sand or, possibly, that artificial heat in a hotbed was used to bring this tender vegetable to fruition in the middle of winter. Jefferson himself never documented the use of hotbeds at Monticello.[34]

Bagwell, Squire's son-in-law and a quarter farm resident at Tufton when Jefferson died in 1826, was also a major supplier of fresh produce. He sold Jefferson sixty pounds of hops for twenty dollars in 1818. A woody perennial, hops require an arbor or structure upon which to vine and, most important, suggest the permanence that perennial crops lend to a garden. Hops purchases were evident during the beer making days of Jefferson's wife, Martha, and between 1812 and 1820, when Peter Hemings, trained by a professional English brewer, was making a Monticello ale. Bagwell was also the king of the cucumbers and was paid for an astounding fifty dozen cucumbers in 1825. After Jefferson died, Bagwell was purchased by Jefferson's grandson Thomas Jefferson Randolph, who moved him and his wife, Minerva, to Edgehill, the nearby home of Thomas Mann Randolph. The garden of Israel Gillette, a dining room waiter and a carder in the Mulberry Row textile workshop, represented another productive African American family plot. His father, Edward Gillette, sold cucumbers, watermelons, beans, and potatoes, while Israel sold large quantities of cabbage, fifty to one hundred heads at a time.[35]

Of the many fruits and vegetables sold at Monticello, cucumbers were the most common, followed by cabbages, Irish potatoes, watermelons, hops, Cymlings, and greens. Jefferson acknowledged many crops that were introduced or commonly grown by African Americans, such as the potato pumpkin, seeds of which he sent to Jamaica's Samuel Vaughan Jr. from Philadelphia in 1790: "We have lately had introduced a plant of the Melon species which, from it's external resemblance to the pumpkin, we have called a pumpkin, distinguishing it specifically as the *potatoe-pumpkin,* on account of the extreme resemblance of it's taste to that of the sweet-potatoe. It is as yet but little known, is well esteemed at our tables, and particularly valued by our negroes. Coming much earlier than the real potatoe, we are so much the sooner furnished with a substitute for that root. I know not from whence it came; so that perhaps it may be originally from your islands." Jefferson purchased fifty-two potato pumpkins from an unknown source in 1794. He also attributed the introduction of sesame to the slave trade and acknowledged an independent African horticultural tradition associated with the culture and use of this plant. Other vegetables associated with African American introductions and culture include okra, grown liberally around Charleston and New Orleans; eggplant, an early introduction into Africa from the Middle East; sweet potatoes, which, Jefferson observed, "the Negroes tend so generally"; peanuts, a New World species quickly associated with the African groundnut and brought back to the Caribbean on slave ships; field and black-eyed peas, noted in slave gardens at Nomini Hall and other plantations; and the West Indian gherkin, a spiny, round cucumber commonly pickled and grown in the Jefferson garden but brought to Richmond via the Jamaican slave trade (fig. 3.24). Some historians have also attributed the earliest distribution of tomatoes in the Deep South to African-Caribbean introductions.[36]

Neither documentary nor archaeological evidence has shed light on the character of these slave gardens. One exception is an in-

3.24. The West Indian gherkin, a pickling type of cucumber, was among the many vegetables with an African American association grown by Jefferson

triguing landscaping reference, three years after Jefferson's death, to family members distributing peach pits to slaves at Edgehill, a Jefferson family estate adjacent to Monticello, "and thus in a few years there will be two or three trees about every cabin." Travelers' landscape commentaries in the eighteenth and early nineteenth centuries often used the term *plats* to identify the slave gardens, an interesting contrast to the word often used to describe how white Virginian gardens were organized into *squares*. Frederick Law Olmsted, America's first landscape architect and the designer of Central Park, traveled through the South in 1860 and described African American gardens as about half an acre in size. Work in these gardens took place on Sundays or at night after slaves were excused from their field labor. An oral tradition suggests that the slaves illuminated their evening garden work by lighting animal fat in cast-iron pots or pans. One can only speculate about the features of these gardens, such as the nature of pathways, or about cultural practices like fertilization and pest control. Various tools were distributed to enslaved field hands and so were undoubtedly useful for the care of the home garden. Otherwise, as always, gardeners improvised with whatever tools were at hand.[37]

Throughout Jefferson's lifetime, the Monticello vegetable garden demanded the joint efforts of members of the Jefferson household, enslaved men, overseers, and hired European gardeners. While the thousand-foot-long terraced garden was an expression of Jefferson's Enlightenment thinking, the fulfillment of that vision required the considerable efforts of dozens of professional and amateur gardeners, whether free or enslaved. These laborers took on Jefferson's experiment—leveling and preparing the soil, maintaining the plants with hand or hoe, and preserving vegetable crops through drought and pests. It was gardeners like Wormley Hughes and Robert Bailey who adhered to Jefferson's belief that the garden and its produce were "all but experiments; the precept however is wise which directs us to 'try all things, and hold fast that which is good.'"[38]

4.1. "No occupation is so delightful to me as the culture of the earth, and no culture comparable to that of the garden"
—Thomas Jefferson to Charles Willson Peale, 1811

4. The Culture of the Garden

Books on Kitchen Gardening

"IN AGRICULTURE I AM ONLY AN AMATEUR, having only that knolege which may be got from books, in the field I am entirely ignorant, & am now too old to learn." If we take Jefferson at his word or believe the testaments of visitors to Monticello, most of Jefferson's knowledge about gardens was gained from literary sources. The Monticello library included more than a dozen books that either focused on vegetables or included substantial directions on the art of cultivating them. These eighteenth- and nineteenth-century works, both British and American, were manuals of a sophisticated European kitchen garden tradition. The skill of the European gardener was tested by his or her ability to harvest fruits and vegetables out of season through the use of artificially heated hotbeds, hand glasses and bell jars, or hoop houses covered with mats or oiled papers (fig. 4.2). Soils were painstakingly prepared and fertilized with various sophisticated composts: cold-hardy vegetables predominated because of Britain's cool, cloudy climate. In England, brick walls were required to ripen most tree fruits, hotbeds countered the lack of sunshine in order to bring melons and cucumbers into fruition out of season, and fruits and vegetables were forced in winter as a confirmation of one's place in the world. The British kitchen garden defied nature.[1]

Jefferson never possessed the financial resources, labor, or desire to create an elaborate British kitchen garden. The tradition existed in America in the writings of eighteenth-century authors like Robert Squibb and Martha Logan of Charleston and gentleman garden writers like John Randolph and Joseph Prentis of Williamsburg at the time of the Revolution. Gardens of plantation owners such as George Washington and John Tayloe included meticulously edged garden squares and professional gardeners who manicured the grounds and mowed garden walkways weekly. George Washington's gardener filled the Mount Vernon hotbed with fresh

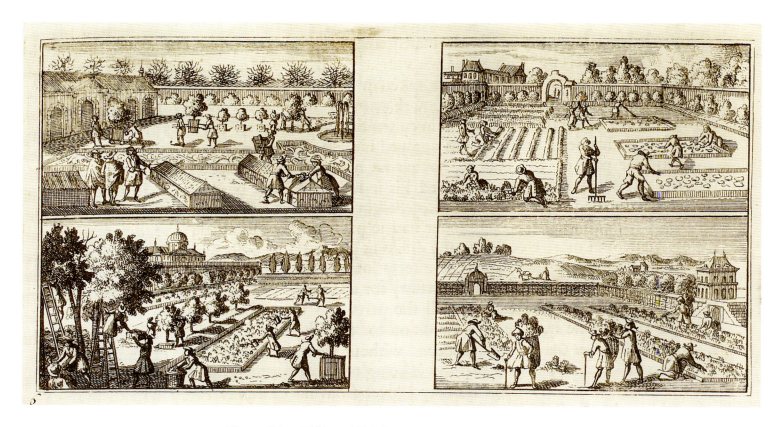

4.2. The traditional Old World kitchen garden from the English edition of
The Compleat Gard'ner, 1693, by Jean de La Quintinie

manure in January 1798 and 1799, while John Tayloe's gardener "made hot beds for mellons" in April 1805 and also mentioned the "framing ground," a larger area devoted to a series of hotbeds. Jefferson's friend and neighbor John Hartwell Cocke constructed a hotbed in his kitchen garden at Bremo, where cauliflower seed was sowed in July 1808 for overwintering with the warmth of fermenting manure. Urban gardeners such as middle-class artisan William Faris of Annapolis—cramped for space and eager for extra income—were compelled to manipulate soils and plants for optimum production in limited areas.

Although he envisioned a different sort of garden at Monticello, Jefferson did consult classic gardening books as references. He owned three editions of Philip Miller's *Gardener's Dictionary*, including the eighth edition of 1768, which described twice as many plants as the first edition (1731) and adapted the Linnaean system of binomial nomenclature for the first time (fig. 4.3). Considered the best source among the Virginia gentry, the *Dictionary* was copied liberally by American authorities including Bernard McMahon in his *Calendar*. Jefferson recorded Miller's observation on cucumbers in the 1769 Garden Book and used the *Dictionary* often as a resource for botanical names and even agricultural advice. Miller's *Dictionary* was exhaustive in its treatment of the kitchen garden, "almost as necessary to a country seat, as a kitchen to a house." On his tour of the Mid-Atlantic colonies before the Revolutionary War, the Swedish botanist Peter Kalm wrote that he had "asked several of the greatest and best horticulturists both in England and in America, what author and what book they had found and believed to be the best in horticulture . . . They all answered with one mouth, Miller's *Gardener's Dictionary* was the best of all." [2]

The art and craft of Philip Miller's model British kitchen garden was best expressed by the methods used to produce vegetables out of season: forcing asparagus in hotbeds for the table in January, harvesting kidney beans early in summertime, and using frames to

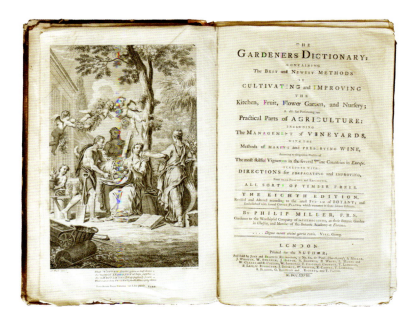

4.3. Frontispiece and title page from Philip Miller's *Gardener's Dictionary*, 1768

hasten bearing. He wrote, "England is better furnished with all sorts of esculent plants . . . than in the gardens of our neighbors, which is owing to our skill in Hot-beds." The typical hotbed was an eleven-by-four-foot wooden frame, pitched from back to front, with three glass sashes or "lights" atop the frame and angled to the south (fig. 4.4). The base of the frame, or "box," was excavated for as much as three feet and filled with piles of fresh horse manure, often mixed with leaves, tanbark, and other organic ingredients. After a week or so, the fermenting compost was leveled and covered with a foot of garden soil, sometimes placed in ridges or hills depending on the crop, and the frame covered with the "lights." The decomposing manure was usually sufficient for as long as two or three months, but often, to sustain the warmth, beds were lined with green manure along the edges.[3]

The authors of American kitchen garden publications, commonly claiming that their directions were better adapted to the climate and soils of eastern North America, likely provided Jefferson with more relevant information. John Randolph's *Treatise on Gardening* was published posthumously in Richmond in 1793, years after he had left the colonies as Virginia's attorney general in 1775. Jefferson owned multiple copies and recommended it to others. According to Nicholas P. Trist, husband of Jefferson's granddaughter Virginia, Jefferson kept "a great many notes at the end" of this tiny, pocket-sized publication. Originally printed anonymously by "A Citizen of Virginia" (1765) on a limited basis for friends in Williamsburg, Randolph's *Treatise* was the first gardening guide published in Virginia. A dictionary more than a calendar, the *Treatise* borrowed unapologetically from Miller, who is mentioned on nearly every other page. Randolph occasionally challenged Miller on, for example, the proper date for cauliflower sowings, but usually he simply repeated or modified the directions in the *Gardener's Dictionary*. Randolph advised readers to cover celery plants from the Virginia summer sun and discussed New World crops like Jerusalem artichokes and lima beans, as well as the latest introduced melon varieties. His vegetable palette was limited, however, and the *Treatise* omitted such essential Virginia crops as sweet potatoes, watermelons, crowder peas, okra, tomatoes, peppers, and squash. Randolph's summer garden would have been bare indeed.[4]

On January 7, 1805, President Jefferson sent his daughter Martha "a book of gardening which I believe has merit. It has at least that of being accommodated to our seasons." *The American Gardener*, published in 1804 in Washington, was written by John Gardiner and Alexander Hepburn and served as an abridged version of the English kitchen garden manual. However, it broke new ground

4.4. Demonstration hotbed in Colonial Williamsburg

by giving instructions on growing "love apples," or tomatoes, okra, and sweet and hot peppers; it pointed out the necessity of watering cucumbers three times a week in a hot Washington summer; and it cautioned readers about the ravages of cucumber beetles, probably unknown in England, on melons, squashes, and other cucurbits. Jefferson forwarded a personally indexed copy of this "excellent" work to his sister-in-law in 1813, adding his own brief calendar of planting times that was eventually published in the *American Farmer*.[5]

Bernard McMahon, an Irish political refugee with a modest but thriving nursery and seedhouse in Philadelphia, sent President Jefferson a copy of *The American Gardener's Calendar* soon after its publication in 1806 (fig. 4.5). Jefferson responded, "It will be found an useful aid to the friends of an art, too important to health & comfort & yet too much neglected in this country." This exchange set off eight years of correspondence consisting of thirty-seven letters. McMahon dispensed vegetable garden seeds and ornamental flowers and shrubs to Monticello, while Jefferson awarded the nurseryman and author the latest horticultural prizes of the Lewis and Clark expedition. The 648-page *Calendar*, modeled on a traditional formula, provided month-by-month instructions on planting, manuring, and soil preparation with an emphasis on kitchen gardening. It was the most comprehensive horticultural work published in the United States in the first half of the nineteenth century. Although McMahon claimed that traditional garden guides "tend to mislead and disappoint the young *American* Horticulturist," the *Calendar*'s structure, style, and kitchen gardening directions—adapted somewhat to harsher winters and hotter summers—still mimic the works of both Miller and Abercrombie. The renowned English garden writer John Claudius Loudon reviewed McMahon's *Calendar* in his *Encyclopaedia of Gardening* (1825) and suggested its derivative character: "We cannot gather from the work any thing as to the extent of American practice in these particulars."[6]

4.5. Presumed portrait of Bernard McMahon by an unidentified artist, ca. 1812

To his credit, McMahon championed the use of native American ornamentals in the flower and pleasure garden. His chief contribution to the American kitchen garden was his celebration of numerous unusual vegetables, from sea kale to liquorice and Swedish turnips to Fuller's teasel. McMahon was a singular influence in promoting tomatoes, okra, hot peppers, rhubarb (both medicinal and esculent), Brussels sprouts, Swedish turnips, endive, and sea kale.

The presence of these crops in the retirement garden of Thomas Jefferson at Monticello attests to the influence of McMahon's endorsements. Although it might be an exaggeration to describe McMahon as Jefferson's gardening "mentor" and the *Calendar* his "bible," when Jefferson planted sea kale seeds in 1819—"6. rows 100. f. long, 16 I. apart, & the seeds 16 I. dist. in the row making 6. rows of 75. holes each = 600. holes or plants. 6 seeds in each hole"—he was following the exacting specifications given by McMahon.[7]

Garden Layout

On paper, Jefferson's drawings and surveying notes for the garden in the late 1770s, in 1806, and in 1809 and later—the beds, walkways, and squares—describe a geometric grid, parallel to the house and Mulberry Row, with the pavilion erected in 1812 at the midpoint of the terrace. Garden authorities such as McMahon and Miller organized their recommended gardens in a similar way—geometrically in "quarters," based on the universal four-square medieval garden—and virtually all Virginia plantation kitchen gardens were arranged in this manner (fig. 4.6). Richard Henry Lee, George Washington, Francis Taylor, and John Hartwell Cocke all use the term *square* to refer to a sizeable garden compartment and designed their gardens with basic geometry in mind. Most Virginia gardens had a "main walk" and adjacent cultivated "squares" of vegetables. In *The Pleasure Gardens of Virginia,* garden historian Peter Martin, frustrated by the limited examples of ornamental gardens in eighteenth-century Virginia, concluded that "planters who could afford to go in for ambitious landscape schemes generally did not abandon the central motif of a large rectangular, rigidly fenced, and symmetrically planted enclosure lined up axially with the house. From Bacon's Castle to Carter's Grove, that was the pattern."[8]

McMahon's ideal kitchen garden was laid out in the British

4.6. The seventeenth-century garden at Bacon's Castle in Surry, Virginia, was laid out in a typical arrangement of squares, walkways, and borders

model, and it was generally adapted by Virginia gentleman gardeners like Jefferson (fig. 4.7). According to McMahon, "The ground must be divided into compartments for regularity and convenience. A border must be carried round, close to the boundary-walls or fences, not less than five . . . feet wide, the better, both for raising various early and other kitchen crops . . . Next to this border a walk should be continued also all round the garden . . . then proceed to divide the interior parts into two, four, or more principal divisions and walks . . . a straight walk should run directly through the middle of the garden; and another, if thought necessary, may be directed across the ground, intersecting the first" (figs. 4.8, 4.9). McMahon also emphasized the use of the borders for small fruits and early vegetables, and the planting of

4.7. Jefferson's organization of squares, walkways, and borders (northwest border in foreground)
was typical of American kitchen gardens

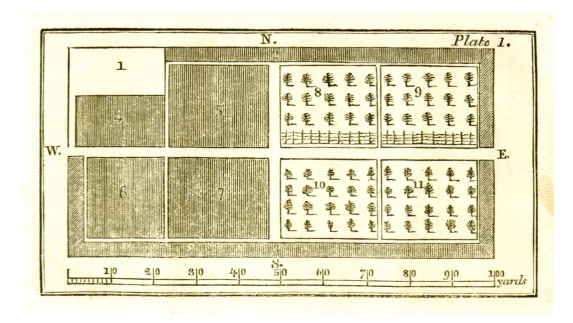

4.8. William Cobbett's kitchen garden from *The American Gardener,* 1821, provides a no-nonsense design of garden squares, including four for fruit trees

squares with the "large principal" crops: beans, cabbage, cucumbers, potatoes, artichokes, and lettuce. Jefferson adapted his basic functional plan to the long terraced plateau, but he added numerous discrete compartments—submural beds, circular terraces, and the northwest border—to adapt soils and align planting beds to the shifting needs of specific vegetables. Other contemporary gardeners such as Francis Taylor and Joseph Hornsby adapted crops to different-sized beds, borders, squares, and even irregular "patches." Their gardens were divided into impromptu squares and beds that prioritized the horticultural requirements of selected crops instead of the order found in geometric arrangements. They used compass points, bed widths, walk locations, and designated crop sites to identify where plantings occurred. Hornsby, for example, recorded how he "sow'd in a long 4 foot wide bed, S. of the Onion Bed & next the Main Walk, 10 feet with Early Cauliflower Seed, then 2 feet space, then 10 feet Latter Cauliflower Seed." Francis Taylor "had Cimbling patch planted by Potatoes patch and planted Cucumber seeds round potatoe patch." Although in each case the main garden was laid out with a central walk and adjacent squares, both Taylor's and Hornsby's gardens sprawled outward into fields and around farm buildings.[9]

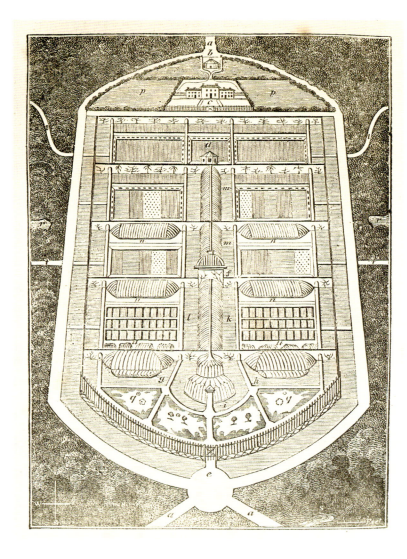

4.9. John C. Loudon's ideal kitchen garden in *Encyclopaedia of Gardening*,
1825, contrasts dramatically with Cobbett's

Margaret Bayard Smith mentioned the turfgrass walkway along the southeastern edge of the Monticello garden on her visit in 1809, but the composition of other pathways—the wide crosswalks, the narrow, two-foot alleys, and the long interior walk dividing these squares from the northwest border—has not been ascertained (fig. 4.10). Most writers believed grass paths to be impractical in wet weather and inevitably doomed by the wear and compaction of constant traffic; for Miller they were "unsightly," for McMahon, "improper." Joseph Prentis's Williamsburg garden walks were paved with gravel, but John Randolph's asparagus bed paths were grassed. Archaeological excavations in Williamsburg uncovered garden paths of oyster shells or mixed brick and stone rubble. Some gardens had both types. The turf walkways in Tayloe's Mount Airy kitchen garden were regularly mowed and grass was pulled from the routinely raked gravel paths; turf walks at Mount Vernon were also mowed and gravel paths were "dressed." Joseph Hornsby sowed blue grass seed in the "two foot wide Walks in the Garden." At Monticello, the archaeological answer to the nature of interior walkways was plowed away after Jefferson's death. Perhaps they were packed clay, or perhaps all the squares and walkways were defined by grass. Gardeners inevitably use the convenient materials available.[10]

McMahon's insistence on neatly formed and edged walks, firm and straight, likely went unheeded at Monticello, where gardening labor was insufficient to groom a garden of this size. In contrast, the gardener working at Mount Airy in 1805 frequently edged garden squares, and William Faris's gardeners routinely "clean[ed] the walks," which likely involved edging beds to straight lines. McMahon noted that, at least in smaller kitchen gardens in America, quarters or squares were edged with boxwood or hardy herbs like thyme and savory. Jefferson used unique plant combinations for the borders he documented in the Monticello vegetable garden. In 1813 he noted planting okra as an "edging" to square X, which was planted with

4.10. On her visit to Monticello in 1809, Margaret Bayard Smith mentioned the garden's turfgrass walkway along the outside (or south) edge of the garden, but evidence about other pathways is inconclusive

tomatoes, while the carrot square XIII was bordered by sesame. The use of the tall-growing okra and sesame as edging contrasts with conventional borders, which are traditionally low and compact. The okra and sesame borders are reminiscent of the castor bean row that was planted around the Monticello nursery in 1811. Mature castor bean plants create an enormous enclosure, as high as twelve feet, which may function as a barrier; their reputation as a mole deterrent possibly inspired this planting, but they could also prevent marauding domestic animals from destroying the young novelties within the nursery (fig. 4.11). The squares, borders, and beds within a typical kitchen garden around 1800 may have been edged with construction materials like brick or wooden boards, or even narrow logs harvested from nearby forests. Archaeological excavations of the northwest border at

Monticello in 1980 revealed what appeared to be borders of both brick and small logs.[11]

Soils

The native soil at Monticello was the soil of choice among the first settlers to the western Piedmont region of central Virginia. The heavy, rich clay, technically described as "Davidson," arose from the unique rock formation, Catoctin greenstone, along and just east of the Southwest Mountain chain upon which Monticello rests (fig. 4.12). Because of its sticky structure, clay soil binds together, particularly when moist, while sand, with its larger particles, drains most effectively. The Monticello soil's strong reddish hue, a striking feature for visitors to the Virginia Piedmont, is the result of the high iron oxide content within the native rock. The soil's most undesirable quality is its propensity to harden after being worked or planted or walked upon—to form heavy, hard chunks the consistency and color of brick, the tiny clay particles baked together by the hot Virginia sun. Although the Monticello soil is inherently rich in minerals and nutrients, experience has shown that its red clay is a challenge for gardeners seeking a friable, easily worked, humus-rich soil.

Questions arise about the nature of the Jefferson-era terracing. Digging perpendicularly into the slope on the upper side of the garden required penetrating into as much as fifteen feet of barren, rocky subsoil. Presumably, Edmund Bacon and the crew of enslaved laborers covered this subsoil with loose, fertile earth to provide workable soil; the alternative, barren hardpan, would support only the most tenacious soil-ameliorating crops. The lower fill section of the terrace would offer a significantly deeper soil, but inevitably, another problem would have occurred here: the fill dirt sinking or even collapsing, a certain result whenever one piles up and fails to compact loose ground. Jefferson may not have understood the need to

4.11. Jefferson used the castor bean as a border
around his nursery in 1811

treat garden soil as a living, breathing, organic substance or the consequences of gardening in subsoil. In a letter of 1811 to John Dortie, a progressive French farmer, he seems to exaggerate the depth and quality of local soils: "The vegetable mould of which is from 6. to 12. inches deep, & below that, many feet of fertile loam without any sand in it." McMahon testified to the problems of the heavy soil found at Monticello: "A clayey, strong, stubborn soil, is the worst of all earths, and must be mended by sandy materials, ashes, and other loosening, light substances."[12]

In 1793 Jefferson wrote from Philadelphia to his daughter Martha, in response to a letter from Martha's husband, Thomas Mann Randolph, who had complained of the ravages inflicted on the Monticello vegetable garden by grubs, grasshoppers, and "volatile" insects. "We will try this winter to cover our garden with a heavy coat

of manure. When earth is rich it bids defiance to droughts, yields in abundance and of the best quality. I suspect that the insects which have harassed you have been encouraged by the feebleness of your plants, and that has been produced by the lean state of the soil. We will attack them another year with joint efforts." Jefferson's rallying cry on the remedial value of manure—the horticultural rewards of soil improvement—is a stirring endorsement of the organic gardening movement. Manure, or "well-rotted dung," was the favored fertilizer, soil amendment, and compost among most American and European gardeners and garden writers. Following much of the terrace leveling in 1808, Jefferson's directions to overseer Edmund Bacon reflect his reading of McMahon: "6 waggon loads are first to be laid on the old asparagus bed below the wall, which Wormley must immediately spread even & then fork it in with the three pronged garden fork, taking care not to fork so deep as to reach the crown of the Asparagus roots. Then begin at the S.W. end of the garden, and drop a good wagon load of dung every five yards along a strait line through the middle of the garden from the S. W. to the N. E. end. This will take between 60. & 70. loads in the whole, which will do for the first year." An extravagant investment, the manure was hauled with two mule-driven wagons from Jefferson's landholdings at Milton, four miles east of, and downhill from, Monticello along the Rivanna River.[13]

Jefferson was aware of the current literature on the ability of manure and other amendments to perform the dual role of providing nutrients like nitrogen, phosphorus, and potassium to cultivated vegetables and improving the soil structure of nearly impervious clay. He wrote his granddaughter Anne in 1808 after she bemoaned the "unpromising" strawberries that "if some sand and stable manure were put on the earth, the waterings would carry both down into the clay and loosen & enrich it." Perennial vegetables like asparagus, artichokes, and sea kale rightfully received the most attention at Monticello. In 1793 Jefferson recorded covering the asparagus beds

4.12. Monticello's distinctive red clay soil was evident during archaeological excavations in 1980

Garden authorities recommended an unrelenting program of manuring the ground, particularly for perennial crops and such heavy feeders as cabbage family species, artichokes, asparagus, and celery. John Randolph of Williamsburg advised that asparagus beds receive six inches of manure every October. Joseph Prentis advocated horse dung for asparagus, cabbage, and artichoke beds and a general garden manuring every fall in his "Monthly Calendar." Miller wrote lengthy essays on dung and manure; he favored cow and hog dung for light soils and sheep, horse, and mule dung for heavy soils. Miller's manure of choice, however, was London street and drain cleanings, especially for cold, heavy soils. Fresh tanbark, wood chips, and various dungs were used to heat hotbeds in the winter. Following fermentation, the resulting product was then ideal for the garden.[15]

Although manure was the soil amendment and fertilizer preferred by Virginia gardeners, other organic materials were also used. The Mount Airy gardener routinely "wheeled" manure into the garden, especially during the dormant season, but he also "made up compost" on occasion, suggesting a more refined use of fertilizer. Work reports at Mount Vernon record how slaves "wheeled dung into the gardens," presumably with wheelbarrows, on seventy-four Mondays in the later years of the 1790s, and William Faris's enslaved gardeners implemented an unrelenting program of "wheeling" manure. As at Monticello, asparagus beds generally received the most attention in Virginia gardens. The only mention of manure in Francis Taylor's diary was a reference to its application to the asparagus square: Taylor believed in the remedial effects of fire in providing plant nutrients and burned the dried garden refuse every year before planting. William Faris regularly "dressed" or manured his asparagus beds, and John Hartwell Cocke imported sandy river-bottom soil to create his eighteen-inch-deep asparagus beds at Bremo.[16]

with a combination of manure and tobacco suckers, the unusable lower leaves of the plant. At the same time he "gave a greendressing of tob.[acco] suckers to the three Westernmost squares of the garden, trenching them 10.I. deep & 2. f. wide at intervals of 2 feet, filling the trenches with green suckers and covering them with earth." A greendressing is an unrotted mulch that, when encouraged to decompose by trenching and burying, will provide both latent fertilizing and soil conditioning. In the 1812 "Calendar for this year," Monticello's seasonal chores included "bring in manure and trench it into hills," and "dress" and "litter" asparagus. To dress or litter a bed is to mulch it; litter is unprocessed compost, such as crop refuse, woodland leaves, or loose branches (fig. 4.13). Dressings might be more refined or decomposed, such as aged sawdust, rotted wood chips, or composted manure.[14]

4.13. Jefferson gave directions for "littering" (mulching with fresh organic debris) his asparagus square

Hills and Drills, Beds and Patches

Although exceptions abounded, Jefferson generally sowed vegetable seed in forty-foot rows, or drills, running north and south (technically northwest to southeast), therefore providing a variety of light angles for the passage of the sun across the sky (fig. 4.14). According to the Garden Book Kalendar, garden squares were often segmented into numbered rows, running west to east. Efficiency dictated that squares planted with large-seeded crops like beans and peas be planted in rows rather than broadcast generally, which was probably the technique used in the earlier Monticello garden when sowing "patches"

or even "beds" of peas. More typical were Jefferson's directions for planting asparagus bean seed: "2/3 pint sow a large square, rows 2 1/2 f and 1 f. & 18. I. apart in the row, one half at each distance." Successively planted vegetables like radish and lettuce sometimes required a division of the rows into north and south halves, and when seed was short, rows were split into different vegetables, as Jefferson did with broccoli and cauliflower in 1812.[17]

Jefferson noted that in 1811 he planted lima beans in "hills," a practice common with some pole beans, but also with melons, squashes, cucumbers, sweet potatoes, and other vining vegetables. In Jefferson's "Calendar" for 1812, one of the gardening tasks was to "bring in manure and trench it into hills." Watermelons, cantaloupes, and pumpkins were documented as planted in "hills" in 1774, and Garden Book notations mention hills for cucumbers. McMahon's hills were typical, formed by mixing six or seven inches of manure to create a raised one-or-two-foot-diameter circle of amended earth. Seeds of lima beans or watermelons were sowed along the edges of the hill and then later thinned to two or three plants. Joseph Hornsby, Francis Taylor, and William Faris planted their trailing or climbing vines like lima beans, melons, cucumbers, and squashes in hills, and Hornsby planted individual tomato plants in hills. Creating hills was a practice likely adapted from American Indian gardens. Gardeners imbued with more of an Old World sensibility, such as those overseen by George Washington and John Tayloe, never mention the practice in their documentary records.

Although seed of most vegetables was sown directly into the garden, Jefferson would, at least in his most energetic seasons, mention sowing northwest border beds or "boxes" for later transplanting into garden squares. Tomatoes, eggplant, celery, kale, cabbage, broccoli, cauliflower, cucumbers, a few choice lettuce varieties, and, somewhat surprisingly, onions and leeks were documented transplants (fig. 4.15). This enabled him to "force" the growing season,

4.14. Aerial view of north/south rows in Monticello's garden squares

4.15. Jefferson transplanted cabbage plants to get a jump on
the season and to assure proper spacing

space plants more efficiently, and fuss over smaller seeds sometimes
difficult to germinate. Transplanting seedlings was a common practice advocated by writers, particularly the Europeans who were so
committed to hotbeds and artificially extending the harvest season,
but was also a technique occasionally mentioned by Virginia gardeners for crops like cabbage, cauliflower, lettuce, and peppers. Jefferson
removed the "transplanted" column from the Kalendar after 1813 as
he began streamlining the cultural practices in the garden.

Jefferson frequently gambled with what modern gardeners
call "frost dates" and consistently planted tender vegetables like tomatoes and cucumbers months before they were safe from freezing
temperatures. Even his early sowings of peas, often planted in early
to mid-February, were risky. The "warm beds" or northwest border
were well suited for such an early sowing; however, some crops were
planted so early, like the tomatoes usually sowed in March, as early
as February 22, that artificial warming was compulsory. The "boxes"
Jefferson mentioned in 1812 for seedlings of cucumbers and tomatoes

4.16. This sketch, "The portable Frame for Ridges," resides in the
Jefferson papers at the University of Virginia. Such a structure could
be used as a hotbed to start seedlings and extend the growing season.
"Ridges" were specially prepared, amended soils.

are a mystery. A sketch of what would be considered a hotbed frame,
titled "The portable Frame for Ridges," resides among Jefferson's
papers at the University of Virginia (fig. 4.16). Although not in his
handwriting, the drawing shows what could be Jefferson's "box": a
wooden frame, fourteen by four feet with handles at each end. The
notes accompanying the sketch explain how to create artificial heat
with fermenting fresh dung, on which planting ridges of "good Earth"
were formed to grow cucumbers and melons.[18]

Jefferson violated standard horticultural practice most egregiously by planting the same crops in the same squares, year after year. From 1809 to 1824, he doggedly adhered to his 1812 "fruits, roots, and leaves" scheme. Peas were reserved exclusively for squares and border beds I–IV, and snap beans for V and VI, sometimes VII. Other "principal" crops like cucumbers, beets, lettuce, and cabbage family vegetables were only somewhat less rigidly designated. Although leguminous crops like peas and beans are not especially greedy in their demands, soil nutrients specific to these vegetables would inevitably decline, while soil-borne pathogens and other pests would build up over the years. Miller, for example, firmly stated that "the ground should not be sown or planted with the same crop two years together, but should be changed annually," and "fresh land always produces the best crops." Elaborate crop-rotation systems were the cornerstone of Jefferson's agricultural policy during his efforts to revive Monticello's farms in the 1790s, so his failure to do this in the garden is surprising. Nevertheless, despite this departure from conventional practice, Jefferson continued to plant and successfully harvest peas and beans from the same soil year after year.[19]

Another questionable Jefferson practice, deliberate or not, occurred in the early 1774 garden, and in 1809 and 1813, when watermelons, cantaloupes, pumpkins, squashes, and even melons were planted next to one another. Cross-pollination inevitably occurred, perhaps resulting in confused and inferior fruit. In 1806 Bernard McMahon thanked Jefferson for seeds "of the Cucurbita you were so kind to send me, some grew to the length of five feet five inches. I have one of them now in my shop window." Was this showcase specimen from Jefferson an example of Monticello plant breeding? Wittingly or not, Francis Taylor commonly planted his cucumbers, squash, and melons around, and next to, one another between 1787 and 1799. A more conventionally accepted technique employed by Jefferson, like Richard Henry Lee at Chantilly in northern Virginia and Joseph Prentis of

Williamsburg, involved sowing quick-germinating radish seed mixed with lettuce. The emerging radish plants clearly outlined the rows of the slower lettuce seedlings and were harvested a month earlier so as to free up space for the lettuce. Francis Taylor not only mixed radish seed with his cabbage and turnip seed but also blended cowpeas with turnips and mixed cabbage, onion, and turnips together. Jefferson planted adjacent rows of Purple, White, and "Prickly" eggplant; purple, green, and white broccoli; Bell, Bullnose, and Cayenne peppers; and many other generically comparable types, the adjacencies enabling him to easily compare the varieties and winnow out the inferior sorts. Jefferson's deliberate experimentation with companion planting was unique among Virginia gardeners.[20]

Staking

Jefferson supported his lima and runner beans and his asparagus peas with four-to-six-foot-high "sticks." As he explained, it was necessary to "stick the plant ["long haricot" runner beans] with flat prongy bushes, which will let you go between the rows [to weed or harvest]." Presumably, tall-growing peas were supported by "sticking" or "rodding" them along the rows in a similar manner (fig. 4.17). This was an essential practice advocated by most garden writers. McMahon said that "peas are never so productive as when rodded," and he suggested a brush fence along either side of the row. Jefferson also proposed an "arbor" along the outside walk of the terrace for scarlet runner beans, perhaps because six-foot-high brush is often inadequate for "pole" beans. Miller recommended placing ten-foot-high "poles" for rows of runner beans, while McMahon suggested that lima beans be planted in hills so as to ascend two or three poles, also ten feet high. "Sticking" beans and peas was a common seasonal chore for gardeners at Mount Vernon, Midland Plantation, and Bremo. Joseph Hornsby planted lima or sugar beans at the base of fenceposts, and William

4.17. "Pea sticks," in this case peach tree prunings, are ideal for training vining crops like runner beans, peas, and cucumbers

Faris complained in 1794 that the "poles" found by his gardener were at first "too small," then "too big." The gardener at Mount Airy reported "making Bean Poles and Pea Stick[s]" in February 1805.[21]

Seed Saving

Vegetable seeds were carefully saved from year to year at Monticello. Robert Bailey's extensive list of varieties from the 1794 garden indicates that an organized, systematic program was pursued. Jefferson may only grudgingly have purchased seeds that he could not raise himself. He wrote Louis Hue Girardin, a neighbor and French émigré, that he was unable to satisfy a request for seeds of Early York cabbage, "He [Jefferson] has ceased to cultivate it because the seed cannot be raised in this country." After seeds had been carefully

cleaned, dried, and preserved, Jefferson distributed them to friends and neighbors. For example, he sent his brother Randolph preserved seeds of twelve favorite vegetables in 1813; however, he did not include radish, cucumber, and others, as he could not spare "my own stock." Supplies being limited, Jefferson noted in his 1813 Kalendar that the April 7 sowing of Brown Dutch lettuce was reserved "for seed." Seed preservation involved a methodical process. The first step was to allow plants, usually the most vigorous in the row, to go to seed rather than being harvested. Some open-pollinated crops like melons, beets, cabbage, carrots, and cucumbers had to be isolated; others, like the biennial cabbage, had to be protected or brought into cellars during the winter so the plant's life cycle could reach fruition. When ripe, the seeds were collected on a dry, sunny day and then preserved in an arid space (fig. 4.18). Gardiner and Hepburn recommended "drawers or paper bags." At some point, the beans and peas needed to be shelled; other crops required "cleaning" by carefully separating the seed from the chaff, vegetable debris, stalks, leaves, and flower parts, perhaps by means of sieves or fans.[22]

Later, the seeds were stored in containers: pint and quart glass jars for the larger pea and bean seeds, tin canisters and glass vials for smaller vegetable seeds. The portable seed rack described by

4.18. Seed pods of Texas bird pepper set out to dry

Smith during her visit to Monticello in 1809 held hundreds of glass vials and tin canisters containing garden seed. On another visit she suggests that this portable frame may have been stored inside: "His cabinet and chamber contained every convenience and comfort, but were plain . . . He opened a little closet which contains all his garden seeds. They are all in little phials, labeled and hung on little hooks. Seeds such as peas, beans, etc. were in tin canisters, but everything labeled and in the neatest order." The "little phials" were glass apothecary vials, commonly available at that time. In May 1809 Jefferson asked his grandson Thomas Jefferson Randolph, who was studying in Philadelphia, to obtain "a gross of vial-corks of different sizes, and 4 dozen phials of 1. 2. 3. and 4. ounces, one dozen of each size. The largest mouthed would be the best as they are for holding garden seeds." Small blown-glass vials in several sizes were imported from England in large quantities during the eighteenth century and were being produced in New Jersey glassworks by the mid-1700s.[23]

Seed saving was an essential endeavor at Monticello, necessary to preserve a collection, and a common practice among Virginia kitchen gardeners. Landon Carter alluded to "preparing" seeds in February 1757, implying that this was the process of cleaning the seed for both planting and sharing. Richard Henry Lee sowed an entire garden square with "seed peas" in 1794, and George Washington's gardener documented collecting garden-dried seed of peas, beans, carrots, parsnips, and beets in August 1798. Jefferson's friends John Hartwell Cocke and George Divers relied on their personal seed stock for exchanging with others. Joseph Hornsby's extensive seed saving efforts were expressed in a 1798 diary entry listing seventy-two kinds of vegetables—some grown in his garden, others received from friends or purchased from seed houses—organized into six paper bags. As well as being an essential means of preserving cherished vegetables, sharing seeds fostered relationships among people with common interests and so promoted a sense of community.[24]

4.19. The Rivanna River at the base of Monticello Mountain, about a mile and a half from the main house at Monticello

Water

Of all the inconveniences involved in placing one's house on a mountaintop, water scarcity seems the most serious. Jefferson's failure to develop a watering system was the most critical flaw in the Monticello vegetable garden. He spent a lifetime searching for water at Monticello, and it came, at least sporadically and inconsistently, from a well, springs, cisterns, and possibly the Rivanna River, one-and-a-half miles down the mountain (fig. 4.19). The Monticello well was dug next to the south pavilion in 1769, the year this structure, popularly known as the "Honeymoon Cottage," was constructed. The well was dug by William Beck, a handyman Jefferson often employed for odd jobs. It was sixty-five feet deep and took Beck forty-six days to dig. Never quite satisfactory, the well went dry during droughts, failing six times from 1773 to 1803 and often after that. Jefferson observed in 1818 that "the well is found to have in it a plenty of water, and very fine. It had been several years out of use." The well may have been functioning 60 percent of the time during Jefferson's residency at Monticello, but its limited supply forbade use for wholesale irrigation of the two-acre garden.[25]

Springs, a more certain source of water, were not nearly as conveniently located. The 890 acres that composed Monticello Mountain included fifteen springs that were named for the points on the compass or individuals who lived nearby—slaves such as Edward Gillette or Abram, overseers like Jeremiah Goodman, and gardeners such as Robert Bailey ("Bailey's Spring"). The North Stone Spring along the fourth roundabout was the closest of these and served as the site of an elaborate Jefferson fantasy for a grotto composed in his 1771 Account Book. He planned to "spangle it with translucent pebbles from Hanover town and beautiful shells from the shore at Burwell's ferry. Pave the floor with pebbles. Let the spring enter at a corner of the grotto, pretty high up the side, and trickle down, or fall by a spout into a bason from which it may pass off thro' the grotto." The North Spring is hardly a trickle today, and one wonders how abundant a water source it was in the Jefferson era. A more certain source, the South Stone Spring, was also along the fourth roundabout, three hundred yards down the mountain. Other springs were either inadequate or too far away. Jefferson was fascinated with their temperature, and in 1817 he took and recorded the water temperature of all fifteen springs on a seventy-degree day in June. Water from springs was, presumably, brought up the mountain in barrels loaded on a wagon, a highly impractical way of watering the entire Monticello garden.[26]

Jefferson's most intriguing effort to garner a dependable source of water was through the use of cisterns (fig. 4.20). Construction of four eight-foot cubes lined with brick began in 1808 at the four corners of the terraces. Each was designed to hold 3,830 gallons of

4.20. The cistern along the south terrace, one of four Jefferson had constructed

water, supplying 540 gallons a day. In his inimitable way, Jefferson compiled the mathematical calculations that went into the cistern construction in the Weather Memorandum Book. He recorded the gallons coming in and out as well as the square footage capturing the water. Water was collected and guttered from the roof of the house, perhaps using underground moats, and from the pavilion roofs and the terraces. Spouts were installed to lead the water from the southwest cistern to the kitchen and laundry, from the southeast to the vegetable garden, from the northeast to the house, and from the northwest cistern to the bathing room (uncompleted) in the coldest site the Spartan Jefferson could find.[27]

Completed in 1810, the cisterns began to leak water in later years, and it was not until the 1820s that Jefferson began using hydraulic or "Roman" cement to seal them more effectively. After the first batch was applied, Jefferson optimistically wrote that one of the cisterns had "4' 3"" of water in it; another had only two feet, but he blamed this deficit on flawed gutters. Jefferson tried an additional shipment of the hydraulic cement, but it completely dissolved in water and proved to be worthless. After this failure, the cisterns were abandoned. Jefferson's granddaughter Anne reported watering her strawberries, the soil "baked as hard as a brick," with a watering can that had been "standing in the sun." Otherwise, Jefferson never documented watering a garden plant at Monticello, and his scheme for the southeast cistern was his only surviving plan for doing so.[28]

Other Virginia gardeners, such as John Tayloe, built garden cisterns, and some made heroic attempts to water their vegetable gardens during droughts. Landon Carter's slave force represented an unparalleled labor supply in mid-eighteenth-century Virginia, but during a drought in May 1758, Carter wrote, "I water night and day" but "we can't long determine on any method. Sometimes the watering seems to be bad, sometimes Covering [presumably, with shades or mulch] is good, sometimes it seems very pernicious." Mount Vernon's gardens included cisterns, but during a drought in the summer of 1785, Washington complained that the gardens were "parched . . . not withstanding they had been watered (as it is said) according to my direction." Williamsburg's John Custis in 1738 "kept 3 strong Nigros continually filling large tubs of water . . . but abundance of things perished notwithstanding all the care and trouble." No matter how many slaves were directed to water vegetable plants, presumably with watering cans, such an exhausting effort—whether for two hundred cabbages or a square of twenty-five hills of cucumbers—would prove frustrating for a vegetable garden of any size. From his perch on Long Island, William Cobbett observed that garden irrigation "is a thing of very doubtful utility . . . and in most cases, of positive injury." Although the naturalist John Bartram dug canals through his orchards outside Philadelphia in the 1740s, channeling manure-laced spring water to specific trees, such an elaborate canal system was probably beyond the means, or imaginations, of most Virginia kitchen gardeners around 1800. In Annapolis, William Faris developed such a system from a well in his small garden, flooding irrigation channels or "water tables" through his rows of vegetables. Virginia gardeners were at the mercy of the elements, but because of Monticello's mountaintop setting, none were so exposed as Thomas Jefferson.[29]

Pests

Jefferson elegantly expressed his philosophy of pest control to his daughter Martha in 1793, when he blithely proclaimed that a heavy dosage of manure would "[bid] defiance" to "the insects which have harassed you." The month before, Thomas Mann Randolph had reported on the difficulty of protecting vegetable seedlings from hungry predators. "Our young vegetables have been separated from the root under ground by grubs, or eaten in the seed-leaf by a very minute tribe of grasshoppers and two species of still more minute volatile insects, or devoured in whole squares when farther advanced by immense swarms of insects resembling a good deal the fire-fly tho wanting its phosphorus." Randolph's "grubs" were probably cutworms, the "immence swarms" of "fire-fly" were perhaps flea beetles, commonly called "turnip flies" in the early 1800s, and the two species of "more minute volatile insects" or the "very minute tribe of grasshoppers" could have been squash bugs or cucumber beetles (fig. 4.21). In 1809 Jefferson recorded that his Windsor beans were "killed by bug," surely aphids or "black flies," still a common problem today.[30]

Modern horticultural historians often suggest that gardens and plants enjoyed a virgin age of innocence, free from pestilence, in early American horticulture. Their appraisals were based on the writings of eighteenth-century natural historians—from Robert Beverley and William Byrd in Virginia to John Lawson and William Bartram in the Carolinas—whose promotional descriptions of a New World Eden included deep virgin soils and pest-free airs. A sampling of early American garden literature before 1820 reveals only scattered references to pest problems in either ornamental or functional gardens. William Cobbett, the most forthright, outspoken, and entertaining nineteenth-century American garden writer, wrote in *The American Gardener* in 1821, "Fine trees, fine fruit, and large crops may be had in a country where blights are almost unknown."[31]

A few early writers disagreed, offering a more realistic assessment of pests in America. The eloquent eighteenth-century New York farmer Hector St. John Crèvecoeur noted, "Our country teems with more destructive insects and animals than Europe." Complaints about pest problems increased through the 1800s. New York governor DeWitt Clinton wrote in 1819, "Greater attention ought to be paid to the . . . destruction of these noxious insects and worms which have injured [our gardens] beyond measure." In 1823, James Worth, a frequent contributor to the Baltimore agricultural periodical, *American Farmer,* predicted a famine because of the pervasive spread of destructive insects. He wrote, "All the evils that are upon us are of our own doing, and the moment we turn from the error of our own ways, we shall be blessed with the proper remedy." Across the Atlantic, English horticulturist J. C. Loudon wrote in his *Encyclopaedia of Gardening* (1825), "The insects which infest plants are almost as numerous as the plants themselves." American garden books of the 1830s and 1840s began to include chapters on "vermin," "insects," and "diseases."[32]

Nostalgia for a virgin past in which soils were more fertile and pests nonexistent is a persistent theme that continues to the present day. According to the anonymous "Veritas," writing for the *American Farmer* in 1821, in "the early years of our country the earth needed only the seed to be sown to produce a rich harvest, for its bosom was softened and enriched by natural manure. The case is now different—it

4.21. Known as the "turnip fly" in the early nineteenth century, flea beetles infest a variety of plants

has been skimmed by grandfather, father, and son, twice or thrice repeated until its face is sadly wasted." Many of the worst insect pests in the modern vegetable garden are twentieth-century introductions, mostly from Asia, and include exotic invasives like the harlequin bug, Mexican bean beetle, and Colorado potato beetle. Other insects such as Randolph's "minute" and "volatile" tribe—leafhoppers, thrips, and spider mites—have built up in the garden due to decades of cultivation and, perhaps, global warming, and were unlikely as serious in Jefferson's garden. The worst garden pest today, the eastern white-tailed deer, is native but rare enough in the early nineteenth century that Jefferson and other plantation owners like John Tayloe at Mount Airy kept them within deer parks. An exception was Sabine Hall's Landon Carter, who planted a special field of spinach in 1778 as a decoy to divert grazing deer from another planting sowed for the family dinner table. Robert Beverley also wrote in the early eighteenth century about the white-tailed deer's preference for peas, probably field or black-eyed, "which they love extremely."[33]

Garden pests were mentioned only rarely in the diaries of Virginia gardeners around 1800. "Bugs" destroyed the melons of Francis Taylor in 1788, and what were likely flea beetles damaged his cabbage, onions, and turnips in 1795. Joseph Hornsby's radishes were "destroyed with the flies," or flea beetles. Landon Carter and Richard Henry Lee only briefly discussed strategies for the control of damaging insects. Further documentation is provided by two popular agricultural journals. The *American Farmer,* an oracle of progressive farming, was first published in 1819 under the editorial direction of Baltimore's postmaster general, John Skinner. Typical articles in the *American Farmer* focused on reviving the country's depressed farming economy with new technology, crops, and agricultural methods. Rural well-being required a knowledge of gardens, and correspondents throughout the country contributed letters addressing issues and successes with their fruit, flower, and vegetable gardens. Many described pest problems and asked for possible solutions. Charleston's *Southern Agriculturist,* first issued in 1828, resembled the *American Farmer* but dealt with specific regional farming issues. Editor J. D. Legare also had an interest in horticulture and authored a monthly kitchen garden calendar that appeared beginning in 1829. Both publications devoted space to editorial letters, a "chat" page in which correspondents alerted fellow readers to their problems with weeds, insects, and diseases.[34]

Jefferson confronted the two most commonly mentioned insect problems before 1832, the "turnip fly," or flea beetle, and corn cutworm. Although both could be considered agricultural rather than vegetable garden pests, the "turnip fly" was mentioned by distinctly horticultural authors. Bernard McMahon was perhaps responsible for popularizing the technique of rolling the garden soil in order to elimi-

nate clods and clumps of earth, the reputed hiding place of this flea beetle. The damage wrought by the corn cutworm was, as described by some authors, so universal as to move from the field to the garden. Many writers in the *American Farmer* felt the best solutions for cutworm control involved timely plowings to disrupt its life cycle—for example, turning the earth in the fall to expose the insects to winter cold.[35]

The grim trio of cucumber family pests—the squash vine borer, cucumber beetle, and squash bug—continue to plague gardeners today. The sneakiest, most insidious, and best camouflaged of the three, the squash vine borer, was not precisely or scientifically documented in the early nineteenth century; however, the damage described by correspondents to the *American Farmer* suggests that the vine borer was universal. One writer recommended covering young melons with muslin-roofed boxes to isolate the plants from "the Depredations of the Bugs," a popular technique used currently by organic gardeners. The squash bug and striped cucumber beetle were clearly described by numerous *American Farmer* contributors, including James Worth of Bucks County, Pennsylvania, who in 1823 cataloged fourteen garden insect pests and suggested protective measures for their control. The squash vine borer, cucumber beetle, and squash bug were sometimes picked off the plants; three times a day was best, according to one author. Gardiner and Hepburn's *American Gardener* included numerous warnings about cucumber beetles on squash, melons, and other cucurbits; readers were advised to "kill by hand or spread soot, wood ashes, or unslacked lime."[36]

Although Jefferson acknowledged that weeds were a major agricultural pest, he never documented the essential task of weeding the Monticello garden. The American literature on weeds, often defined as "plants out of place," was more extensive before 1832 than for other pests. Weeding played a dominant role in the work reports of gardeners at plantations like Mount Vernon, Mount Airy, and Sabine

Hall, where Landon Carter complained that the "weeds have every advantage of us possible. They outgrow us and seem to flourish on our removing them." Weeds have plagued North American gardeners since their arrival from Europe. John Smith noted the appearance of "all manner of herbs and roots we have in England" in the fields about Jamestown in 1629. Peter Kalm, who journeyed through the Mid-Atlantic colonies from 1748 to 1750, identified the native pokeweed (*Phytolacca americana*) and the European jimsonweed (*Datura stramonium*) as the "worst weeds," but he also included wild onions, mullein, native brambles, yarrow, and dandelions among the "weeds that are everywhere in fallow land" (fig. 4.22). In a letter to Philip Miller in 1759, John Bartram described thirty-five "troublesome" plants, both native and introduced, growing wild in the fields and coming up in the gardens of eastern Pennsylvania. Richard Parkinson observed crabgrass and foxtail, both European introductions, as problematic around Baltimore in 1800.[37]

European weeds adapted more quickly to American garden soil than exotic insect or disease pests. Wild onions and Canada thistles were most commonly complained about in the *American Farmer,* while Bermuda grass, reputedly introduced into North America in the bedding of slave ships, was mentioned frequently in the *Southern Agriculturist.* Some of the most dreaded agricultural weeds, such as Bermuda grass, narrow-leaved plantain (called "ribbon grass" in the 1820s and "dugg" from William Faris's garden), and crabgrass, were initially described with alarm but eventually began to be accepted by some writers as desirable pasture and forage plants for livestock. The laissez-faire approach to weed control was also expressed by William Byars of Virginia in the *American Farmer.* He recommended leaving burdock plants uncontrolled, and after three years they would be covered by "fine grass." Another author concluded, "Weeds are good servants, but like fire, bad masters," in urging a benign neglect approach to their management. Many theories were postulated on the

4.22. American pokeweed from Philip Miller, *Figures of the Most Beautiful, Useful, and Uncommon Plants Described in the Gardener's Dictionary,* 1755–60

most effective way to rid fields of wild onion or Canada thistle, "like a pert clown, sure to intrude where it is least wanted." William Cobbett complained about the "twin vegetable devils," burdock and dandelions: "nothing but absolute burning . . . will kill their roots."[38]

Cobbett also condemned goldenrod, or "plain weed, the torment of the neighboring farmer," presumably on Long Island (fig. 4.23). He documented this North American native's adoption by London gardeners and described a flower border of goldenrod at Hampton Court that was thirty feet wide and a half-mile long, acclaiming it "the most magnificent walk in Europe." Jeremiah Simple's analogy in the *American Farmer* captures the inevitable issues that arise when trying to differentiate between transplanted weeds and ornamental flowers: "Thus it is that what we most despise here as more than useless, is cultivated with care in Europe, and our most noxious plants are returned to us as treasures, and perhaps too in a degenerated state. Something like some of our dashing young bucks who visit Europe to be refined, and return to us greater fools than they were before." Beginning in 1808 an annual shipment of as many as seven hundred species of garden seeds was sent to Jefferson by André Thöuin from the Jardin des Plantes in Paris. Although some were reserved for the gardens at Monticello, most were sent to more capable gardeners like Bernard McMahon. In 1822 Jefferson passed Thöuin's shipment to the Albemarle Agricultural Society. The members formed a committee to identify the seeds and determine what to do with them. After deliberation, the head of the seed committee, Peter Minor, wrote, "I feel much at a loss to decide what would be a *suitable* answer to Monr. Thöuin seeing that he has sent us mostly the weeds of our own country. Should we pay him in kind, or not?"[39]

As outlined in his letter to Thomas Mann Randolph extolling how manure-enriched soil "bids defiance" to pests of all kinds, Jefferson believed in a holistic approach toward the tension that inevitably exists among weeds, destructive insects, diseases, and the cul-

4.23. The American native goldenrod, according to William Cobbett, was a show-stopping ornamental in the flower beds at London's Hampton Court in the 1820s

tivated garden. No documents survive indicating any active defense against pests except for his advocacy of soil improvement as a means to developing resistant plants. When Jefferson confirmed that his son-in-law John Wayles Eppes was growing wheat infested with Hessian flies, he suggested that "the advantageous remedy is to sow no more . . . than can be well manured." Pest control is presently the most expensive and complex horticultural task facing commercial and, to a lesser extent, home gardeners. Philosophies of pest control varied in the early nineteenth century as much as they do today (fig. 4.24).[40]

Benjamin Smith Barton, the country's most respected botanist around 1800, wrote an influential essay on pest control entitled "Of the Usefulness of Birds." Barton insisted on the need to study the life cycle of destructive insects and celebrated the effectiveness of insect-devouring birds: wrens, bluebirds, woodpeckers, even vultures. In 1819, many years after the first publication of the essay, Barton's pioneering ideas were hailed by DeWitt Clinton and by editor

John Skinner in the *American Farmer*. In 1823, James Worth, like earlier writers such as Peter Kalm, bemoaned dwindling bird populations and added, "This increase [in insect pests] has come upon us in consequence of our wanton destruction of the feathered tribe, which is that link in creation that seems intended to keep the insect race within bounds."[41]

Gardeners in the early nineteenth century creatively used whatever household materials available to combat garden pests. Biological control was often the first line of defense. Of course, weeds were usually easily pulled up or hoed down, larger insects were simply picked off leaves, and disease could sometimes be isolated by cutting it away from the main body of a plant. Williamsburg's Joseph Prentis planted radishes as a "trap" to divert the cabbage root maggot from his precious cauliflowers. Landon Carter also mentioned how he left weeds in his garden to serve as decoys for his choice vegetables. In a speech before the Albemarle Agricultural Society in 1824, Thomas Mann Randolph, Jefferson's agriculturally astute son-in-law, discussed how he rid a hundred-acre pasture of horse nettle by timing the grazing of his sheep to coincide with the flowering of this pasture weed. Although the leaves and stems are inedible, the flowers essential to the plant's reproduction were eagerly consumed, and the pasture became nettle free.[42]

Various concoctions, usually referred to as "washes" and often containing effective insect and disease repellents such as soap, lime, sulfur, wood ashes, and tobacco, were extolled by the most serious early nineteenth-century horticulturists. Tobacco was a popular and effective pesticide for numerous problems and was sometimes soaked for days in water, which was applied as a spray. Tobacco dust, as well as sulfur, wood ashes, and soot, was more easily dusted on vegetable crops to control insects such as aphids, cucumber beetles, squash bugs, "pea flies," and flea beetles. The use of chinaberry leaves in Southern gardens anticipated the use of the currently popular insec-

ticide, Neem, by two hundred years, and tan bark mulch was another surprisingly clever recycled deterrent. Richard Henry Lee recorded in 1780 how he "used a strong infusion of Green Elder [the flowers of elderberry, a native shrub] in water, sprinkled over cabbages to keep away flies and lice." Physical barriers, such as muslin-covered boxes over young melon plants or paper bags placed around ripening grapes to block black rot invasions, though labor-intensive, provided lasting solutions to difficult problems. On the one hand William Cobbett acclaimed the New World's pest-free gardens in the *American Gardener*, but he also sarcastically conceded that pests and pesticides were an inherent part of early nineteenth-century horticulture: "As there are persons who have a delight in quackery, who are never so happy as when they have some specific to apply, and to whom rose cheeks and ruby lips are eye sore, it is perhaps fortunate, the vegetable world presents so many patients."[43]

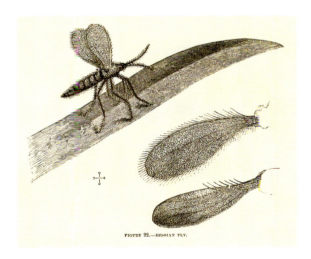

4.24. The Hessian fly or barley midge was a widespread pest of wheat around 1800. From *Harper's Magazine*, 1859

5.1. "I am constantly in my garden or farms, as exclusively employed out of doors as I was within doors when at Washington, and I find myself infinitely happier in my new mode of life"—Thomas Jefferson, 1809

5. The Garden Restored, the Garden Today

The Garden Restored

I WAS HIRED AS MONTICELLO'S SUPERINTENDENT of grounds on December 1, 1977, after serving over three years as the horticulturist for Old Salem, a restored eighteenth-century Moravian town in Winston-Salem, North Carolina (fig. 5.2). This was an exciting time to be involved in historic landscape preservation. During the 1970s, a revival of interest in historic landscapes led many American public history sites to realize that the gardens and landscape around a historic house deserve the same attention as the architecture and furnishings within. Colonial Williamsburg, renowned for its Colonial Revival gardens, began reevaluating the authenticity of its landscape. The Colonial Williamsburg Foundation sponsored scholarly studies on colonial Virginia gardens, and a state-of-the-art program in historical archaeology, led by Ivor Noël Hume, uncovered new information about vernacular gardens. Archaeologists at nearby Carter's Grove unveiled the structure of a colonial kitchen garden through the excavation of fencepost stains that defined its perimeter. Other institutions, including Old Salem, Old Sturbridge Village, and Plimoth Plantation, demonstrated a renewed concern about the documented accuracy of their gardens and the fences, outbuildings, pathways, and other landscape accessories that provided the pulse of a working plantation and a clearer portrait of the past. As garden history became a legitimate field for serious scholarship, historic sites throughout the country hosted conferences on historic gardens and landscape preservation. A nostalgic interest in heirloom plants, along with a more serious concern about the loss of genetic diversity in agricultural crops, inspired organizations such as Seed Savers Exchange, founded in Decorah, Iowa, in 1975 as a seed bank for the preservation of historic and heirloom vegetable varieties.

In the fall of 1976, just before I arrived at Monticello, the Monticello Board of Trustees adopted a resolution for the long-term restoration of the mountaintop to its appearance

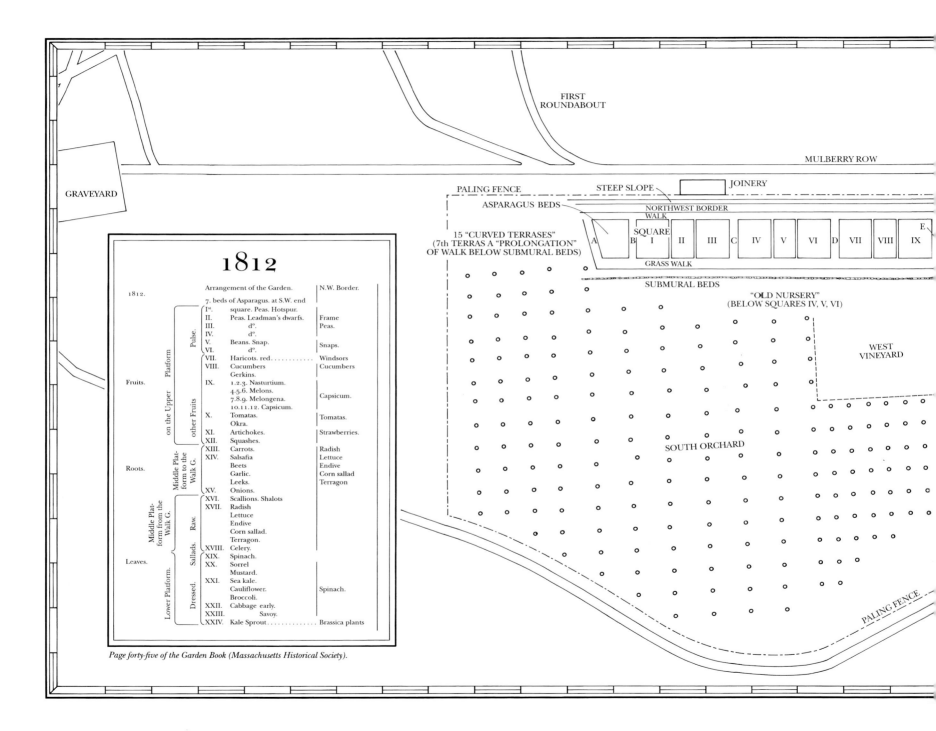

FIRST ROUNDABOUT

MULBERRY ROW

GRAVEYARD

PALING FENCE STEEP SLOPE JOINERY

ASPARAGUS BEDS

NORTHWEST BORDER WALK

15 "CURVED TERRASES"
(7th TERRAS A "PROLONGATION"
OF WALK BELOW SUBMURAL BEDS)

A
B I II III C IV V VI D VII VIII IX E
SQUARE

GRASS WALK

SUBMURAL BEDS

"OLD NURSERY"
(BELOW SQUARES IV, V, VI)

WEST VINEYARD

SOUTH ORCHARD

PALING FENCE

1812

1812.	Arrangement of the Garden.	N.W. Border.
	7. beds of Asparagus. at S.W. end	
Iᵃ.	square. Peas. Hotspur.	
II.	Peas. Leadman's dwarfs.	Frame
III.	dᵒ.	Peas.
IV.	dᵒ.	
V.	Beans. Snap.	
VI.	dᵒ.	Snaps.
VII.	Haricots. red	Windsors
VIII.	Cucumbers	Cucumbers
	Gerkins.	
IX.	1.2.3. Nasturtium.	
	4.5.6. Melons.	
	7.8.9. Melongena.	Capsicum.
	10.11.12. Capsicum.	
X.	Tomatas.	Tomatas.
	Okra.	
XI.	Artichokes.	Strawberries.
XII.	Squashes.	
XIII.	Carrots.	Radish
XIV.	Salsafia	Lettuce
	Beets	Endive
	Garlic.	Corn sallad
	Leeks.	Terragon
XV.	Onions.	
XVI.	Scallions. Shalots	
XVII.	Radish	
	Lettuce	
	Endive	
	Corn sallad.	
	Terragon.	
XVIII.	Celery.	
XIX.	Spinach.	
XX.	Sorrel	
	Mustard.	
XXI.	Sea kale.	
	Cauliflower.	Spinach.
	Broccoli.	
XXII.	Cabbage early.	
XXIII.	Savoy.	
XXIV.	Kale Sprout	Brassica plants

Fruits. — Pulse — on the Upper Platform — other Fruits
Roots. — Middle Platform to the Walk G.
Middle Platform from the Walk G. — Raw. — Sallads.
Leaves. — Lower Platform. — Dressed.

Page forty-five of the Garden Book (Massachusetts Historical Society).

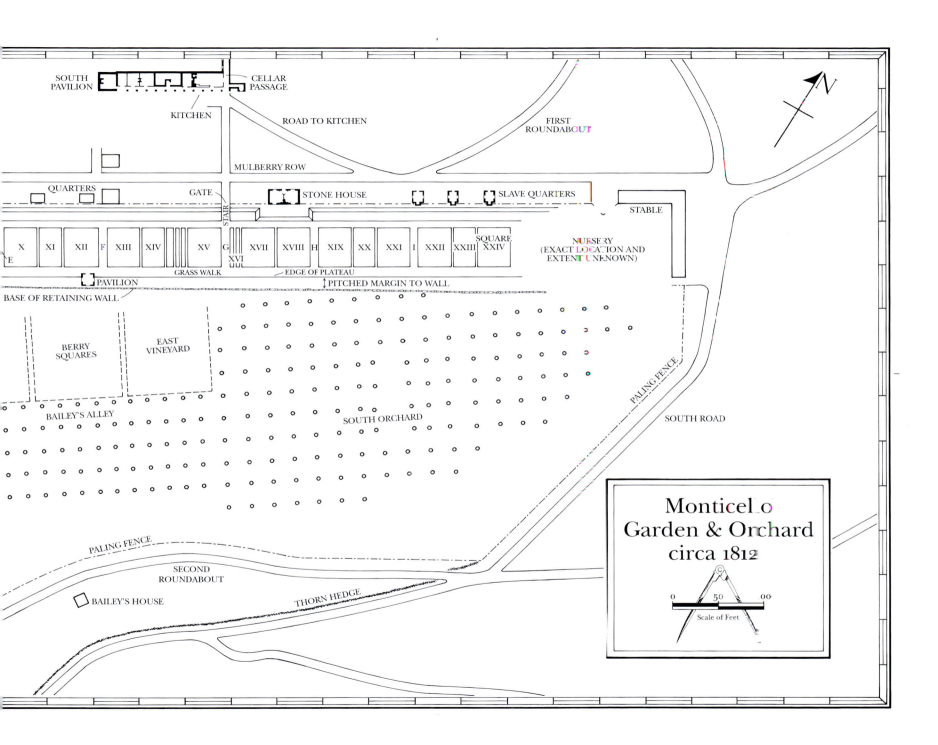

SOUTH PAVILION

CELLAR PASSAGE

KITCHEN

ROAD TO KITCHEN

FIRST ROUNDABOUT

MULBERRY ROW

QUARTERS

GATE

STONE HOUSE

SLAVE QUARTERS

STABLE

STAIR

E X XI XII F XIII XIV XV G XVI XVII XVIII H XIX XX XXI I XXII XXIII SQUARE XXIV

NURSERY (EXACT LOCATION AND EXTENT UNKNOWN)

GRASS WALK

EDGE OF PLATEAU

PAVILION

PITCHED MARGIN TO WALL

BASE OF RETAINING WALL

BERRY SQUARES

EAST VINEYARD

PALING FENCE

SOUTH ROAD

BAILEY'S ALLEY

SOUTH ORCHARD

Monticello
Garden & Orchard
circa 1812

0   50   100

Scale of Feet

PALING FENCE

SECOND ROUNDABOUT

BAILEY'S HOUSE

THORN HEDGE

5.2. The author pulling weeds in spring 1980

in the years following Jefferson's retirement from the presidency. The focus of the Thomas Jefferson Foundation, the nonprofit organization formed in 1923 to preserve Monticello, had been on the restoration and preservation of the house and on accommodating as many as half a million annual visitors. Although the flower beds and borders around the house had been re-created by the Garden Club of Virginia between 1939 and 1941, restoring the Jefferson landscape within the second roundabout had not been a priority. Under the leadership of Monticello's architectural historian William L. Beiswanger, Connecticut landscape architect Rudy J. Favretti developed a plan to re-create Jefferson's eighteen-acre grove, an ornamental forest on the west slope of the mountain. My initial role was to execute Favretti's scheme for Jefferson-inspired tree plantings on the edge of the west lawn and to clear and thin a mature forest, the appearance of which Jefferson envisioned in an 1806 letter to Philadelphia plantsman William Hamilton.

I assumed my position at Monticello eager to meet the challenge of restoring Jefferson's vegetable garden, his chief horticultural achievement. Before gardening could begin, however, a series of projects demanded my attention, including the planting of the "grove" in 1979. Soon after, Beiswanger prepared a program for the re-creation of the terraced garden and the "fruitery" that lay below it. Garden archaeology, although revelatory at places like Pompeii where carbonized seeds and an arid climate have unveiled gardens as clearly as an architect's scaled drawing, was still a relatively young field in the United States. Beiswanger, however, believed it could be helpful in defining the structure of the vegetable garden—fence lines, walkways, gates, beds, walls—and in confirming that Jefferson's plans were executed, always a question at Monticello. Jefferson's plans and notes on the layout of the garden terrace between 1806 and 1814, along with his copious Garden Book records, offered evolving and conflicting evidence about the nature of the garden's design. The character of the wall, then buried beneath the earth, and the remnants of the foundation of the garden pavilion at the halfway point of the terrace, had been partially excavated in 1958 by Harvard archaeologist Vladimir Markotic, but questions remained. Beiswanger also argued that, by its very nature, the cultivation of the land is inherently destructive—plowing and digging deep holes disrupts soil stratigraphy and scatters artifacts. In 1981 he wrote, "No restoration which involves the excavation of the site should be approved if important archaeological evidence might be lost." Pre-restoration archaeology was essential to save the existing historic fabric beneath the ground.[1]

In 1978 the garden terrace existed as a general approximation of the original and had been cultivated off and on since Jefferson's death (fig. 5.3). The fruit orchard and fences had long disappeared, and the foundations of the garden pavilion and wall were buried beneath the eroded earth. Now a flower garden, the terrace featured rows of zinnias, roses, and peonies; at that time, horticulture at Monticello meant the growing and displaying of cut flowers. The garden layout was based on the 1806 plan, composed by Jefferson but never executed. The cultivated part of the terrace was curtailed by an asphalt parking lot at its northeastern end, and the parking areas extended into two more platforms leading virtually up to the lawn on the east front of the house. A future garden restoration would offer the bonus of removing these modern intrusions from the mountaintop.

Beiswanger, ever meticulous in the Jefferson tradition, began assembling the documentary evidence for the garden and orchard, consulted with garden historians and archaeologists at Colonial Williamsburg, and hired surveyors to stake out Jefferson surveys. He also began preparing a detailed base map of the garden and orchard that compiled the Jefferson documentation. William Kelso, a protégé of Ivor Noël Hume and the lead archaeologist in the discovery of the garden at Colonial Williamsburg's Carter's Grove, was hired to find the garden and illuminate its features. His mission was to discover "the precise *location,* materials, and construction *details* of these garden elements and which elements planned by Jefferson were actually built." Kelso began laying out garden test plots on June 17, 1979.[2]

Kelso and his crew were unusually efficient in opening the way to a garden restoration. The archaeologists immediately discovered that years of garden cultivation—plowing and digging—had destroyed most evidence of the central garden beds and walkways. For a gardener like me, this meant that the plate had been scrubbed clean of

5.3. The "cutting" garden at Monticello in 1977 included rows of daffodils, tulips, and roses for flower arrangements in the house

5.4. Aerial photograph in 1979 showing the location of archaeologically uncovered fencepost stains (lower) around one side of the garden and of tree-hole stains (center) from the original Jefferson plantings in the south orchard. The fence also divided the garden from Mulberry Row (along left side of garden).

the past and was ready to be used again. Fortunately, Kelso and his crew uncovered the locations, visible as circular soil stains, of the fenceposts that marked the garden gate, perfectly aligned with the axis of the house and its underground passageway. This new information enabled Beiswanger to use the Jefferson surveys to precisely lay out the location of garden squares and walkways. Soon Kelso and his team found details of the northwest border, revealing a sloping surface and curious mix of edging materials, including bricks and possibly logs. Above the garden, on Mulberry Row, regularly spaced soil stains caused by the rotted black locust posts still marked the presence of 850 feet of paling fence 160 years after its construction (fig. 5.4). Excavations of the remains of the garden wall revealed a fascinating two-tiered construction in its highest twelve-foot section below the middle of the terrace, and also that the rock wall was almost as thick as it was tall because of the structural need to support the Jefferson-era backfill of thousands of tons of earth.[3]

The earlier archaeologically excavated foundation of the garden "temple," or pavilion, was also uncovered (fig. 5.5). Although the structure's brick foundation had been removed in 1958, the stone footings that were tied into the garden wall remained. It was a big step forward when Kelso found

5.5. Archaeological excavations of the garden wall remnants and stone foundation for the pavilion, 1980

tree-hole stains for fifty-seven fruit trees in the south orchard, the pattern corresponding clearly to a Jefferson drawing from the 1770s where the trees formed a regular grid. Preliminary excavations revealed posthole stains on the site of the northeast vineyard and a protective ditch, described by Jefferson as a "ha-ha," along the uphill side of Mulberry Row. Fortunately, these discoveries about the pavilion, wall, disturbed garden, and fence closely matched our predictions. Kelso recommended reconstructing the wall and ha-ha under the supervision of archaeologists, performing further testing on the fence line and vineyards, and postponing the archaeology for the northwest border because of its complexity.[4]

After the completion of Kelso's archaeological survey in 1981, the Thomas Jefferson Foundation engaged a team of diverse professionals, under the leadership of Beiswanger, to begin the structural re-creation of the garden. Rudy Favretti was commissioned to oversee the reconstruction of the thousand-foot-long garden wall, a complex task requiring the interpretation of the varying character of the buried original wall and the creation of a structurally sound rebuilt one. Favretti also detailed a bean arbor for the southwestern end of the garden, basing its form on one devised by Jefferson, and designed a rustic barrier to prevent visitors from stepping off the garden wall. In addition, he plotted the terrace elevations at the critical midpoint of the garden, adjacent to the pavilion where the highest terrace platform sloped into the middle platform. Kelso continued as the director of Monticello archaeology, expanding excavations to include the buildings on Mulberry Row, roads, and a dry well and walkway in the kitchen yard below the house. Archaeologist James Deetz, noted for his excavations at Plimoth Plantation, declared that Kelso's work in the garden at Monticello was "on a scale rarely if ever encountered before in historical archaeology." Floyd Johnson, a highly respected Charlottesville architect, was hired to produce the working drawings for the reconstruction of the garden pavilion. Anticipating the

re-creation of the garden and south orchard, I researched and began to assemble a collection of Jefferson fruit and vegetable varieties. Beiswanger's proposal for the restoration was approved by the Monticello board in April 1981, perhaps in part because of his uncharacteristic boast that "the evidence gleaned through archaeology studied in light of an unparalleled wealth of documentation presents an opportunity to make this the most accurate garden restoration of its kind in America."[5]

The first step of the reconstruction project was to restore the garden wall, 117 feet of which the archaeologists had already uncovered. Some sections were virtually intact, others provided clues as to the original's varying construction, and in still others, the wall had virtually vanished, leaving piles of rubble. The team developed a theory that the "garden wall may have been robbed," removed by the Levy family, the owners of Monticello in the nineteenth century, and the rock reused to construct a retaining wall along the present-day exit road that passes the family cemetery. Expert analysis revealed that the properties of rock were similar; the exit road stone thus provided a convenient and historically accurate source of rock for the reconstruction. A team of archaeologists and students began uncovering the rest of the original wall in the spring of 1981. Following photographic documentation, the wall remains were dismantled, leaving the large base stones in place. Another crew collected the stones from the exit road wall and delivered them to the site, where Shelton Sprouse, a local mason, began reconstructing the garden wall. The goal was to create a wall that was "both rustic and sound," as faithful to the appearance of the original wall as possible. Only two sections of the original wall were judged as sufficiently stable to be allowed to remain, one below the garden pavilion and another below the "stone house," or Weaver's Cottage.[6]

Beiswanger's goal, "to make this the most accurate garden restoration of its kind in America," was expressed in the exacting thoroughness of his daily journal, kept through-out the project in his tiny, grammatically correct hand. Beiswanger's questioning of every minute point regarding grades, slope angles, and elevations might have tried the patience of a less dedicated team, but his indefatigable devotion to precision, logic, and reason resulted in decisions worthy of Jefferson's Enlightenment ideal. His ringing mantras, "less is more" and "do no damage" to the historic fabric of the landscape, emphasize the sincere conservatism that marked the restoration's methodology. By the close of 1981, four hundred linear feet of wall had been constructed, and the last stone was laid by Sprouse on June 9, 1983, after three years of work (fig. 5.6). The wall, like the garden, is massive in its scale and scope—one thousand feet long, twelve feet high in its tallest section, and punctuated at its midpoint by the garden pavilion. The wall contains some five thousand tons of rock.[7]

During the fall of 1981, the restoration team was challenged by the need to integrate the stone retaining wall with the construction of the garden pavilion, including an extant wall section that it was hoped could be preserved. Although the original temple had stood atop, and was supported by, the stone wall, its demise was due to the lack of foundation support. Jefferson's 1810 notes on the pavilion's construction were a

5.6. Restoration work in process showing segment of the "double wall" needed to support the large amount of fill dirt to create the garden terrace

5.7. The restoration of the garden pavilion was completed in 1984

model of clarity, but questions arose about the pavilion's awkward integration into the stone wall. Other difficult decisions were made about how to interpret floors, ceilings, and triple-sash windows, and the logic behind the Chinese railing atop the roof (fig. 5.7).[8]

As the restoration team slowly proceeded with the pavilion during the spring of 1982, I began to lay out the garden squares and beds. After such intense planning and research, it was a relief to finally begin work in the garden. Almost immediately, however, I confronted some interesting challenges. Although documentary references assured the team that the outside walk of the garden next to the wall was turfgrass, a question remained about the character of interior walkways and alleys. It was decided to create grass walkways throughout the garden to reinforce the nature of the outer walk and to provide a unified appearance (fig. 5.8). An irrigation system was also installed along the length of the garden, and Favretti's adaptation of a Jefferson-designed arbor was constructed. A documentary reference mentioned an arbor based on "locust forks" for the south walk of the pre-1806 garden. This was used as the basis for a one-hundred-foot-long structure supported by black locust posts, forked at the top and providing a resting place for wooden cross-pieces that would support the twining vines. The newly laid out garden, effervescent with its freshly seeded turf pathways, was planted with vegetables for the 1982 season while construction proceeded on the wall, the pavilion, and the northeast or lower platform.[9]

Decisions were postponed about re-creating the original width of the northwest border, now buried at the bottom of the steep slope below Mulberry Row. It would be archaeologically complex to strip off the soil on such a radical incline and environmentally unwise to re-create the unusually steep grade of the Jefferson era. A narrower version is annually cultivated with a diversity of garden crops. Practical issues also abounded regarding the rebuilding of the ten-foot-high paling fence that ran for more than three thousand feet, enclosing the entire 7.2-acre fruit and vegetable garden. Many observers were disturbed by the way it blocked the "sea view" from Mulberry Row to the east; others were considering the extensive labor required to maintain such an enormous wooden structure. Also, because the Jefferson-era fence was constructed with pales or thin boards riven from American chestnut, a species near extinction, wood sources were scarce. The best alternative, white oak, was more difficult to split into narrow five-and-a-half-foot-long strips. A one-hundred-foot-long sample of the paling fence, from the stone house (now

5.8. Although the documentation confirmed only an outer walk of turfgrass, this photograph shows how all the paths were initially planted in grass. In 2002 earthen walkways were installed along the inner walk to reduce maintenance.

5.9. Monticello vegetable garden, November 2010

known as the Weaver's Cottage) to the Levy tomb along Mulberry Row, was eventually rebuilt in 1993 with the aid of craftsmen from Colonial Williamsburg.[10]

Following the removal of the parking lots, the entire garden was extended into the lowest platform, referred to as the "new section" by Monticello's gardeners, in the spring of 1984. Although this area was terraced by Bacon and his crew, Jefferson left no recognizable document that identifies planting in this northeastern section. Two tiers of parking above the garden were also removed, opening the door for the possible restoration of Mulberry Row and the first roundabout around the east front of the house. This dramatic removal of an intrusive modern convenience—tour buses had spewed diesel fumes and ghostly mechanical sounds within two hundred feet of the east front portico—radically enhanced the visitor's experience of the Monticello landscape. In a ceremony on Jefferson's birthday, April 13, 1984, the garden pavilion was dedicated and the Monticello vegetable garden finally restored to an accurate rendition of its 1812 appearance (fig. 5.9). Significant later additions included the northeast vineyard in 1984, the submural beds in 1985, the berry squares in 1986, the southwest vineyard and the paling fence sample in 1993, and the "old nursery" in 1994.

Jefferson's documentary record and the archaeological research had not provided all the answers. Although ambitious efforts were made to define the bones of this landscape feature, the garden at Monticello is both a restoration and an exhibit. Strictly defined, the terms *restoration* and *re-creation* do not account for the mutable qualities of a garden, always evolving with each year's horticultural decisions. Beiswanger's dedicated oversight, the specificity of the Jefferson documentation, and the miracle of archaeological discoveries combined to provide a model for future work in the field of historic landscape preservation.

The Garden Today

Michelle Obama declared in 2010 that the White House kitchen garden "has been one of the greatest things I've done in my life so far." The garden is a central feature of the First Lady's "Let's Move" initiative to encourage healthier lifestyles by combating childhood obesity, improving school lunch programs, and introducing children to the joys of gardening and fresh vegetable cuisine (fig. 5.10). Her campaign to support Wal-Mart's move to healthier food selections, rally behind local farmers' markets, and send White House chefs to speak and cook at elementary schools is also part of this far-reaching initiative.[11]

In 2009, Sam Kass, senior policy adviser for Healthy Food Initiatives, was placed in charge of the White House Kitchen Garden. Kass, the Obama family chef when they lived in Chicago, called me one day and pronounced the Monticello garden "the most beautiful garden I've ever seen." He visited Monticello on April 4, 2009, and returned to Washington with plants of Jefferson's favorite vegetables and plans to reserve a discrete section of the White House garden in honor of Thomas Jefferson. The seeds and plants included Tennisball and Brown Dutch lettuce, Prickly-seeded spinach, Choux de Milan cabbage, Green Globe artichoke, and Marseilles fig. White House executive pastry chef William Yosses, described by President Obama as the "crust master," began overseeing the Washington garden along with Kass and also visited Monticello before the fall planting season. He returned with Monticello seeds and plants of cool-weather vegetables to plant a fall garden. Interviewed by a Charlottesville television news station, Yosses said, "Monticello and Thomas Jefferson were an inspiration for us from the very beginning." He added. "It's really the soul of our garden here.' In 2010 Michelle Obama, after visiting Monticello with her children, echoed these sentiments, saying that Monticello "is just incredibly beautiful, and that beautiful garden that he

5.10. First Lady Michelle Obama breaks ground on the
White House Kitchen Garden, March 20, 2009. At right is Dale Haney,
White House grounds superintendent.

planted there is three times the size of anything that you'd ever do. It brings it to life, not just for my kids but for me." I helped plant the spring White House garden in 2010 and 2011, joining schoolchildren, White House chefs and gardeners, and the First Lady in a celebratory planting of Thomas Jefferson's favorite vegetables. In a tumultuous world, the opportunity to go to the White House, the center of the Western world, and plant vegetables with children was an affirmation of the inherent optimism of the gardening process.[12]

Thomas Jefferson's legacy in food, wine, and gardening provides an engaging model for today's interest in local food, vegetable cuisine, organic gardening, and sustainable agriculture. Jefferson's vegetarian inclinations, his endorsement of French cuisine and the latest trends in innovative cookery, and the enduring model offered by his Garden Book lend credence to his emerging reputation as this country's "First Foodie." With its initial stirrings by Alice Waters in the 1960s at Chez Panisse in Berkeley, California, and then bolstered by Michael Pollan's *Omnivore's Dilemma,* the local food movement has profoundly influenced the food and lifestyle choices of millions of Americans. Jefferson's garden has attracted pilgrims of this movement—Alice Waters herself, Rosalind Creasy, the founder of the edible landscaping movement, and Walter Staib, among others. An internationally known chef at Philadelphia's City Tavern, Staib filmed four segments of his Emmy-award-winning PBS show, *A Taste of History,* in the newly restored Monticello kitchen using vegetables from the garden. The Heritage Harvest Festival, hosted by Monticello every September, uses the Jefferson garden legacy in a celebration of heirloom and historic vegetables, sustainable farming, and local food.[13]

Jefferson's stirring endorsements of market gardening and holistic horticulture inspire not only cooks and gardeners but artists in a variety of media. The whimsical paintings of Anne Bell Robb translate the Monticello landscape into lasting souvenirs that have been sold in the Monticello museum shops for two decades (fig. 5.11). Chicago artist Laura Nicholson Foster wove tapestries of the Monticello garden and its produce in 1993 for exhibitions in Chicago and Michigan (fig. 5.12). They offer a stunning and unique perspective on the linear character of the vegetable garden. The celebrated Annie Leibovitz used the vegetable photography of Charles Jones as a model for her captivating images of Monticello root crops taken in November 2010. A Charlottesville botanical illustrator, Lara Call Gastinger, has used Monticello vegetables as subjects for a series of watercolors on cultivated crops (see fig. 5.16).

The artist and naturalist Charles Willson Peale wrote to Jefferson in 1812, "Your garden must be a Museum to you." Few topics tell us more about Thomas Jefferson than gardening, and the restored Monticello garden thrives as a living exhibition of his scientific and aesthetic sensibility. Today, most visitors enter the garden through the site of the original garden gate; the terrace, garden pavilion, and "sea view" are hidden by the ten-foot-high paling fence. The surprise encounter with the garden elicits exclamatory gasps and sudden expressions of wonder as visitors first set eyes on the one-thousand-foot-long garden. Many are then impressed by the tidy rows of crops; most are shocked by the arresting orangish red clay that is the native soil; others marvel at the expansive view; but the question most commonly asked is, "What happens to the vegetables?" This question reflects the practical-minded American, always curious about how things work. Many varieties are seed crops, their rows designated with labels that read, "preservation seed plot." Saving seed demands that the plants— whether fruits, roots, or leaves—are allowed to mature through their natural life cycle. Most of the produce, however, is harvested and distributed twice a week, either to the hundreds of employees who work at Monticello on a summer's day, or else to the Café at Monticello, which features garden vegetables in soups, sandwiches, and salads.[14]

The gardens and grounds department regards itself as a horticultural academy and includes a staff of gardeners devoted to caring

5.11. Anne Bell Robb's whimsical depiction of the garden

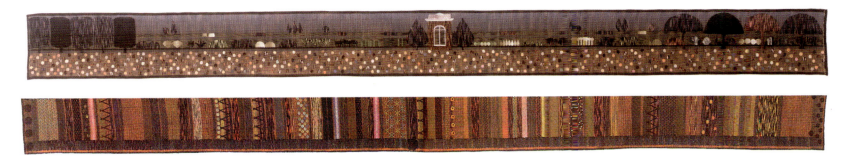

5.12. *Thousand Foot Garden: Elevation and Plan,* by Laura Foster Nicholson, 1993, handwoven wool with cotton, each approximately 12 in. × 110 in.

5.13. The garden today functions as a seed bank of Jefferson and historic varieties of vegetables. Vegetable seed is harvested from the garden, packaged by the gardens and grounds staff, and distributed through the Thomas Jefferson Center for Historic Plants.

for the Thomas Jefferson Foundation's 2,400 acres, restoring Jefferson's gardens, preserving an early nineteenth-century plant collection, and interpreting the landscape to Monticello's 450,000 yearly visitors. Research focuses on Jefferson and the history of plants in American gardens. The Thomas Jefferson Center for Historic Plants, begun in 1987 as a culmination of Monticello's commitment to garden plant preservation, is a satellite program with both interpretive and commercial goals. Seeds collected from the garden or historic plants propagated at nearby Tufton Farm are sold through Monticello's museum stores (fig. 5.13). By sharing these tangible links to the past—from seed of Tennis-ball lettuce to seedlings of original trees that date

to the early nineteenth century—Thomas Jefferson and Monticello are brought to life in gardens around the world.[1F]

Another commonly asked question is, "Who takes care of this garden?" Many visitors, at least initially, fail to link the vegetable garden with Monticello or with Jefferson but perceive it as an unrelated market garden. In fact, the Thomas Jefferson Foundation employs a skilled vegetable gardener, who oversees at least one gardener in the spring and fall, and other helpers during the busiest summer months. We sow the garden with peas, spinach, and fava beans in February and intensive planting continues with leaf and root crops through March and April to produce a spring garden in May and June of cold-hardy crops. Summer plantings begin in April with beans and cucumbers, then transplants of tomatoes, "melongena" or eggplants, and peppers, plus hot-weather crops like melons, sweet potatoes, and okra. May is a choice time to visit for lush rows of peas, lettuce, cabbage, beets, and artichokes; the full flush of Mediterranean herbs like rosemary and lavender; and impending harvests of more than thirty vegetable species (fig. 5.14). Vegetable gardening at Monticello is at its height in July: bean poles laden with scarlet runners, caracalla beans, "snaps," "long haricots," and lima beans; the red soil hidden beneath rampaging vines of sweet potatoes, "cymlin" squash, "tomatas," "peendars" (peanuts), and melons; and the garden further punctuated by rambunctious mounds of "topinambours" (Jerusalem artichokes), castor beans, hop vines, and "bene" (sesame). Fall vegetables are sowed and transplanted in August and September as harvest season continues into Virginia's most idyllic and tranquil season. Monticello enjoys the best of all vegetable worlds—cool-season spinach and cabbage are harvested at the same time as heat-loving okra, lima beans, and squash. It is a long season and a big garden: two acres of cultivated ground, organized into twenty-four squares and a seven-hundred-foot-long northwest border, planted for three seasons of harvest, some 175 plantings a year.

5.14. Monticello garden in spring 2011

Monticello is a museum, not a living historical farm. House interpreters are regarded as scholars explaining the past and are not dressed in period clothing. Guides use the third person in their tours, and demonstrations of crafts by nineteenth-century interpreters are scheduled only occasionally. Although the garden reveals some historical techniques—the "rodding" of peas, cucumbers, and beans with dormant brushy sticks and the use of "hills" for vining crops like melons, squashes, pole beans, and cucumbers—gardeners use modern shovels, rototillers, and an electrically pumped irrigation system to cultivate the soil and care for the crops. Watering the garden regularly through the summer months and working the soil with a tractor-operated rotovator are not the only historical compromises. The garden is planted with more variety and intensity than is suggested in Jefferson's Kalendar. Squares are planted with three to seven different vegetables over the course of the season instead of being devoted to a single crop of peas or "snaps." Because today's visitors encounter only a snapshot of an hour of a day of a month of a season of a year, the garden includes almost twice as many plantings—175 versus Jefferson's 94 in 1809—to illustrate the breadth of Jefferson's garden experience over a lifetime of experimentation.

Gardening is gambling, whether undertaken in 1809 or 2012. Although we do not deliberately repeat Jefferson's "failures," the garden today is nevertheless a victim of similar devastating calamities, some resulting from the vagaries of the Virginia climate, others from the damaging effects of disease, destructive insects, and unruly weeds. An uneasy relationship invariably results between historical authenticity and horticultural re-creations. We find it impossible to reproduce the drought season of 1809, the precise character of the clay content in the original terraced soils, or, in many cases, the exact variety of bean cultivated by Thomas Jefferson two hundred years ago. Nonetheless, a growing cultivated garden provides the ideal classroom to explain the past and compare the historical record with the garden displayed today.

Seed saving is integral to the preservation role of today's Monticello garden. Philip Mazzei wrote Jefferson in 1805 and described the ephemeral state of cherished vegetables. "In the environs of my birthplace they used to grow delicious melons weighing about 100 English pounds, the seed of which has been lost. The same is true of a variety of lettuce superior to any other. People like change, fashion rules food as it does clothes, and self-interest compels farmers to subserve it." Mazzei's complaint describes the plight of today's preservationists concerned for the fate of historic vegetables. Unlike fruit trees, which often live a hundred years, most vegetables are annuals, and their seed has a restricted viability. When Jefferson wrote about his effort to "select only one or two of the *best* species or variety of every garden vegetable," he was describing the scientific process so essential to his experimental garden. The proliferation of varieties enabled him to selectively eliminate inferior types, so he could declare the Carnation cherry "so superior that no other deserves the name of cherry," or that the Arikara bean "is one of the most excellent we have had." Just as Jefferson would discard an inferior bean, so have many other vegetable varieties been lost over the past 150 years, overlooked

because of an inferior taste, a lack of productivity or resistance to disease, or, more recently, an inability to adapt to mechanized methods of culture, harvesting, or transportation. Other older varieties are the lost parents of our modern hybrids, and their genetic character lies buried within the super-bred varieties of today's seed catalogs.[16]

Only a hopeless romantic would disparage the progress in plant breeding that has resulted not only in miraculous disease and insect resistance but, in many cases, in tastier vegetables that feed more people than ever before. Nevertheless, Philip Mazzei's lost hundred-pound watermelon is an example of the regional and community vegetables so worthy of preservation. For years writers have discussed the need to broaden the genetic base of our agricultural and horticultural crops to prevent a recurrence of a disaster on the order of the nineteenth-century Irish potato famine or the Southern

5.15. Tomato tastings are held yearly in August as part of the Saturdays in the Garden series of natural history walks, lectures, and workshops

corn blight of the early 1970s. The efforts of organizations such as the Seed Savers Exchange and the National Seed Storage Bank are to be applauded. A broad spectrum of diverse varieties provides insurance against a virus-induced plague afflicting the high-strung hybrids that dominate world agribusiness. Older varieties are more primitive and, in some ways, more resilient; they are also genetically akin to their wild ancestors, native plants that have persisted without human efforts and have survived centuries of nature's pestilential attacks so successfully. Heirloom vegetables taste better, too.[17]

Today, the Monticello garden serves as a seed bank of early American varieties. Noteworthy seeds are saved, dried, cleaned, packaged, and then sold as a means of preserving the ephemeral genes of the past. Special varieties of pea include Prince Albert, an 1840s variety identical to Jefferson's Early Frame; Blue Prussian, named for a fashionable paint color; Champion of England, the oldest wrinkled pea still in cultivation; and Marrowfat, a later and starchier pea usually grown for soups or drying. Four lettuces—including Jefferson favorites Brown Dutch and Tennis-ball, along with Spotted Aleppo and Bath Cos, Romaine-type lettuces common in early nineteenth-century American seed houses—are featured during the cool-weather growing season. Monticello also offers a nineteenth-century collection of tomatoes, including Purple Calabash, reputedly a pre-Columbian tomato with a rich, acidic flavor, and Costoluto Genovese, a heavily lobed and convoluted Italian variety. These tomatoes are rated by the public during August tomato tastings that feature dozens of heirloom varieties (fig. 5.15). Cow's Horn okra, Whippoorwill crowder pea, and Anne Arundel melons were important varieties in the early 1800s, while Monticello might be the only source for Prickly-seeded spinach, a winter variety with smooth leaves, unique for its sharply burred seeds. Varieties from the Monticello bean collection are ever popular. These include two ornamental species, the hyacinth bean and the caracalla or snail flower, for Jefferson "the most beautiful flowering

5.16. Tennis-ball lettuce, watercolor by Lara Call Gastinger

bean in the world." Both were popularized in the restored garden at Monticello and have since become commercial successes in corporate American seed houses and nurseries.

Sources for the vegetable collection at Monticello today are as varied as they were for Thomas Jefferson. In 1980 we obtained seed of the Tennis-ball lettuce, originally a French variety that evolved into a typical Boston type, from the National Seed Storage Laboratory in Fort Collins, Colorado, a repository of "vegetable germplasm" (fig. 5.16). We planted a tidy row of greenhouse-raised plants in the garden. The foundation's executive director, using a Jeffersonian superlative as only a Monticello scholar could, announced that he'd never tasted better lettuce. Soon, a rapacious band of lettuce thieves (it was surely an internal job perpetrated by Monticello employees) had harvested, and presumably consumed, our row of Tennis-ball lettuce. I didn't object to our employees' right to a delicious vegetable, but

5.17. Hyacinth beans planted on the re-created bean arbor

there were now no plants left to form seed, a necessary ingredient for the regeneration of this precious Jefferson variety. Instead of admitting my failure to the Seed Bank (it was in some ways a loan, the interest being the return of the seed), I found a surrogate to reapply for more Tennis-ball lettuce. Our efforts were eventually successful, our seed crops became more plentiful, and we soon began selling the seed of Tennis-ball lettuce around the globe.

Other acquisitions were the result of serendipitous fortune and good friends. The Red Calico lima bean arrived unannounced from a seed collector in east Tennessee who had documented the passage of seeds through generations of the Thweatt family since 1793. The Oxheart cabbage, mentioned by Jefferson while in Paris, was sent to us by another casual visitor to the garden, as was the Cow's Horn okra, sometimes referred to now as "Monticello okra." Hyacinth bean, although not a documented Jefferson bean variety, was a gift from the gardens of Mount Vernon by way of a recommendation from the Colonial Williamsburg grounds director (fig. 5.17). Garden and culinary historian William Woys Weaver contributed exciting acquisitions in the Anne Arundel melon, which he documented in Peale family paintings, and Brown Dutch lettuce, a delicious, floppy

5.18. Four hundred and fifty thousand visitors enjoy the Monticello gardens annually

nest of reddish-tinged green leaves. The late Robert Becker of New York, a career scientist in modern horticultural technology, passed on the Prince Albert pea, and Colonial Gardener Wesley Greene of Colonial Williamsburg has helped us replenish our historic pea collection. The Seed Savers Exchange has contributed numerous "heirloom" and traditional vegetables to the collection.

Rob Brown, former vegetable gardener, often remarked to his young apprentices that gardening would be easy if it weren't for the bugs, the weeds, and the diseases. Controlling the eastern white-tailed deer has been the modern Monticello gardener's most frustrating challenge. Author and natural historian John McPhee famously labeled deer "rats with antlers, roaches with split hooves, denizens of the dark primeval suburbs," and with their populations increasing exponentially over the past century, gardeners are giving up the art and craft of horticulture. On the suggestion of Mount Vernon horticulturist Dean Norton, Monticello began a program in the mid-1990s of using dogs to chase away poaching deer. The modern garden has also inherited the legacy of Jefferson's water problems. Summer drought, exaggerated by the garden's mountaintop setting, climate change, and the terraced southeastern exposure, often defines the growing season. Another horticultural challenge inherent to a restored, historic garden is the inevitable increase of pests—disease, insects, and weeds—over decades of intensive cultivation. Soil-borne pathogens, insidious insects, and even new weeds thrive now with a warming and changing environment. The garden is a hothouse of pests, an experimental museum demonstrating how a reasonably sustainable ecosystem from the age of Jefferson confronts the ravages of modern horticultural plagues.[18]

The philosophy of the Monticello vegetable garden restoration is based on the wisdom of Thomas Jefferson (fig. 5.18). Although we repeatedly invoke his gardening mantra, "the failure of one thing repaired by the success of another," modern gardeners also use Jefferson's avowed methods of soil regeneration through the incorporation of composts as a means of enriching the soil and thwarting pestilence. The two-acre garden is covered annually with compost, rotted leaves, or barnyard manure to sustain long-term tilth, basic fertility, and bacterial balance in the soil. Gardeners at Monticello also maintain a high tolerance for superficial pest infestations. Garden interpreters point out silver goosegrass, worm-ridden cabbage leaves, or yellowing squash plants as a way of discussing the evolution of pests in American gardens. We strive for a professional garden while finding both solace and inspiration from the past. Jefferson's echoing epiphanies about soil regeneration, plant experimentation, and the essential balance of the cultivated garden and the natural world are as uplifting as his real-life struggles with drought, pests, and failure are comforting.[19]

Gardens are always changing as plants flourish and fade through the seasons. Similarly, gardeners come and go. The Monticello vegetable garden features a broad range of eighteenth- and nineteenth-century historic vegetable varieties, the preservation of which is an ongoing challenge for the modern gardener. The garden restoration of the early 1980s set a high standard in the field of landscape preservation and provided new perspectives on the genius of Thomas Jefferson. Since then, educational programs have linked the garden to Jefferson and his world. Today the Thomas Jefferson Foundation has embarked on another major project—the restoration of Mulberry Row—which will finally help us to create a fuller picture of the Monticello plantation community, its kitchen, and its garden. There is no final act to the unfolding of the garden's dramatic play. This is reassuring to a gardener who has worked in this garden for thirty-five years. The failure of one thing will be repaired by the success of another as future horticultural curators find new goals and confront fresh challenges. A gardener's work is never done.

PART II

FRUITS, ROOTS, AND LEAVES

A CATALOG OF SELECTED MONTICELLO VEGETABLES

Prologue

W HEN THOMAS JEFFERSON CREATED HIS "Arrangement of the Garden" in 1812, he organized the Monticello vegetable garden into "fruits," "roots," and "leaves"—a satisfying way of cataloging culinary vegetables according to which part of the plant was to be harvested. He divided fruits into "pulse"—beans and peas—and further classified leaves by their preparation: "dressed" (cooked) like cabbage and spinach and "salads, raw," presumably fresh vegetables such as lettuce, radishes, and celery with a salad dressing. Part II of *Thomas Jefferson's Revolutionary Garden* features "vegetable portraits" depicting the fruits, roots, and leaves essential to the Monticello garden. The vegetables are described not only by their role at Monticello—how they were grown and prepared—but also by how they arrived in North America and their place in the gardens of Jefferson's contemporaries.

As Part I of this book has shown, Jefferson's experiments with a diverse range of species and varieties often meant adapting Old World techniques to the growing conditions of his native Virginia. Although distinct American varieties of fruit trees, particularly apple and peach, emerged in the colonial period and their numbers exploded early in the nineteenth century, the golden age of vegetable breeding in America did not occur until the latter half of the nineteenth century. Earlier gardeners, such as Jefferson, relied on mostly European vegetable sources. When returning home to his crowning glory, the terraced vegetable garden of his retirement, Jefferson brought as many as thirty vegetable varieties he had purchased on February 1, 1809, from seedsman Theophilus Holt of Washington. These legendary British varieties—from the Brown Dutch and Silesia lettuce to the Charlton Hotspur and Leadman's Dwarf pea—were repeatedly mentioned in the historic garden literature. At the same time, Jefferson grew a small but significant selection of promising American-developed vegetables like Cooper's Pale Green asparagus and Carolina lima bean.[1]

In contrast to these much discussed English varieties, many of the vegetables Jefferson received from friends and neighbors remain unidentified. For example, Jefferson's two favor-

Caseknife bean

Rows of sesame in square XIV, July 2011

The Fish pepper, adopted by African Americans in the twentieth century, represents the motley tribe of American *Capsicums*

ite kidney beans, selected from a long trial involving the cultivation of thirty-six varieties were "long haricot" from General Thomas Sumpter of Georgia and "grey snap." Unfortunately, Jefferson's nomenclature was too vague to give us a picture of what the "grey snap" or "long haricot" actually looked like, other than that the seed was "grey" or the pods were "long." Jefferson consistently described vegetables by the source of his seed ("Mazzei bean"), the place of its origin ("Miami melon"), or a basic physical description like "long haricot" or "early" cauliflower. The abundance of regional vegetables that were never described or even listed in the kitchen garden literature of the day offer a teasing promise of a revolutionary horticultural breakthrough in the development of distinct American vegetable varieties.

Other Mid-Atlantic gardeners in Jefferson's circle, such as John Hartwell Cocke, assembled intriguing collections of new and unusual vegetables. Cocke grew sunflowers and purple tomatoes not documented in the Monticello garden, along with novelties like sea kale, eggplant, okra, and tomatoes. Francis Taylor's garden included curiosities like white asparagus, blue potatoes, and red pulp and white cucumbers, plus an array of local, vernacular varieties such as Goose-craw and Saddlestrap bean, "Royster's" watermelon, and an unusual collection of cow or field peas. William Faris documented growing rare Brussels sprouts and eggplants in the nineteenth century, and even Joseph Hornsby on the Kentucky frontier mentioned African American crops like potato pumpkins, as well as recent introductions such as okra, tomatoes, and *Capsicum* or "Guinea pepper." Despite the creative experimentation of his gardening contemporaries, the range of vegetables grown in Jefferson's garden—the unique blend of cool-weather stalwarts from the English kitchen garden and pioneering American, African, and Asian crops suited to a hot Virginia summer—was an unprecedented horticultural achievement.

6.1. "Planting is one of my great amusements, and even of those things which can only be for posterity,
for a Septuagenary has no right to count on anything beyond annuals"
—Thomas Jefferson to Dr. Samuel Brown, 1813

Artichoke: The Gentleman's Elegant Thistle

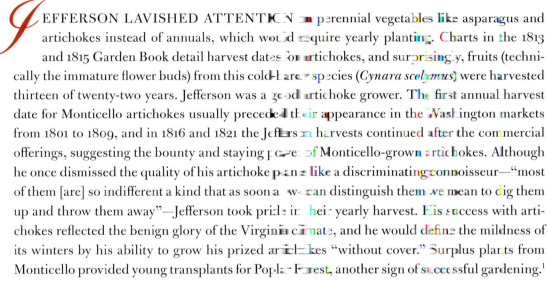

JEFFERSON LAVISHED ATTENTION on perennial vegetables like asparagus and artichokes instead of annuals, which would require yearly planting. Charts in the 1813 and 1815 Garden Book detail harvest dates for artichokes, and surprisingly, fruits (technically the immature flower buds) from this cold-hardy species (*Cynara scolymus*) were harvested thirteen of twenty-two years. Jefferson was a good artichoke grower. The first annual harvest date for Monticello artichokes usually preceded their appearance in the Washington markets from 1801 to 1809, and in 1816 and 1821 the Jefferson harvests continued after the commercial offerings, suggesting the bounty and staying power of Monticello-grown artichokes. Although he once dismissed the quality of his artichoke plants like a discriminating connoisseur—"most of them [are] so indifferent a kind that as soon as we can distinguish them we mean to dig them up and throw them away"—Jefferson took pride in their yearly harvest. His success with artichokes reflected the benign glory of the Virginia climate, and he would define the mildness of its winters by his ability to grow his prized artichokes "without cover." Surplus plants from Monticello provided young transplants for Poplar Forest, another sign of successful gardening.[1]

Statuesque shrubs with robust, silver foliage crowned by the pineapple-like heads of incipient purple flowers, artichokes are the most ornamental of all vegetable plants: "a thistle upon a gigantic scale," according to garden writer William Cobbett (fig. 6.2). Jefferson reserved the centrally located square XI to showcase the artichoke at the center stage of his retirement garden, flanking the garden pavilion. Bernard McMahon sent seeds to the President's House of red and white globe artichokes in February 1807, and Jefferson recorded planting the resulting seedlings in the Monticello nursery in two four-foot-wide beds, each with three long rows. On May 31, 1808, Jefferson counted the 35 red and 40 green artichokes that had germinated, and McMahon forwarded more plants in June. The plants were later transplanted into their perma-

6.2. Artichoke from Bacilius Besler,
Hortus Eystettensis, 1613

6.3. Green Globe artichoke

nent garden square on March 22, 1810, and the heads were harvested the following year on May 15 (fig. 6.3). Artichokes were likely prepared at Monticello similarly to the recipe of Mary Randolph: the harvested flower heads were boiled for one and a half to two hours, the heads presented on a plate with the leaves trimmed and served with accompanying cups of melted butter for dipping, so that "each guest may have one." [2]

Artichoke cultivation was a fine art, at least as articulated by both British and American garden authorities in the age of Jefferson. Philip Miller's directions on the crucial task of protecting artichokes in winter were detailed, copied slavishly by early American writers, and adapted by Jefferson at Monticello. In November, artichoke rows were covered with wide earthen ridges, surrounding the plants but exposing their leafy heart; when extreme cold arrived the plants were further covered with pea haulm, tan bark, long [rotted] dung, or straw. Landon Carter's artichokes were severely damaged during the winter of 1770, but John Tayloe's gardener removed the winter covering of manure on March 23 to reveal thriving basal leaves in 1805. Aside from the dressing of artichoke plantations with soil-improving manure, the other key to perpetuating plants involved separating slips, or suckers, from older plants in the spring to propagate new plantations, often a yearly task. Landon Carter passed on 456 young artichoke plants to Richard Henry Lee of Chantilly in 1772, and John Hartwell Cocke received "slips" from a friend in 1822.[3]

In 1629 English herbalist John Parkinson bragged about the superiority of English artichokes and wrote that their preparation was "well known to the youngest Housewife," but the artichoke was more a gentleman's trophy vegetable in eighteenth-century Virginia. Although artichokes were known in Virginia gardens as early as 1648, William Hugh Grove observed in 1732 that only the "gentry sometimes rayse a few." William Byrd mentioned them as a Virginia product in 1737, and Philip Fithian ate artichokes on July 2, 1773, at Nomini Hall, the Robert Carter plantation on the northern neck of Virginia. John Hartwell Cocke and George Washington cultivated artichokes, but they were one of the few vegetables absent from the Annapolis garden of middle-class artisan William Faris around 1800. Because artichokes were more commonly propagated from established plants, seeds were uncommon on commercial seed lists.[4]

Corn: An American in Paris

Indian corn (*Zea mays*) was essential to the subsistence plantation economy of Monticello, used internally to ward off hunger and to feed livestock, but a marginal figure in the vegetable garden. Jefferson recorded planting experimental corn varieties along the outskirts of the garden, below the garden wall in the south orchard and vineyard, and in specially prepared test plots like the "island" or "circular" beds. Sweet corn was a late nineteenth-century improvement and was slow in taking its place with beans and cabbage as a standard kitchen garden vegetable. Although the staff of American life from the founding of Jamestown, the essential "bread for the laborers" at Monticello, and

everywhere grown by European colonists as a field crop, corn was nearly absent from American garden literature around 1800. Corn varieties began appearing on commercial seed lists only in the 1820s. Pioneer horticulturist Bernard McMahon was the first authority to advocate planting "the small early kinds" in the American vegetable garden of 1806, and Jefferson was ahead of his time by recommending the April planting of "forward" corn in his published "General Gardening Calendar" of 1824. Corn was also sold in the Washington farmers' market, probably as a result of Jefferson's initiative in passing out choice seed varieties to local market gardeners. Indian corn, used at the table as roasting ears, was a garden vegetable in the age of Jefferson, but only barely.[5]

On the farm, Jefferson was a reluctant corn planter, at least in theory. Corn, along with pork, was integral to the diet of Monticello slaves, used in bread, meal, hominy, pone, hoecakes, mush, and various cakes and as roasting ears. Corn was also fed to Monticello's livestock—oxen, sheep, horses, and cows—and was a central ingredient in Jefferson's plans for crop rotation. Like tobacco, corn feeds heavily off the land and robs the soil of its fertility, and it involved large-scale plowing and soil-eroding cultivation along hillsides. Jefferson wrote, "Good husbandry with us consists in abandoning Indian corn and tobacco," yet corn remained a critical crop throughout Jefferson's tenure at Monticello. Forty acres a year were usually reserved for Indian corn on the Monticello farms (fig. 6.4), sometimes more at Poplar Forest. Jefferson paid for the leveling of the top of Monticello Mountain with twenty-four bushels of corn; he outlined charts detailing the distribution of the year's corn crop to slaves and livestock; and he built a merchant mill along the Rivanna River as a potential profit center. A corn crop compromised by drought, floods, or weevils was a cause for anxiety. Jefferson wrote his son-in-law Thomas Mann Randolph in 1796, "There's vast alarm here about corn . . . We shall

6.4. Corn in square XXIII, 2011. Today squares XIX–XXIV are planted in field crops
such as corn, potatoes, pumpkins, and sweet potatoes.

starve literally if I cannot buy 200 barrels, & as yet I have been able to find but 60." Jefferson's aspiration "towards the recovery of our lands" by replacing corn with diversified crops of potatoes, clover, or legumes was never successful.[6]

Perhaps because of its familiarity, Indian corn and its essential products—hominy and cornmeal—were surprisingly absent from the Jefferson family culinary manuscripts. Mary Randolph's *Virginia House-wife*, however, contains numerous recipes for either hominy or cornmeal, used in breads, puddings, johnnycakes, and mush. The only specific references to Jefferson's consumption of Indian corn occurred while he was in Paris in 1787, when he wrote home to Nicholas Lewis and asked for "homony-corn . . . which we used to make 20. barrels a year for table use, green, in homony, and in bread." Jefferson added, "I cultivate in my garden here Indian corn for the use of my own table to eat green in our manner." This reference suggests Jefferson's affinity for "rosten ears," unshucked ears that were commonly moistened, set in the banked ashes of a kitchen hearth, and then eaten American style on the cob.[7]

The experimental character of Jefferson's vegetable garden was expressed by the corn varieties he tested, many of which were Lewis and Clark novelties collected from Northern Plains Indian tribes. The Mandan, Hidatsa, and Arikara villages, depicted so vividly by the landscape artist George Catlin in the 1830s, were along the bluffs of the Missouri River and its tributaries, in what is today North Dakota. Here the Lewis and Clark expedition spent the winter of 1805 after constructing Fort Mandan from cottonwood trees. The winter was harsh, averaging four degrees Fahrenheit and plummeting to minus forty-five. As supplies of buffalo and deer meat diminished, the corps was sustained through the trading of corn. At first they bartered with ribbons, mirrors, and beads, but as their supply of trinkets became limited, they built a forge to repair Indian tools and sharpen axes. The expedition's blacksmith then constructed iron tools such as

hoes, axes, and tomahawks, and these were traded for corn—a sheath of iron for seven to eight bushels of corn. According to popular historian Stephen Ambrose, "It was Mandan corn that got the men through the winter." Fifty percent of their subsistence and economy was based on cultivated vegetable varieties that had been developed for the cold weather, short season (ninety days), and limited rainfall (ten inches a year).[8]

Jefferson's goal was to find a short-season variety, and he compared the Native American varieties, improved for centuries to withstand the brief growing season, cold temperatures, and arid conditions of the Northern Plains, with the Quarantine (or forty-day) variety obtained from his European contacts J. P. Reibelt and André Thöuin. Jefferson wrote that the Quarantine was "a present of real value . . . to furnish early subsistence after a year of scarcity." Although the Plains Indian corn varieties reflected an advanced horticultural improvement of an essential economic crop, they failed to compete effectively with the Quarantine. At Monticello, Quarantine was planted in four-to-five-acre plots on bottomland along the Rivanna River, and it produced "rosten ears" in eight weeks. Jefferson's plantings of Mandan were less satisfactory and the variety was abandoned at Monticello. He, however, stubbornly persisted with the Pani, "the finest and forwardest corn I have ever tried," and advertised as a six-week bearer. The Kalendar documents plantings in 1812, 1813, 1814, and 1820 despite records that suggest a decidedly longer season than the Quarantine. The "remarkably fine" Cherokee corn was planted in the south orchard, but it also took more than two months to produce a crop. Jefferson's drive to find an early corn variety was expressed by the names of other varieties planted below the Monticello garden: "forward corn from Caxton," "forward yellow," "forward white," "Maryland forward corn (white) planted by Mr. Biddle." This obsession is puzzling because Jefferson also documented the arrival of corn in the Washington markets as early as July 4, an early date compared

6.5. Indian corn from Leonhard Fuchs, *De Historia Stirpium,*
1542, perhaps the first European color
rendering of *Zea mays*

to when fresh sweet corn could be expected today. How instant must a gardener's gratification be?[9]

Corn was, and continues to be, the fundamental food of American civilization (fig. 6.5). An annual grass native to Central America, corn was depicted in plots cultivated by Virginia Indians by John White in 1585, and Jamestown residents ate Powhatan's corn and bean succotash. In 1730 William Hugh Grove wrote that children and the gentry breakfasted on cornbread, while the "middling-sort" ate corn mush. According to Grove, "all their [Virginia colonists] Care is for Tobacco & Little Else Minded Except Corn." Thomas Anburey, an eighteenth-century traveler, described the hominy and hoecakes prepared by Virginia slaves: "The former is made of Indian corn, which is coarsely broke, and boiled . . . until it is almost a pulp. Hoe-cake is Indian corn ground into meal, kneaded into dough, and baked before a fire, but as the negroes bake theirs on the hoes that they work with, they have the appellation of hoe-cakes." Around 1800 Richard Parkinson of Baltimore wrote that the "better sort" made corn cake with eggs and milk, while other Americans made johnnycakes, corn mixed with water to create a paste that was baked on a board or shingle. Although universally used in countless culinary concoctions, "Indian meal" was not introduced into national cookbooks until 1796, when New England's Amelia Simmons broke ground in her *American Cookery.*[10]

Indian corn at the turn of the eighteenth century was usually considered a field, rather than a garden, crop. Colonel Francis Taylor of Orange County planted his turnips in the "corn field" in 1786 and then rotated his corn into the "turnip patch" in 1790. Although Annapolis's William Faris sowed a few kernels of "small Indian corn" in his parsnip beds, he purchased his "Roasting Ears" from a market, while John Hartwell Cocke was unusual in sowing "garden corn" with other kitchen vegetables in 1821. The introduction of corn into the garden was largely a result of the development of sweet corn, a breeding process whereby the starch within the kernel is condensed. In *The History of Horticulture in America,* U. P. Hedrick describes how corn found its place in the vegetable garden only after 1850, with the development of Stowell's Evergreen, not particularly sweet by today's standards. Hedrick also placed the arrival of sweet corn to 1799, when an army officer brought a few ears from an Indian plantation along the Susquehanna River to Plymouth, Massachusetts. Jefferson provided an intriguing reference to the sowing of "sweet or shriveled" corn in the south orchard in 1810. Shriveled kernels suggest that sugar may have been relatively concentrated.[11]

Cucumber: Death by Cucumber

Cucumbers (*Cucumis sativus*) were a popular crop in the Monticello vegetable garden and for Jefferson "a great favorite." Planted routinely and yearly in the retirement garden in a central location in square VIII, Jefferson diligently sowed seeds in boxes in February for later transplanting into the garden. Yet he may not have cherished this bellwether summer vegetable as passionately as his contemporaries, for whom this most refreshing of vegetables represented a harbinger of summer harvests. The race to harvest the first summer cucumber, as with the pea, was an acknowledged goal of both gardeners and garden writers (fig. 6.6). Even though Jefferson regularly referred to his cucumbers as "early," "forward," or "frame," his earliest documented date for a cucumber harvest, June 22, is a modest accomplishment compared to the professional truck farmers in Washington who brought their fruits to the market, surely using artificial hotbeds, as early as April 23. According to Jefferson's great-granddaughter in 1866, a family tradition held that Jefferson never recovered from eating cucumbers a few days before his death on July 4, 1826. Isaetta Randolph Hubard wrote to her mother, the wife of Jefferson's grandson Jeff Randolph: "Tell Papa I had a great ambition to have cucumbers before the 4th. of July as

6.6. The first cucumber was a refreshing harbinger of summer harvests

I had often heard him say that in the year his Grandfather died he brought some in from his little garden at Monticello and his Grandfather eat them and never was well afterwards, he died you recollect on the 4th." Other Virginians like John Custis and Landon Carter complained of "bilious Complaints" caused from eating cucumbers.[12]

Cucumbers were the vegetable most commonly purchased from slaves at Monticello. Anne Cary Randolph bought more than 550 cucumbers between 1804 and 1807, and the granddaughters' accounts between 1823 and 1825 document massive purchases, including a transaction involving fifty dozen cucumbers in 1825. This suggests the cucumber's importance to the kitchen and its role as an everyday staple when cured and preserved. Pickles, especially the small gherkins Jefferson praised to his brother, Randolph, in 1813, were added to Monticello soups. When Anne Cary Randolph purchased seven dozen cucumbers from Bagwell (the typical purchase was two or three dozen) in 1808, they were likely intended for the pickle barrel rather than the salad bowl, as were the five hundred gherkins purchased by Etienne Lemaire in 1806, "a little barrel," perhaps for guests to the President's House.[13]

6.7. The long gourd is a candidate for Jefferson's "mammoth" Ohio cucumber. Treasured in Italian gardens, it is known as "Guinea bean" among Charlottesville area residents today and prepared and eaten like squash.

Jefferson also displayed his characteristic horticultural playfulness when he sowed seeds of Early and Long Green cucumbers in hogsheads or barrels "by the middle gate of the garden" on April 13, 1811. This was one of the few plants Jefferson documented as growing in a container at Monticello, and its placement at the garden entrance, an embellishment with a functional theme, was for Jefferson a typical statement about combining beauty and utility. Early cucumbers were grown in hogsheads again in 1812 on February 22 and March 8, suggesting how Jefferson was gambling by planting this tender vegetable months before the last frost date in mid-April. The resultant plants were transplanted on two dates in June, but the absence of a harvest date implies that this experiment, commonly advocated and practiced in Britain, was not worth the effort. Cucumbers are "juicy" plants, quickly wilted by a hot June sun, and so transplanting them is difficult without a convenient source of water. Although the 1812 Kalendar suggests that cucumbers were sowed in "rows," in 1774 seeds were planted in "monticini," or "little hills," a more typical method.[14]

Jefferson played the character of a boyish elder in a letter of November 29, 1825, to the governor of Ohio, Thomas Worthington, asking for seeds of the "mammoth cucumbers" he had read about in the *Cleveland Herald*. The eighty-two-year-old Jefferson posted the article at the head of the letter: "And the object of my letter is to ask you if this text is really true? and if it is to request further that you will procure for me and send in a letter by mail half a dozen seeds of these mammoth cucumbers. one of 4. 6 I long, and another of 4 f. 5 3/4 should afford so many seeds as to spare a few to a beggar. although giants do not always beget giants, yet I should count on their improving the breed, and this vegetable being a great favorite of mine, I wish to take the chance of an improvement" (fig. 6.7). Worthington came through with the seeds, and Jefferson, six weeks before his death, prudently forwarded a small sample to his neighbor George Divers "to multiply chances of securing it." The rector of Charlottesville's Christ Church, Frederick W. Hatch, reportedly produced an eighty-eight-inch-long cucumber from the Monticello stash of seeds a few years after Jefferson's death.[15]

Giant cucumbers were a source of wonder and even inspired a controversial mock civil war during the late 1730s. The English plant collector and merchant Peter Collinson sent his gardening mentor, John Custis of Williamsburg, seeds of "Turkey cucumber" in 1736. Custis passed on three seeds to his son, Daniel Parke Custis of New Kent County, and the ensuing cucumbers were three feet long. Parke Custis wrote, "To the astonishment of many; severall people rid many miles to see . . . there are more people begd some of the seed; than 10 cucumbers can afford." Collinson himself reported that they "grew in one night three inches in length" as confirming evidence of "the effects of so fine a climate on so rich a soil." The *Virginia Gazette* announced that the fruits were "ribb'd almost like a Musk-melon, colour'd like a Watermelon; and taste much like the common Cucumber" (fig. 6.8). A skeptical Boston writer read the *Gazette* announcement and offered up an equivalent-sized watermelon harvested from a Cambridge garden, more than a yard in circumference and thirty-six pounds in weight: "This rarity we send to Virginia, in Return for

6.8. The Armenian cucumber is another possible example of the "mammoth" cucumbers Jefferson obtained from Ohio in 1825

their Cucumber." In the *Virginia Gazette* of August 25, 1738, a Williamsburg correspondent, Mr. Parks, retorted, "If the Author of this Paragraph was ingenuous and candid in his Account, we receive his Present very kindly: But if he intended wittily to impose upon us an overgrown imaginary Watermelon, for a real Cucumber, supposing our Account to be false, we must beg leave to assure him, that the Description we gave of that Cucumber was true . . . As we have undeniable Proofs of the Truth of this Account, we venture to send it to the Northward, for Improvement, or Admiration." Garden historian Wesley Greene identifies both the Ohio and Williamsburg cucumbers as *Cucumis flexucsus*, the serpent, snake or Armenian cucumber, more a melon than a cucumber and mentioned by John Randolph in 1793 as *Cucumis oblongus* "cultivated only in curious gardens, and . . . remarkable for their length and fewness of seed."[16]

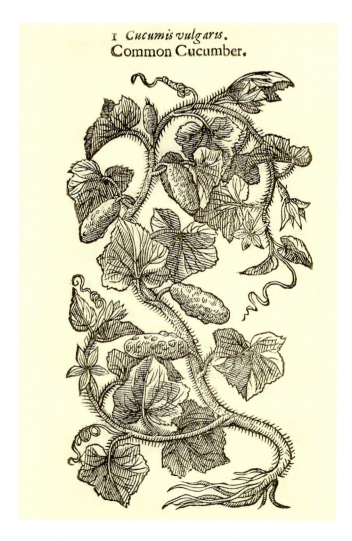

I *Cucumis vulgaris.*
Common Cucumber.

6.9. The lumpy, misshapen cucumber illustrated in John Gerard's *Herball,* 1633, varies dramatically from the smooth-skinned, torpedo shapes we know today

Cucumbers were cherished by the Greeks and Romans, but even by 1633 John Gerard's *Herball* depicts an unappealing, lumpy, potato-shaped fruit (fig. 6.9) that was eaten out of the garden with salt, oil, and vinegar. Introduced into the New World by Columbus in 1494, cucumbers, perhaps mistaken for forms of squash or pumpkin, were observed in American Indian gardens by the earliest explorers. Although not abundant in late eighteenth-century Virginia seed lists—they were sold by Miles Taylor and Minton Collins in Richmond, by Peter Crouwells in Alexandria, and in Williamsburg stores—cucumbers were a staple of the summer vegetable garden. Francis Taylor of Orange County mentioned the planting of cucumber seeds more than any other Virginian, averaging six sowings a year between 1787 and 1799.[17]

Cucumbers thrive in warm, sunny Virginia with only casual attention, as documented by the out-of-the-way sites like the "potato patch" and "about the cherry stump" where Francis Taylor planted them. Nevertheless, American garden writers doggedly followed tradition and recommended lavish attention upon them. Monticello cucumbers in 1813 "failed from drought," and writers such as John Randolph emphasized the need for carefully formed "basons" around plants to trap and hold moisture in the Virginia heat. From Washington, John Gardiner and Alexander Hepburn in *The American Gardener* (1804) suggested watering cucumbers three or four times weekly in August. Bernard McMahon's instructions for cucumber culture were consistently the first chore in his monthly advice on kitchen gardening, and his 1806 *Calendar* included eight varieties, which garden historian U. P. Hedrick wrote were "little like" those grown today. Most early nineteenth-century varieties had a blunt rather than torpedo-like shape, as well as short spines running longitudinally down the fruit.[18]

Jefferson's modest "gerkin" (*Cucumis anguria*) was a surprisingly common crop in the late summer Monticello garden, planted in six seasons between 1812 and 1824, sometimes in July, when few vegetables are sown. Jefferson recommended it to his brother, Randolph, in 1813: "The season being over for planting everything but the Gerkin . . . It is that by which we distinguish the very small pickling cucumber." This was likely the West Indian gherkin, a native of Africa brought to the Caribbean through the slave trade, then reputedly introduced from Jamaica by Minton Collins in his Richmond store in 1793. McMahon identified the "round prickly" cucumber as *Cucumis anguria* in 1806. The West Indian gherkin is an aggressive vine with smallish leaves that are lobed like a miniature watermelon leaf. The three-inch-long plump fruit are round, firm, and covered with blunt spines.[19]

Eggplant:
The Mischievous Mad Apple, the Lusty Brown Jolly

Eggplants were a novel but prized vegetable planted in the retirement garden in 1809, 1810, 1812, and 1814 but first obtained by Jefferson from a Monticello neighbor, Peter Derieux, in 1796. Three years earlier Jefferson had written to Derieux, a French emigrant schoolteacher and husband of Philip Mazzei's stepdaughter, that "the Melonzone (Solanum Melonzo[ni] of the botanists) is unknown to me. I expect they will be to be found only in possession of Mr. Bartram who keeps a botanical garden some miles in the country [outside Philadelphia]." Later that June, Jefferson's daughter, the gardening novice Martha, proudly wrote her father from Charlottesville, "I . . . have the promise of an egg plant from Mr. Derieux" (fig. 6.10). Not until July 1796 in a letter to Derieux did Jefferson acknowledge delivery of the "promise": "P.S. I was so pleased with the egg-plants brought by Peter, and his dressing according to the directions you were so good as to give, that I must ask some seed, and advice how to cultivate them." This Peter was Monticello's African American cook Peter Hemings, who

6.10. Eggplants ("melongena" to Jefferson) produce abundantly in the warm microclimate of the Monticello garden

had been trained by his brother James. Despite Jefferson's endorsement of Peter's eggplant preparation, no record of eggplant cultivation survives until the 1809 Kalendar, when seeds were sowed in a row in square IX on April 21. These "failed" owing to that year's cold and drought. Undeterred, Jefferson planted seed again in 1811 on June 1, and the resultant seedlings were transplanted two weeks later. They may also have perished, because Jefferson requested seed from Bernard McMahon in 1812, when the Kalendar cited plantings of White, "Prickly," and Purple "Melongena" in adjacent rows in square IX.[20]

6.11. "Mala insana" illustrated in Leonhard Fuchs's *De Historia Stirpium*, 1542, suggests how the English name for *eggplant* may have originated

Although not matched by recipes in the Jefferson family documents, Mary Randolph's directions for preparing eggplants reflect an exuberant culinary wisdom. "They are delicious," she wrote, "tasting much like soft crabs." She first recommended dipping sliced "young and fresh" purple ("the purple are best") eggplants in egg yolk and bread crumbs to "fry them a nice brown." Alternatively, skinned and seeded eggplants could be parboiled, filled with a meat stuffing, and then stewed in a "well seasoned gravy."[21]

The eggplant (*Solanum melongena*), long distributed in Asia, Africa, and the Middle East, was first illustrated in Europe by Swiss naturalist Leonhard Fuchs in *De Historia Stirpium* (1542; fig. 6.11). His "Mala insana" has glistening white fruit shaped and colored like a chicken's egg. Only in English does the name refer to this likeness. Fuchs wrote, "Those who have some interest in sanity, those at once terrified by its very name, will avoid using these." The dubious reputation of eggplant, the "fruit the bignesse of a goose egge," was also expressed by English herbalist John Gerard. "The people of Tolledo do eat them with great devotion being boiled with fat flesh . . . But I rather with English men to content themselves with the meate of sauce of our owne Countrey, than with fruit and sauce eaten with such peril; for doubtlesse these apples have a mischievous qualitie, the use whereof is utterly to be forsaken." Already stigmatized by its classification in the deadly nightshade family, *Solanum*, the eggplant was thought to be native to the area around the Dead Sea, reputedly the home of Sodom and Gomorrah. The "apple of Sodom" consumed by John Milton's fallen angels in *Paradise Lost* (1687) was "with spattering noise Rejected." By 1768, Philip Miller had winnowed out the mythical associations, except for the fruit's propensity for "provoking lust." He said the Brown Jolly, as this "esteemed delicacy" was called in the British Caribbean, was only a curiosity in England, where garden authorities banished it to the flower garden.[22]

6.12. White eggplants in the garden, July 2010

Some authors have suggested that the eggplant was introduced to the colonies by Africans through the slave trade with the West Indies. William Byrd may have been alluding to eggplants in 1737 when he mentioned a "Guinea" melon in Virginia gardens. Lady Jean Skipwith, a skilled gardener who lived near the North Carolina border at Prestwould, recorded planting "Brown Jelly" in 1793, and William Faris of Annapolis sowed "egg plant" seed as an ornamental in pots. Bernard McMahon sold seeds of both White and Purple eggplant in 1804, but he listed them with ornamental flowers rather than with vegetables. John Gardiner and Alexander Hepburn in *The American Gardener* (1804) provided the first advice for growing culinary eggplants in the United States, but McMahon may have enhanced their popularity in 1806 when he recommended this "delicious" fruit be sliced and "nicely fried," producing a dish "nearer to that of a fried oyster than perhaps, any other plant." Urban seed companies sold eggplant seed, including the White (fig. 6. 2), regarded more often as an ornamental, the Purple, and the "large new prickly." "Prickly" is a reference to the spiny calyx where the stem merges into the fruit.[23]

6.13. Hops vines on poles in the submural beds below the garden terrace

Although one of Jefferson's most persistent horticultural legacies is as a failed grape grower and winemaker, homemade beer, along with apple cider, was produced with such success that it became a regular "table liquor" in Monticello's dining room. Hops (*Humulus lupulus*), native to northern Europe, were necessary to flavor and preserve beer. The dried fruit was purchased in large quantities from Monticello slaves, and in 1812 perennial vines were planted in the submural beds below the garden wall in a bed as long as one hundred feet. This planting was probably in response to the increased demand for hops made by Captain Joseph Miller, an experienced London brewer whom Jefferson had hired to train Peter Hemings and whose Monticello ale became the toast of the community (fig. 6.13).[24]

Breweries were well established in large American cities around 1800, but in rural Virginia homemade beer was an integral part of life. From his arrival at Monticello, Jefferson reserved room in the cellars for the making and storage of beer, and his books included Michael Cornbrunie's *Theory and Practice of Brewing* (1801). Jefferson's wife, Martha, was Monticello's first brewer, in the 1770s overseeing the brewing of fifteen-gallon batches of a simple "small beer" made from molasses and hops every two to three weeks. Captain Miller arrived in Albemarle County, where he had nearby relatives, after being shipwrecked along Virginia's Atlantic shores at the onset of the War of 1812. Jefferson welcomed the arrival of the British brewer, writing "I wish to see this beverage become common instead of the whiskey which kills one third of our citizens and ruins their families." Miller settled at Monticello during the brewing season of 1813, malt was purchased from a neighbor, and he produced three sixty-gallon casks of what Jefferson referred to as "ale," suggesting it was a light beer. Peter

6.14. Thomas Jefferson grew hops at Monticello for brewing beer and also purchased them in large quantities from local slaves

Hemings, who possessed "great intelligence and diligence," according to Jefferson, took over the brewing, and Jefferson moved to plantation-grown Indian corn as a source for the malt. Neighbors, including James Madison and former Governor James Barbour, asked for Jefferson's ale recipe (which he never actually wrote down) or requested that one of their workers be trained in the process.[25]

Hops were known to the ancient Romans, perhaps as an esculent vegetable (the young shoots can be cut and prepared like asparagus), but as an ingredient in beer making, hops date to Germany in the eighth and ninth centuries. Hop gardens, as they were known, were common in eighteenth-century Kent, and Philip Miller devotes five pages to their cultivation for brewing in *The Gardener's Dictionary*. The earliest reports from Jamestown documented how "their Hops are faire and large, thrive well," and the Moravians in Salem, North Carolina, cultivated the species on a large scale in the late eighteenth century. William Cobbett was probably the first to consider hops as a kitchen garden crop for brewing in *The American Gardener* (1821). He compared English-grown hops "kept in a garden state," with the commercial hops grown more casually along the Susquehanna River, where the vines were riddled with weeds

6.15. Anne Arundel muskmelons in a northwest border bed

and grazed by sheep. Cobbett concluded that "in America any *stick* will carry enough to supply a family" (fig. 6.14).[26]

Muskmelon: "Multiplying the good things of life"

Although he wrote from Paris that "muskmelons, such as are here, are worse than the worst in Virginia," and he sent to Charlottesville for seed of "fine Cantaloupe melon" for his Parisian garden to show off to his French friends, Jefferson regarded muskmelons (*Cucumis melo*) as only a casual crop in the Monticello garden (fig. 6.15). Melons were seldom planted, and when they were, they shared space in the major squares with such other vegetables as okra, nasturtiums, and squashes. Jefferson hinted that muskmelons failed to thrive at Monticello. In 1800 he thanked America's most prominent physician, Benjamin Rush, for melon seeds, writing warily that he would "try

whether the climate of Monticello can preserve them without degeneracy." Jefferson may have failed to remedy the "degeneracy" issue, at least in his early season plans for the 1813 garden, when he planned in his "Agenda" to sow melons with squashes, a sure recipe for cross-pollination. He often deflected gifts of melon seeds to more proficient gardeners. In 1810 he sent "a very fine melon," the winter melon, to Judge William Johnson, because "I think it will be more likely to do well with you than here," and in 1816 Jefferson acknowledged a gift of Persian melons from Baltimore's John Campbell White but emphasized, "especially to dispense it among his [Jefferson's] most careful acquaintances." Jefferson added, "It is by multiplying the good things of life that the mass of human happiness is increased." These are two succinct confirmations of Jefferson's ultimate gardening role as a facilitator. Whether because of the Virginia humidity, the heavy clay soil, or the skills of the gardener, fine and tasty melons are only occasionally harvested from the restored Monticello garden today.[27]

Few vegetable harvests produce a fruit so sweet and juicy, and a ripe muskmelon from the garden has been a treasured prize since the early seventeenth century, in part because of its reputation for being difficult to grow. A native of the Old World tropics and associated with the Middle East, the muskmelon was deemed a rewarding crop by the earliest English writers, such as John Parkinson in 1629, though challenging to grow in the cool and cloudy English garden: "Many have tried and endeavoured to bring them to perfection, yet few have attained unto it." By the eighteenth century no vegetable in the English kitchen garden received such exaggerated attention as the muskmelon. In 1768 Philip Miller devoted eight thousand words to its culture, prescribing elaborately made up hotbeds for February sowings and successive transplanting and an exact and unforgiving formula for planting soils.[28]

The Spanish introduced muskmelons into North America, and like the Old World cucumber, they were often recorded in Ameri-

6.16. Mary Randolph's *Virginia House-wife*, 1824, includes a recipe for ice cream made from citron melon

6.17. Seeds of the popular Nutmeg melon, "which I know to be fine," were sent by Jefferson to his son-in-law John Wayles Eppes in 1811

can Indian gardens, perhaps mistaken for gourds or pumpkins. William Hugh Grove wrote in 1737, "Musk Melons are plentifull Enough but they [Indians] plant them among their Corn in the shade & ordinary ground with out any care as our Gardeners use & have not the Advantage of Soyl or sun & Consequently the high flavor of our Engl Melons." Richard Parkinson noticed the same companion planting—corn with melons—in fields around Baltimore in 1800. Landon Carter complained that "not a melon of any Kind can be kept" because of thievery at Sabine Hall in 1773. Francis Taylor planted melons in "hills" bordered by cucumbers in the tobacco nursery or "plant patch." "Bugs" destroyed his melons in 1788. In contrast, John Tayloe's gardener planted muskmelons more deliberately in hotbeds at Mount Airy in 1805, evidently following the cultural advice of writers like McMahon and Miller. While Washington market gardeners used hotbeds to force cucumbers, the late date of August 2 suggests that melons were grown only in the open ground. This confirms William Cobbett's view that in America melons were casually "brought into market in wagon loads and . . . tossed down in immense heaps," not "carried by twos or threes with as much care as a new-born baby." Melon seed was consistenly offered by Virginia seed merchants in the eighteenth century and by urban nurseries in the early 1800s, but they were sometimes simply sold generically, as "melons," and varieties were not as abundantly listed as for other traditional English kitchen garden fare.[29]

   At one time or another Jefferson documented a notable array of melon varieties. Citron, "green," Pineapple, and "Venice" melons were "objects for the garden" in 1794. Mary Randolph offered a recipe for citron ice cream, and William Cobbett wrote that the citron "was the finest by far" of all muskmelons (fig. 6.16). Pineapple melon, a likely descendent of the citron line, was a cherished variety by the early 1800s with small, netted olive green skin, and a sweet, perfumed green flesh. Seeds of the "very fine" winter melon from Malta, probably from André Thöuin, were sowed in the 1809 garden. Jefferson wrote, "The fruit is gathered before the danger of frost . . . put away in a warm, dry place [so] it will go on mellowing as an apple. it is eaten through the months of Dec. Jan. & February." Seeds of the popular Nutmeg melon, "which I know to be fine," were sent by Jefferson to his son-in-lawn, John Wayles Eppes, in 1811 (fig. 6.17). These fragrant, oval-shaped, heavily netted, green-fleshed melons were commonly distributed by seed merchants.[30]

Nasturtiums: For the "Garden of Delight"

Nasturtiums are a multi dimensional esculent vegetable as well as a cherished ornamental. The young leaves are a spicy addition to fresh green salads, and the brightly colored orange and yellow flowers are also edible and provide a dashing garnish to any dish. Jefferson's inclusion of nasturtium among his "fruits" in 1812 suggests that he primarily harvested the seeds, which were pickled as an aromatic substitute for capers. Nasturtiums were popular at Monticello, and seed was sown yearly from 1812 to 1824, usually in square IX, center stage in the garden, and apparently occupying the entire sixteen-hundred-square-foot bed. This would produce a staggering number of nasturtium plants. Mary Randolph directed her readers to cover ripe nasturtium seeds with salted boiling water, let them stand for three or four days, then drain and cover with vinegar, adding whole peppercorns and "a few blades of mace." Some writers such as Bernard McMahon thought that nasturtiums were "better" than capers, and Randolph endorsed

6.18. Jefferson included nasturtium among the "Fruits" in his "Arrangement of the Garden," 1812, using the seeds as pickled capers

their substitution in her recipe for a caper-based butter sauce. Jefferson also acknowledged the nasturtium's place in the ornamental realm at Monticello when he included them in his 1782 "Calendar of the bloom of flowers" (fig. 6.18). By 1812 nasturtiums shared square IX with rows of melons, eggplants, and peppers—a pleasing blend of colorful fruit and flowers, a tidy marriage of the New and Old World for the warm-season vegetable garden.[31]

The two species of trailing and dwarf nasturtium, *Tropaeolum majus* and *T. minus*, were collected by the earliest Spanish explorers in the Peruvian Andes. As late as 1629 John Parkinson, though he acknowledged that the larger-growing "Indian Cress" or "yellow Larkes heeles" were grown as a salad in southern Europe, confined nasturtiums to his "Garden of delight [which] cannot be unfurnished of it." Miller described the "finer appearance" of "Indian cress" and endorsed eating the "very wholesome" orange and yellow flowers, as well as the pickled seeds. In Virginia, nasturtiums, or "Indian cresses," appeared in seed lists as early as 1768. John Randolph found the flowers "superior to a radish in flavour" and planted three seeds to a hill with a pea stick in the middle for support. Jefferson grew nasturtiums in "35. little hills" in 1774. Philadelphia plantsman William Hamilton used the vining nasturtium to hide the unsightly dead cedars at his renowned horticultural showcase, the Woodlands, while Kentucky's Joseph Hornsby planted ten-foot-long beds, not as large as Jefferson's but a significant investment of garden space. Bernard McMahon's focus was also on the flowers for "their excellence in salads" and the pickled seeds, rather than the leaves.[32]

Okra: From Slave Food to the South's Melting Dainty

Okra's yearly appearance in the retirement garden, as well as its central role in Monticello soups and stews, reinforces the garden's revolutionary role as a culinary melting pot of African, West Indian, and French traditions (fig. 6.19). Jefferson sowed this African native (*Abelmoschus esculentus*) from 1809 until 1823 (except for 1814), and in 1813 okra was planted as "edging" to the internal rows of tomatoes in square XII, next to the garden pavilion. Jefferson steadily moved his retirement plantings to earlier dates in the spring, before the standard April 15 frost date, a puzzling decision for a crop so suited to Monticello's warm and humid summer season. A recipe for okra soup, actually gumbo, has been attributed to Jefferson's daughter Martha. In this stew sliced okra pods were boiled with Cymlings or Pattypan squash, small Irish potatoes, an unusual gumbo ingredient, peeled "tomatas," lima beans, onions, parsley, and bacon. Chicken was added later. Martha's daughters Septimia Meikleham and Virginia Trist contributed variations that focused more on the meat preparation, and they added veal, corn, and green pepper. Randolph's *Virginia House-wife* also

6.19. The showy hibiscus-like flowers of okra with the young and mature pods

6.20. Rows of young okra plants in square XIV, September 2010

has recipes for both okra soup and "Gumbs—A West India Dish," essentially steamed okra pods served with melted butter that "are very nutritious and easy of digestion." *Gumbo,* a word derived from the Angolan *kingumbo,* meant okra, but *gumbo* later became a reference to the thick, mucilaginous quality of soups, traditionally provided by the gummy okra, but later artificially created with flour (fig. 6.20).[33]

Widely distributed in prehistoric Asia and Africa and first grown in Europe in southern Spain, okra was adopted in the West Indies by the 1780s. Natural historian Sir Hans Sloane wrote that okra was flourishing in Jamaica in 1707 in both European and slave gardens. In 1768 Philip Miller, who had grown this handsome relative of the hollyhock for years, observed that in the West Indies the harvested pods "add a thickness to their soups, and renders them very palatable." Okra was grown around Charleston and New Orleans in the eighteenth century, but it was rarer in Virginia than such other uncommon vegetables as eggplants, tomatoes, and cayenne peppers. Enslaved African Americans are generally credited with introducing okra, and the means in which it was prepared, into the colonies. In a surprisingly early record of 1748, Peter Kalm noticed how okra in Philadelphia gardens was made into a soup "as thick as porridge. This dish is reckoned a dainty by some people and especially by the negroes." In 1787 Charleston's Robert Squibb provided full directions on the plant's need for "low" ground and a lot of space. In 1802 William Faris sowed "ocro" in as many as sixty-two specially prepared hills in his outlying "Lott" in order to harvest seeds that were dried and ground into a coffee substitute, which Bernard McMahon described as "much superior to foreign coffee." McMahon offered okra seed for sale around 1804, and it became more common thereafter, sold regularly in urban seed establishments.[34]

Peppers: "Planting is one of my great amusements"

Jefferson grew various forms of Bell, Bullnose, sweet, and cayenne pepper (*Capsicum annuum*), as well as Texas bird pepper (*Capsicum annuum* var. *glabriusculum*). His documented sowing of cayenne pepper seed at Shadwell in 1767 is one of the earliest references to this form of *Capsicum* in North America (fig. 6.21). Later, in the 1812 "Calendar," "Major," "cayenne," and "Bullnose" (marked by a crinkled noselike appendage on the blossom end) were planted in adjacent rows in square IX. The Texas bird pepper, obtained from Dr. Samuel Brown of Natchez through acquaintances near San Antonio, was among Jefferson's most exciting introductions. Jefferson planted

6.21. Jefferson first planted cayenne peppers at Shadwell, his birthplace, in 1767 and included them among the hundreds of plants listed in his garden calendar for 1812

6.22. Cayenne pepper illustrated in Leonhard Fuchs's
De Historia Stirpium, 1542

bird pepper seed in the garden and with a dibble in flowerpots, and relayed the seed to Bernard McMahon in 1813. Green (also called Bell and Bullnose) peppers appear in the Jefferson family manuscripts as additions to tomato pickles and gumbo soup, while cayenne peppers were added to Virginia Randolph Trist's tomato soup and Septimia Meikleham's salad dressing. The Monticello family physician, Dr. Dunglison, prescribed a red pepper gargle to relieve the sore throats of Jefferson's granddaughters. Culinary historian Karen Hess called the use of hot peppers in traditional Virginia cooking "highly skilled and discrete."[35]

The motley tribe of *Capsicum annuum* are New World natives that were often described and illustrated in sixteenth- and seventeenth-century European herbals. Swiss herbalist Leonhard Fuchs depicted a long red cayenne pepper in *De Historia Stirpium* in 1542 (fig. 6.22) and discussed a block-shaped sweet pepper. John Gerard reviewed three principal sorts, and Richard Bradley listed twenty varieties in 1728. In an early edition of *The Gardener's Dictionary,* Philip Miller said that peppers were "of no great use in England" despite extolling "the wholesomest Pickles in the World" made from bell-shaped peppers. By 1768 he was recommending peppers chiefly for ornamental gardens and flowerpots but also praised the cake-like pepper pots made in the West Indies that reputedly relieved flatulence.[36]

Peppers may have been brought into North America by coastal traders or slaves born in the West Indies, where European explorers described the use of hot peppers to enliven native dishes. Travelers described Jamaican Indians pickling bell-shaped peppers in the 1600s. Swedish botanist Peter Kalm observed "guinea peppers" and "*piment*" in gardens near Philadelphia in 1748 and Albany in 1749. He was impressed by the versatility of this "spice" when pickling cucumbers, flavoring stews, and preserving peppers with salt and vinegar in bottles. The North Carolina Moravians, immigrants

6.23. With its rich foliage and shiny fruit, Texas bird pepper is an attractive ornamental

from Pennsylvania, brought "Spanish peppers" to Salem as early as 1759. John Randolph in his *Treatise* around the Revolution and Gardiner and Hepburn in *The American Gardener* (1804) briefly allude to planting peppers for pickling. "Indian Peppers" were planted by Orange County's Francis Taylor in 1791 and 1792; William Faris grew cherry peppers in Annapolis in 1799; and Lady Jean Skipwith mentioned peppers in her Prestwould garden in southern Virginia around 1800. McMahon's seed house offered eight *Capsicum* varieties around 1804, but they were called "Annual Flowers" and sold as ornamentals. Pepper seed was found only occasionally on urban lists of the early 1800s. William Booth of Baltimore, for example, sold three varieties of *Capsicum* for the flower garden in 1810.[57]

The Texas bird pepper is a pretty plant: a tidy, compact mound of rich green foliage capped with petite, sparkling red peppers. Native to northern Mexico and southwest Texas, where it is known as Chiltepin or Chiltecpin, this species is the wild ancestor of many of our cultivated chile peppers (fig. 6.23). Texas bird peppers were used to make pepper vinegar, pepper sauce, and pickles and were the main ingredient of pepper pots. Jean Andrews, in *Peppers: The Domesticated Capsicums,* reports that "originally, the Nahuatl [Aztec] word meaning flea was applied [to the bird pepper] because of the similarity in size and bite." In Mexico, she continues, the flavor is described as "'arrebatado,' an expression that means 'although it is extremely hot the sensation disappears easily and rapidly.'" Chiltepins are still harvested in the wild and sold in Mexican markets, though native colonies of bird peppers in Texas are becoming rare.[38]

In letters to Jefferson, Dr. Brown noted that Spaniards and American Indians used bird pepper as Europeans do salt. He said it had potentially important medicinal qualities, particularly for "disorders of the alimentary canal," and noted that "a tablespoon of the pods will communicate to Vinegar a fine aromatic flavor." Brown added, "The Americans . . . make a Pickle of the green Pods with Salt & . . . I find this taste growing so fast that it will soon become as essential to my health as salt itself." Jefferson was excited by the possibilities and wrote to Brown how, if it proved hardy, the bird pepper would be "a valuable addition to our gardens." He also exclaimed on the initial shipment of seed, "Planting is one of my great amusements." Typically reticent about assuming the full responsibility for preserving Brown's bird peppers, Jefferson forwarded seed to McMahon, to whom he wrote, "They will be more likely however to be preserved in your hands." An oral history tradition credits McMahon with a central role in popularizing the species throughout southeastern Pennsylvania, where the potted pepper plants served as a winter table ornament or as windowsill plants.[39]

Sesame: "Among the most valuable acquisitions"

The horticultural drama of growing bene, or sesame (*Sesamum indicum*), at Monticello expressed many of the themes that defined Jefferson's gardening experiments (fig. 6.24). A whirlwind of excitement arose from his initial sampling of sesame oil in the President's House,

6.24. Rows of sesame in square XIV, July 2010

sent by William Few, a farmer and politician from New York, in 1808. Sesame inspired typical hyperbole, such as "This is among the most valuable acquisitions our country has ever made," in letters Jefferson wrote to his community of agricultural reformers. Jefferson enthusiastically distributed sesame seed to nationally renowned farmers and gardeners, including Bernard McMahon and John Taylor. Failure marked the initial trials at Monticello as an unlucky September frost in 1808 and an unprecedented drought in 1809 diminished the harvest. Indefatigable, Jefferson continued sowing sesame until he was eighty-one years old. This handsome plant combines utility with beauty, and Jefferson used sesame ornamentally, as an edging plant to his garden square of carrots, in 1813. He also persistently experimented with at least three seed presses, one the result of his own design. The Jeffersonian propensity for detailed and exacting measurements is illustrated in a Garden Book entry of April 16, 1811: "1, gill of seed drilled 12. rows of 153. yds on an average equal to 1836 yds. Consequently to drill an acre in 4. f. drills would take 2. gills of seed."[40]

Jefferson's experiments at pressing sesame were ultimately unsuccessful. He underestimated the species' hardiness and the enormous amount of tiny sesame seed required to make a significant quantity of oil, his seed presses really never worked properly, and he found the seed difficult to separate cleanly from the chaff (fig. 6.25). Sesame oil never replaced other vegetable oils or butter on American tables. However, Jefferson's acceptance of a new food tradition is another testament to his open embrace of new plants as a means of transforming society.

6.25. Sesame flowers and the resultant seed capsules form in the axis of the leaves

In January 1808, at the president's table in Washington, Jefferson held a "blind tasting" of salad oils made from both olives and sesame seeds, and the guests preferred the sesame oil. He wrote to William Few that he "did not believe there existed so perfect a substitute for olive oil. Like that of Florence it has no taste, and is perhaps more limpid." He added, "I would prefer to have it always fresh from my own fields to the other brought across the Atlantic and exposed in hot warehouses." Jefferson also freely acknowledged its African origins and the food traditions that sesame, or bene, inspired among Lowcountry slaves, noting that "they bake it in their bread, boil it with greens, enrich their broth, etc." Jefferson copied Philip Miller's extensive information on sesame from *The Gardener's Dictionary* in a letter to James Taylor and disputed McMahon's allocation of the species to the "greenhouse" rather than to the garden or field. On March 22, 1808, Jefferson forwarded seed to his granddaughter Anne Cary Randolph and told her to instruct the enslaved gardener Wormley Hughes to sow "in some open place in the garden by dropping two or three seeds every 10. or 12. I. along a row, and by rows 2. feet apart." Although Jefferson could report the sesame was "growing luxuriantly" on August 20, a record-setting September frost destroyed most of the seed harvest. Nevertheless, a small sample of seed was saved for sowing the next two years, and Jefferson documented producing at least one gallon of sesame oil in 1810, a modest accomplishment.[41]

Jefferson acknowledged that "our cultivation has not yet had entire success" to Georgia governor John Milledge in June 1811, when he also detailed his trials with three different presses to extract oil from the seed. An iron press induced "a brown tinge to the oil," and a wooden press used in flax processing was "troublesome and embarrassing," but Jefferson's own adoption of "a simple mortise in a block . . . answered best of all," at least initially (fig. 6.26). Jefferson also complained about cleaning the seed—separating it from the chaff of leaves and pods—and asked for advice from the experienced

6.26. Dried pods and seeds of sesame

Milledge. Finally, Jefferson unfairly blamed the species' lack of cold hardiness: "Consequently our climate will barely permit us to make enough for family use." Milledge wrote back, agreeing that domestic production for use within a plantation was "as much as can be done." In fact, the growing season at Monticello is easily long enough for raising sesame; the worst problem is the inefficiency of seed production. Jefferson's initial bookish calculations on production—an acre of sesame produces ten bushels of seed, ten bushels produce thirty gallons of oil—were wildly optimistic and surely resulted in a crushing disappointment. Despite such setbacks, Jefferson never gave up, planting seed six times between 1812 and 1824, a gentleman's recreation rather than the salvation of the country's agricultural economy.[42]

Commonly described as "the oldest oil seed plant known by humans," sesame has been distributed throughout Asia, the Middle East, Africa, and the Mediterranean since the beginnings of ancient culture. In a letter that accompanied the precious bottle of sesame oil to Jefferson, William Few discussed sesame's heritage: "The Negroes are well acquainted with it and fond of cultivating it." Although Few believed it was "probably" introduced from the "Slave Coast" of West Africa, he also posited the Mediterranean as another possible homeland. Jefferson, perhaps because he recognized the etymology of the South Carolina Gullah word *bene,* settled the issue by emphatically attributing the seed's introduction to African slaves. *Bene* is a feminine noun in the language of the Bambara of French West Africa and of the Wolof tribe in Senegal and Gambia. Jefferson spelled it four ways: "bene," "benni," "beny," and "benney."[43]

The naturalist Sir Hans Sloane first observed sesame in "negros" gardens in Jamaica in 1687, and Thomas Lowndes of Charleston sent sesame oil to London in 1730, writing optimistically, "This seed will make the Pine Barrens land of equal value with the rice land." William Byrd noted how trials with North Carolina sesame oil met "with good success" soon after. Philip Miller in 1754 reported that sesame culture was common in South Carolina. Miller was impressed that the oil resisted becoming rancid for years and that nine pounds of seed made two quarts of oil, a remarkably efficient productiveness that inspired the English name for the plant, "oily-grain." Miller wrote on the use of the parched seed by enslaved Africans in the Carolinas as a "hearty Food" when mixed with water and stewed, as well as made into puddings similarly to rice. Records in Savannah of the exportation of five hundred pounds of bene in 1774 to an unnamed port suggest some commercial ambitions. Nevertheless, sesame was only a regional commodity in the South, grown by enslaved African Americans for the kitchen and occasionally on plantations for minor oil production. It was absent from American seed lists and garden manuals, except for McMahon's inclusion of "oily-grain" among "Tender Annual Flowers" in his *Calendar.* Jefferson's fascination with sesame helped inspire Southern members of Congress to promote its culture

vocally in 1809, and in South Carolina a gold medal was promised to the largest producer of sesame oil. Although it remains a common ingredient in confections and has been immortalized for its use on hamburger buns, sesame was among Jefferson's unrequited causes in garden experimentation.[44]

Squashes and Cymlings Thomas Jefferson, Plant Breeder?

Jefferson recorded planting a variety of squash, a member of the Cucurbita family of some eight hundred species and one hundred genera of plants, including many vegetables that have been historically confused: melons, cucumbers, pumpkins, and gourds among them. In addition, the squash (usually *Cucurbita pepo*) easily crosses within its species and so has an endless variation of types. In his writings on squash, Jefferson, unfortunately, added further twists to an already muddled botanical and vernacular nomenclature. His favorite was the uniquely southern American Cymling for Jefferson "one of our finest and most innocent vegetables," a white scalloped summer squash known today as Pattypan (fig. 6.27). Pattypans were grown in the retirement garden, purchased commonly from Monticello slave gardens, and both added to family soup recipes and likely boiled and stewed along with butter, salt, and pepper.[45]

By playing around with the cross-pollination of pumpkins and squashes, Jefferson may have developed his own versions of Cymling and other kinds of squash. In 1801 Jefferson wrote Philip Mazzei and urged him to plant Cymlings and pumpkins together: "You will produce the perfect equivalent of the Squash, and I am persuaded the Squash was originally so produced and that it is a Hybridal plant." In 1809 Jefferson planted a submural terraced bed with "soft cymling," "squash from [Washington nurseryman Thomas] Maine," and two varieties of pumpkin, perhaps to encourage the promiscuous prolif-

6.27. Cymlings, or Pattypan, were the squash of choice among Virginia gardeners around 1800

eration of pumpkin-type fruits. In addition, Jefferson commonly used the plural, "squashes" rather than "squash," when recording plantings, in his "Objects for the garden" in 1794 and between 1817 and 1824 in the Kalendar; this diversity of "squashes" would occur if seed was saved from cross-pollinated plants. Intentionally or not, Thomas Jefferson was having fun with squashes. In 1806 Bernard McMahon thanked Jefferson for seeds "of the Cucurbita you were so kind to send me, some grew to the length of five feet five inches. I have one of them in my shop window, perfectly dry . . . they are excellent to use as squashes while young." Was this showcase specimen from Jefferson an example of deliberate Monticello plant breeding? Probably not. Philip Miller wrote in his *Gardener's Dictionary* (1768) about the problem of maintaining varietal purity: "I have cultivated most of the sorts near forty years, and have not been able, with all possible care,

to preserve the varieties longer than two or three years in the same garden."[46]

Pattypan squash, an American native grown and, according to at least one authority, developed by eastern North American Indians, was integral to the gardens of enslaved African Americans, but it also was the universal squash among white Virginians in the age of Jefferson. Providing tangible evidence of a distinctly American product, Jefferson passed on seed to European gardeners like Madame de Tessé and Philip Mazzei. In a letter to Poplar Forest overseer Jeremiah Goodman, Jefferson implied that Pattypans were a common staple among slaves, and they were the fourth most frequently purchased vegetable at Monticello from enslaved gardeners such as Squire and Bagwell. "Cymlins," not "squash," were the ingredient added to Monticello soup, Monticello gumbo, and the Albemarle version of the Spanish dish known as olla. The "squashes" purchased from the Washington markets by Etienne Lemaire on fourteen occasions, usually in late summer and early fall, might have been Pattypan, a summer Crookneck, or, remotely, a form of winter squash. Jefferson grew other squashes, including the "long crooked & warted Squash" that was sent to him by Philadelphia's Timothy Matlack. This squash was probably similar to the yellow Crookneck so abundant today. In 1817 Jefferson recorded planting both "summer" and "winter" squash, finally a simple way of organizing such a confusing tribe (fig. 6.28). Although Monticello squash was harvested as early as June 20, the summer types were picked through July and August.[47]

Forms of *Cucurbita pepo* (summer squash and Pattypans) probably originated in Central America and Mexico. Documented confusingly by the earliest Spanish adventurers, they were soon illustrated and described in early sixteenth-century European herbals. Squash, of course, was among the "three sisters" of North American Indian gardens. In North Carolina in 1709, John Lawson found many tribes within the Cucurbit race: "Pompions yellow and very

6.28. This depiction of a confused squash plant,
from Petri Matthioli's *De Medica Materia,* 1554, suggests how
cross-pollination with other species and varieties might
theoretically result in a multifarious production of fruit

6.29. Green-striped Cashaw is a productive squash for the fall months

large [*Cucurbita maxima*], Burmillions [a variety squash, perhaps eaten "green"], Cashaws, an excellent Fruit boiled [*C. argyrosperma*, in effect, a winter squash] Squashes [probably a summer squash], Simnals [or Cymlings], Horns [a summer or winter Crookneck], and Gourds [not eaten but used for the dried vessel] (fig. 6.29)." Robert Beverley in 1737 was delighted with the diversity of muskmelons, watermelons, and pumpkins in both native and European Virginia gardens, but he was also impressed by "Macocks, sometimes called Cymnels from the Lenten Cake of the Name." Beverley's "Lenten Cake" was a round cake decorated with small balls of almond paste, rounded and scalloped around the edges. He added, "These being boil'd whole, when the Apple is young, and the Shell Tender, and dished with Cream or Butter, relish very with all sorts of Butcher's Meat." William Hugh Grove in 1737 also tried Cymlings and noted that they were requested at the tables of the Virginia gentry.[48]

Squash needs warmth and sun, and London's Philip Miller, while growing scores of squashes variously colored and shaped, wrote, "Their fruit [was] little valued in England." Squash, from the Algonquin word *askutasquash,* or "that which is eaten green," became well established in gardens and garden "patches" in the British colonies and Virginia during the eighteenth century. Peter Kalm in 1748 and 1749 saw squashes ("gourds or melons raised by Indians called squash by the English") planted in "large quantities" throughout New York, New Jersey, and Pennsylvania. They were harvested while green, boiled, and "put on the edge of the dish round the meat." Landon Carter grew "cymlins" in 1778, and Francis Taylor sowed "cymblings" every April or May from 1787 to 1791. William Faris of Annapolis reserved precious space, enough for thirteen hills in 1803, for Pattypan squash in his town garden, yet he purchased "cymlins" twenty-one times at the market, more than any other vegetable. Since most commercial garden seed originated from imported European stock, squash seed was unavailable from eighteenth-century merchants. Squash growing was not included in the eighteenth-century gardening manuals and was mentioned only briefly by writers such as Bernard McMahon.[49]

"Tomatas": The Strange and Sexy Love Apple

Now everyone's favorite vegetable, "Tomatas" (Jefferson's spelling suggests the waning American pronunciation, "toe-mah-toe") were an indispensable ingredient of the Monticello retirement garden. Jefferson was a pioneer grower of this grudgingly accepted, myth-ridden vegetable. Tomatoes (*Lycopersicon lycopersicum*) were planted yearly between 1809 and 1824, often in the centrally located square X, and in 1812 and 1813 in conjunction with okra. Jefferson's appreciation of, and success with, the tomato was best expressed by the "love apple's" presence in the Monticello kitchen. His granddaughters Virginia Randolph Trist and Septimia Meikleham left numerous tomato recipes, including different kinds of gumbo soup, the Spanish olla, cayenne-

6.30. Cross section of a Costoluto Genovese tomato

spiced tomato soup, tomato pickles, preserves, and omelets. Mary Randolph's *Virginia House-wife* marked one of the first appearances of tomatoes in an American cookbook, and tomatoes show up more often within its pages than any other vegetable. Tomato catsup, gazpacho, and stewed and scalloped tomatoes are among her seventeen tomato-based concoctions. Culinary historian Karen Hess writes that the "richness and range" of these recipes "indicates long familiarity with the tomato." In 1806 Etienne Lemaire purchased tomatoes eight times from the Washington farmers' market, where tomatoes were sold between July 16 and November 17 during Jefferson's presidential tenure.[50]

Jefferson's son-in-law Thomas Mann Randolph summarized the place of the tomato in early nineteenth-century Virginia in a speech before the Albemarle Agricultural Society in 1824. He stated that whereas tomatoes were virtually unknown ten years earlier, by

1824 most citizens were eating them, not necessarily for their delicious sweet and tart flavor but because they "kept blood pure in the heat of summer" (fig. 6.30). This supports the thesis of Andrew Smith in *The Tomato in America,* who argues that American's initial experimental use of tomatoes for their medicinal qualities evolved into a gradual acceptance of their flavor and taste. Bernard McMahon, for example, sold love apple seed around 1804 under "Physical Herbs" before writing about their "much admired" flavor in his 1806 *Gardener's Calendar.* Other gardeners, such as the English garden writers of the eighteenth century, or James Middleton of Charleston's Middleton Place, initially grew the love apple as an ornamental, perhaps only to discover that the joys of the eye often lead to the savoring pleasures of the tongue.[51]

Although Jefferson wrote that tomatoes were common in Virginia gardens as early as 1781, Monticello plantings were not documented until 1809. The garden-savvy George Divers provided the seeds (or plants) for "transplants" that were set out in a specially prepared bed in the asparagus square on June 3. Jefferson also received seeds of the "Spanish tomato (very much larger than the common kinds)" from General John Mason of Maryland in 1809 and planted them in the northwest border, opposite square VI. Jefferson continued to plant tomatoes until he was eighty-one, including a "dwarf" variety alongside the "Spanish" tomato in 1817. Tomato seeds were also planted at Poplar Forest in 1811, suggesting the tomato's importance to the Jefferson table even when he was away from Monticello.[52]

Myths abound about Jefferson and the introduction of the tomato. One doubtful story that is still celebrated with a tomato festival was first recounted by W. Asbury Christian in *Lynchburg and Its People* (1900). He wrote how Jefferson, "seeing some Love Apples [in a Lynchburg garden] . . . asked a girl standing near a gate why she did not eat them. 'Because they are poison,' she replied. 'Bring me one,' said Mr. Jefferson, 'and I will eat it.' She gave him one, and, to her great surprise, he ate it. This was the first time tomatoes, or love apples, were ever eaten in Lynchburg." The tomato, scorned for centuries by northern Europeans for "a ranke and stinking savour" and "slimy juice and watery pulp," was an ideal candidate for promotion by a child of the Enlightenment like Thomas Jefferson. In his *Notes on the State of Virginia,* which was in part a promotional tract, Jefferson wistfully included tomatoes as standard garden fare in 1781 Virginia, along with muskmelons and watermelons, okra, pomegranates, and figs. Like the tomato, such garden produce is uniquely sweet, lusciously juicy, and, for the northern European audience he was hoping to impress, singularly exotic.[53]

Few garden vegetables are as dazzlingly sensual as the tomato: a lush, rampant, twining vine with clinging, pungently fragrant foliage and, at least until the end of the nineteenth century, a misshapen but ornamental red fruit: lip-wetting with its juicy, sweetly tart liquid. Historically, the tomato has been too dangerously sexy for its own good. When introduced into sixteenth-century gardens, the tomato overwhelmed and frightened the earliest herbalist commentators, still medieval in their awe of the mysteries of nature. The sheer sensual shock of the tomato—stinky, wobbly, slimy—and the sometimes diabolical associations it received, continued to flavor its reception by gardeners well into the 1800s. Such a strange fruit inspired centuries of European storytelling.

Native to the coastal mountains of South America, tomatoes were encountered in domesticated varieties in 1519 by the Spanish in Mexico, where the Aztecs mixed "xitomatl" with chile peppers and squash seeds to create what we today call "salsa." German herbalist Petri Matthioli first described a yellow tomato, "mala aurea" or "golden apple," in 1544 that was prepared like fried eggplant. Perhaps because Matthioli associated tomatoes with another nightshade family member, the mandrake, which had presumed aphrodisiacal quality due to its entwining roots, or perhaps because Matthioli's "Pomi

6.31. Purple Calabash is distinguished by its dark and convoluted fruit and unique "acidic" flavor

d'oro" became corrupted by the Flemish herbalist Rembert Dodoens to "pomme d'amour," the "golden apple" became known in English as the "love apple." The tomato's earliest botanical name, *Lycopersicon,* or "wolf's peach," may have derived from a similarity between the juice of a yellow tomato and a peach. Further unsavory, mysterious, even devilish associations clouded the reputation of the tomato, already branded with the toxic qualities of the nightshade family. In addition, French author Charles de l'Écluse revived the myth of the Hesperides, Greek keepers of the golden apples, symbols of eternal life and divine fertility. Poisonous, dangerous, an aphrodisiac, the key to immortality—these were all associations that tempered the acceptance of the tomato in both northern Europe and North America.[54]

Well aware of the stories from Continental herbalists, London's John Gerard described "Apples of Love" in England in 1633 but dismissed the species because of "a ranke and stinking savour."

Tomatoes in seventeenth- and eighteenth-century England were regarded primarily as a garden ornamental, and perhaps an ethnic bias or nativist regionalism prevented their appearance in the diets of northern Europeans. John Parkinson described both yellow and red tomatoes with "slimy juice and watery pulp," but concluded, "Wee only have them for curiosity in our Gardens, and for the amorous aspect or beauty of the fruit." Philip Miller, in his *Gardener's Dictionary* (1754), conceded that the English were adding tomatoes to soup. "The Italians and Spaniard eat these Apples, as we do Cucumbers . . . There are some persons who think them not wholesome, from their great Moisture and Coldness." By 1768 Miller dismissed them from the pleasure garden for their ungainly habit and rank-scented foliage (fig. 6.31).[55]

Historian Andrew Smith claims the existence of more than five hundred versions of the introduction of the tomato into North America. The Spanish inevitably brought tomatoes to Florida and other settlements as far north as Parris Island, now in South Carolina, by the early 1700s, and archaeologists have dated tomato seeds near St. Augustine, Florida, to approximately 1740. The slave trade and the influence of French Creole cuisine, both based in the Caribbean, where tomato culture flourished, were two major factors in the early reports of tomatoes in Southern cities like Charleston. A portrait of John de Sequeyra, a Williamsburg physician of the mid-1700s, included a signed note by Williamsburg's E. Randolph Braxton: "Dr. Seccari, an Italian, was family physician to my grandfather Philip Ludwell Grimes. He first introduced the custom of eating tomatoes, until then considered more of a flower than a vegetable." Later, John Augustine Smith, president of the College of William and Mary from 1814 to 1826, wrote that Sequeyra believed that tomato consumption led to immortality, recalling the Greek legend of the Hesperides and the golden apples. Smith also mentioned a personal connection between Jefferson and Sequeyra.[56]

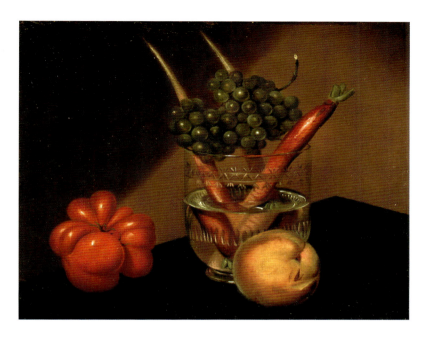

6.32. Raphaelle Peale, *Still Life with Fruit and Vegetables,* ca. 1795

Charleston gardeners, such as merchant and plantation owner Henry Laurens and garden writers like Martha Logan and Robert Squibb, documented tomatoes around 1770, though hawk-eyed botanist Peter Kalm failed to find tomatoes in the Mid-Atlantic colonies at midcentury. The artist Raphaelle Peale depicted a curious tomato in Philadelphia around 1795 in his painting *Still Life with Fruit and Vegetables.* This tomato had been raised by his brother Ru-

bens from French seeds sent to their father, Charles Willson Peale, and its convoluted, heavily lobed, and flattened shape suggests that the culinary tomato of 1300 had changed little since the sixteenth century (fig. 6.32). In 1804 John Gardiner and Alexander Hepburn's *American Gardener* offered advice on raising tomatoes for "soups and pickles," and Bernard McMahon, perhaps exaggerating in order to further the tomato's popularity, wrote in his *Gardener's Calendar* (1806) that it was "much cultivated for its fruit, in soups and sauces . . . and is also stewed and dressed in various ways, and very much admired." By 1821, *The Domestic Encyclopedia,* published in 1821 in Philadelphia, described how tomato culture was rapidly expanding, "where a few years ago it was scarcely known." Love apple seed began to be offered more and more often by urban seed houses throughout the first quarter of the nineteenth century, its popularity gradually moving northward.[57]

Jefferson planted tomato seed early in the season, usually in late March but as early as March 7 in 1814, and he also noted transplanting established plants in 1809. This raises the possibility that Jefferson followed the advice of garden writers such as McMahon by sowing seed in artificial frames, or perhaps indoors, in order to get a jump on the season. Early American writers like McMahon, Gardiner and Hepburn, and William Cobbett focused on the need to properly contain the rampant vines, using stout pea sticks to cage the plants. Jefferson's tomato varieties, "Dwarf" and large "Spanish," possessed the Pattypan shape seen in early European herbal depictions. American tomato breeding in the mid-nineteenth century eventually produced a rounder, smoother fruit.

7.1. "The most beautiful bean in the world is the Caracalla bean"—Jefferson to Benjamin Hawkins, 1792

7. Fruits

Beans and Peas, Jefferson's "Pulse"

A Melting Pot of Beans

LATIN IS SUPERIOR TO THE ENGLISH LANGUAGE in capturing the range of beans grown at Monticello. The common bean before the American Revolution was often the Old World fava, broad, or Windsor bean (*Vicia fava*). Jefferson treasured lima beans (*Phaseolus lunatus*; fig. 7.2), scarlet runners (*P. coccineus*), caracalla beans (*Vigna caracalla*), and asparagus beans (*Vigna unguiculata* ssp. *sesquipedalis*). However, when Jefferson simply wrote "beans" he was referring to the New World kidney or green bean (*P. vulgaris*), which he organized into "snaps," usually green with the chopped-up pod, but sometimes shelled and dried for winter use, and "haricots," either harvested when young and cut lengthwise for boiling fresh or shelled and dried. American kidney bean varieties were passed around the neighborhood or were regional in their culture. Few varieties arrived from England with other kitchen vegetables, and few had been described by either European or American horticultural authorities before 1820. As a result, Jefferson commonly described kidney beans by the individual or geographic source of the seed ("Tulien" or "Roman"), basic physical characteristic ("yellow snap," "long haricots"), or season of ripening ("forward," "early").

Jefferson sowed and savored kidney beans with nearly the same routine avidity he devoted to peas. The retirement garden was planted five to ten times a year with successive sowings of his two consistent favorites, "grey snaps" and "long haricots," along with secondary varieties such as "Bess snaps," "French kidney beans," and scarlet runners. Jefferson conscientiously followed the instructions in his published "General Gardening Calendar," planting snap beans at least three times successively for harvests throughout June and July. Green beans, particularly the "grey snaps," were harvested remarkably early in the season, usually in the first half of June (fig. 7.3). A trophy harvest on June 1, 1813, preceded the earliest snap bean in the Washington market of Jefferson's presidency by four days. Jefferson toyed with the usual mid-

7.2. Lima beans on poles with rows of sesame in square XII, August 2010

April frost date and regularly sowed frost-sensitive snap beans the first week of April or even in late March. He also recorded the dates for seed sprouting, the first flowering, and pod formation; his dutiful notations on kidney bean harvest days suggest consistent success as a bean grower. Beans took up a lot of garden space: squares V and VI were devoted to rows of snaps while square VII contained haricots in the 1812 organizational scheme.[1]

Bush beans, pole beans, and half-runner beans are all the same species, *Phaseolus vulgaris*. Many of Jefferson's snap bean varieties were labeled "dwarf," bush types not requiring any artificial support. In 1809 square V contained about thirteen rows of "grey snaps" and red haricots, the rows two to three feet apart. Jefferson's favorite "long haricots" grew as half-runners, somewhere between a pole and a bush bean. His instructions were to "plant in rows 3. f. apart, & 12 I. asunder in the row. Stick the plants with flat, prongy bushes, which will let you go between the rows." John Gardiner and Alexander Hepburn, in *The American Gardener* (1804), provided the standard admonition, "The better you supply them with sticks the more they will produce," and they recommended poles ten feet high, while Britain's John Abercrombie suggested ten-to-fifteen-foot-high stakes for the running kidney beans. Jeffer-

7.3. Jefferson organized his kidney beans into "snaps,"
shown here, and "haricots," which Mary Randolph advised
should be harvested when very young

son's contemporaries commonly planted their running beans at the base of fences or recorded how poles were brought into the garden for staking them.[2]

"Snap" beans are so called because the green pod is "snapped" in two before boiling. Unless they were harvested when very green or young, nineteenth-century kidney beans also required "stringing." Amelia Simmons in *American Cookery* sliced them in two, then "across" longitudinally, before salting: "Make them boil up quick, they will be soon done and they will look of a better green than when growing in the garden." Mary Randolph discussed "French" or snap beans (as opposed to "English" or fava beans), which should be picked young and prepared with the strings plucked, not "Frenched" by slicing them longitudinally. "Those who are nice," she wrote,

probably to debunk Simmons, "do not use them at such a growth as to require splitting." Harvesting the young, skinny beans before they toughen requires uncommon vigilance in a hot, summer garden, but Jefferson did not seem worried about his haricots getting too big. He wrote James Barbour in 1816 and told him to prepare the "long haricots . . . brought me from Georgia by General Sumpter" by dressing the two-and-a-half-foot-long pods as snaps, "or in all the ways of asparagus." Jefferson also composed a recipe, "to preserve haricot verts for winter use," that involved layering alternate rows of dried beans and salt in a barrel. Another recipe in Jefferson's hand survives for dried beans: "Boil them till done but not mashed, take a bit of butter the size of a walnut ½ an onion chopped fine[.] do them to gether in a frying pan till the onion is done. Dash in a little flour and soup enough to make a gravy[.] put in your beans, let them boil up & season with pepper and salt." Dried bean recipes abound in the surviving Jefferson family recipes. Jefferson's granddaughters left a recipe for Mexican black bean soup and Septimia Meikleham, Martha's youngest daughter, copied a recipe for white bean soup originally received from Gouverneur Morris, who followed Jefferson as minister of France. Beans, the fifth most commonly purchased vegetable at the President's House, were bought from the Washington market twenty-six times in 1806.[3]

With other New World native productions like potatoes and corn, the bean is among the most diverse vegetables on earth. Williamsburg garden historian Wesley Greene has stated that the kidney bean "was perhaps the most popular New World vegetable in the eighteenth-century Virginia kitchen garden" because of numerous American cookbook references. William Cobbett summed up the kidney bean's American universality: "In this fine country the seed is so good, the soil and climate so favourable to the plant, the use of the vegetable so general, the propagation and cultivation so easy, and so well understood, that little in detail need be said about them." Jefferson documented the planting of some forty kinds of kidney beans, a testament to the cornucopia of colors, shapes, and sizes, as well as the growing habits, culinary function, and seasonality, of this all-American vegetable. Philip Miller wrote, "It would be to little Purpose to enumerate all the Varieties of this Plant which have come to Knowledge in this Place; since *America* annually furnishes us with new sorts." Jefferson was discriminating in winnowing out varieties and ultimately selecting his favorite "grey snap" and "long haricot." When he wrote botanist Benjamin Smith Barton, about how "I have found one kind only superior to them ["Ricara" or Arikara bean], but being very sensibly so, I shall abandon the Ricaras," the superior kind was the "grey snap," which was commonly harvested a remarkable eight weeks from planting (fig. 7.4).[4]

The diversity of beans grown at Monticello was expressed in the bustling 1774 garden: some were Italian varieties like "Fagiuoli bianchi di Toscana"; others came from Virginians such as Colonel Theodore Bland, or the family of John Clayton, Virginia's first botanist, or the garden of James Donald in Scotland. The six varieties of bean seeds collected by Robert Bailey in 1794 included Red-speckled snap, probably the widely disseminated Cranberry bean praised by Amelia Simmons as "rich" in 1796, and Golden Dwarf, possibly one of the first references to a wax bean (fig. 7.5). Jefferson also received and planted a "very delicate" red haricot from André Thöuin of the Jardin des Plantes in Paris. Another promising bush bean was "Bess snap," planted annually from 1813 to 1817 and coming "remarkably early . . . to table" on June 17. "Hominy beans," named for their culinary ("suc-

7.4. Shelled Yellow Arikara bean. The "Ricara" bean was among the seeds collected from American Indian gardens in the Northern Plains that were given to Jefferson by Meriwether Lewis.

7.5. Cranberry beans are an example of the distinctively American bean varieties that emerged around 1800

cotash") and horticultural association with corn, were planted in an experimental corn patch in the circular beds at the southwest end of the garden in 1812.[5]

American kidney beans were immediately introduced into European gardens after 1492 and were first illustrated in Swiss herbalist Leonhard Fuchs's *De Historia Stirpium* in 1542. John Parkinson wrote that kidney beans "are esteemed more savory than [the English fava bean]," particularly by wealthier Britons. Philip Miller was rather lukewarm about kidney beans in his 1768 *Dictionary* and like most English writers, perhaps partly because of the confusing abundance of kidney bean names, listed few varieties. The earliest European explorers in North America were impressed by the Indian-grown kidney bean, which they had never seen before. Richard Hariot in 1586 remarked on the kidney beans on Roanoke Island, comparing them to the English fava bean: "They are flatter, of more divers colours, and some pied." Naturalist Mark Catesby in 1736 described the interplanting of corn and beans in American Indian gardens and noted that kidney beans were commonly fed to slaves, "being a strong hearty Food." William Hugh Grove also observed several types of "French or kidney bean . . . one sort called the six weeks bean is striped & from that Planting ripens in that time." Amelia Simmons was perhaps the first to describe distinct American bean varieties in 1793. Three of these are still recognizable today: "Clabboard," a possible candidate for Jefferson's "long haricot" and synonymous with the long-podded Caseknife (fig. 7.6); the "Lazy bean," a rugged grower requiring no staking and related to a variety considered today an heirloom, Lazy Wife; and "Cranbury," possibly Jefferson's "red-speckled snap," the Cranberry bean still popular with bean collectors. Despite the proliferation of names and varieties, beans were beans to many Virginia gardeners. Francis Taylor, more attuned to the "vernacular" Virginia kitchen garden, grew the Saddlestrap and Goosecraw, one of a number of American varieties named for their source in the droppings

7.6. Caseknife beans are grown today to duplicate Jefferson's "long haricot"

of geese or turkeys. The lone kidney bean variety identified by Kentucky's Joseph Hornsby in 1798 was the "hominy," sowed as Jefferson did in rows of corn.[6]

Kidney beans were less common than favas on eighteenth-century Virginia seed lists, but typical commercial varieties included the Canterbury Dwarf and Speckled French Dwarf sold in Richmond by Minton Collins or the White Dutch and Early Negro beans offered by George French of Fredericksburg. Although American in origin, these bean varieties had been tested in European, not New World, gardens. American garden writers like Bernard McMahon and Gardiner and Hepburn followed the English tradition by planting their kidney beans in hotbeds in February, but they continued to describe bean varieties by their most basic physical qualities, suggesting their American vernacular roots: "cream-coloured," "speckled dwarf," "white dwarf." McMahon's advice for beans in the open ground was followed by Jefferson at Monticello. Kidney beans were planted in successive rounds; in April bush beans were sowed in rows, two to two-and-a-half feet apart, the seeds dropped every two inches; in May came the running beans sowed farther apart; sowings continued through August. Virginia and American seed lists, as well as garden writers, failed to express the bounty and diversity of the everyday kidney bean that was grown by families across the economic spectrum and that helped define the beginnings of a unique American tradition in gardening and cooking.[7]

7.7. Shelled scarlet runner beans

Scarlet Runner, the "Arbor Bean" for Both Function and Beauty

The scarlet runner is generally considered a type of culinary kidney bean, at least when harvested very young, but this New World species from Mexico was commonly regarded as an ornamental because of its handsome and typically bright orange flowers. In his Calendar for 1812, Jefferson recorded planting "Arbor beans white, scarlet, crimson, purple. at the trees of the level on both sides of the terrasses, and on long walk of garden." This reference inspired the restoration of the flowering bean arbor at the southwest end of the garden terrace. In 1819 Jefferson also noted sowing "wild goose bean to wit red blossd kidney bean," presumably the "scarlet beans" sowed annually from 1809 to 1824, apparently in the old nursery beds below the garden wall. Although the typical scarlet runner has orangish colored flow-

ers, the color variations are promiscuous, and Jefferson's reference to "scarlet" may refer to the color of the seed, which is beautifully mottled in waves of scarlet and black (fig. 7.7).[8]

Herbalist John Gerard credited plant explorer John Tradescant with introducing *Phaseolus coccineus* into Britain early in the seventeenth century, and by 1754 Philip Miller observed how common it was "for the beauty of its scarlet Flowers," suited for embellishing arbors or shady walks. By 1768 Miller also considered it "the best sort for the table." Scarlet runners grow better than standard kidney beans during England's cool summers and, because they are perennial, were often transplanted to hotbeds or stove houses for winter harvests. The growth of scarlet runners slows drastically in the heat of a Virginia summer, and McMahon, while acknowledging their popularity in European kitchens, dismissed them as "neither productive nor esteemed" but "cultivated exclusively for the beauty of

7.8. Scarlet runner beans were treasured both for the beauty of their flowers and for the flavorful nourishment of the immature beans

it flower." Scarlet runners were absent from eighteenth-century Virginia seed lists, but seeds were sold in the early 1800s by urban seedsmen (fig. 7.8).[9]

Lima Beans: The New Southern Cuisine

Lima beans (*Phaseolus lunatus*) were a hot-weather favorite of Thomas Jefferson and among the most conspicuous vegetables in the garden during the steamy, late-summer months of August and September. Lima beans, native to South America and grown by Virginia Indians were also known as "bushel," "sugar," or "butter" beans in the eighteenth century, and Jefferson even named them "honey beans" in his General Gardening Calendar. He sowed them yearly and often in great quantities. In 1811 square X was planted in "72 hills" of lima beans. Surplus seed was distributed to his brother, Randolph, and friends like Madame de Tessé, to whom Jefferson noted that "I never saw them in France." Jefferson grew a smaller and more tender lima, the Carolina White, saved by Robert Bailey in 1794 and purchased by Etienne Lemaire from the Washington market in 1806. A "larger sort" obtained from Captain William Hilton of Jamaica was the chief type planted in the retirement garden until supplies dwindled,

7.9. Red Calico lima beans

when John Lawson described "a spontaneous growth, very flat, white, and mottled with a purple figure . . . trained on poles" (fig. 7.9). Francis Taylor and Joseph Hornsby grew "sugar beans" on fence posts in their respective gardens, and many of Jefferson's contemporaries, such as John Hartwell Cocke and George Washington, grew limas. Minton Collins sold lima beans in Richmond in 1792, and the Tory John Randolph expressed his Virginia roots by giving directions for growing "Bushel" or "Sugar" beans, "esteemed very delicate, and are of various colours, as white, marbled, green, etc." Lima bean growing became more widespread after 1800. McMahon distinguished the Carolina lima as a smaller and earlier variety and suggested planting this "extremely delicious" vegetable in hills with two to three poles for support. William Cobbett used the term "butter bean," a common term now for the smaller, more delicate varieties of lima, but believed that it was too cool on Long Island for their successful cultivation there.[11]

forcing Jefferson to get replacement seed from George Divers in 1822. Mary Randolph recommended boiling young lima beans until tender, then serving them in a "boat" of melted butter. A frequently mentioned Monticello recipe for the Spanish olla, a spicy version of the Southern Brunswick stew, called for lima beans blended with other vegetables and chicken, pork, or beef.[10]

Lima beans thrive in the warm microclimate of the Monticello garden. While Jefferson mentioned the "72 hills," perhaps staked with large poles, he also referred to growing limas in rows, the twining vines supported with large pea sticks. Lima beans are a distinctly American product, suited to the warmth of Southern summers and difficult to successfully grow in northern Europe. Although they were noticeably absent from eighteenth-century English garden books and scarce in American seed lists before 1800, "bushel beans" were observed in North Carolina Indian gardens as early as 1714,

Caracalla Bean: A Snail's Nest of Sweets

Jefferson expressed his admiration for the richly perfumed and elaborate blossoms of the caracalla bean (*Vigna caracalla*) in a letter to North Carolina's Benjamin Hawkins in 1792: "The most beautiful bean in the world is the caracalla bean, which, though in England a greenhouse plant, will grow in the open air in Virginia and Carolina. I never could get one of these in my life." Also called snail-flower and corkscrew flower, the name *caracalla* derives from *caracol,* a snail, spiral shell, or winding stair. The caracalla bean is a perennial vine to fifteen feet, hardy in frost-free climates, with long, pealike pods that are edible only in their most juvenile stage. Jefferson evidently saw the caracalla bean in Europe, perhaps in a conservatory at Kew Gardens or in Paris (fig. 7.10). Philip Miller said he obtained seeds from the species' native Brazil and that it was widely grown outdoors in Portu-

7.10. The tender caracalla bean requires a long growing season for flower and seed production

The English or garden pea (*Pisum sativum*) is easily considered Thomas Jefferson's favorite vegetable. The legacy of his renowned pea contests with neighbors, the generous amount of garden ground, squares I through V, devoted to this harbinger of spring, and the sheer quantity of pea plantings at Monticello, more than 130, and recorded harvest dates, more than eighty, were signs of favoritism unprecedented among any other garden species. Peas are a joy to grow, easily sprouted in cool earth, the vines abundant, the bluish green leaves translucently pure, the plants simply cultivated by either a casual or a novice gardener (fig. 7.10). Jefferson didn't merely record when his peas were sowed or when they arrived at the dinner table, he noted when they sprouted from the ground, the dates they blossomed, and the day on which the season's first pod formed. The Garden Book started with peas in 1767 and yet plantings actually increased in the later retirement years, again reflecting Jefferson's unabated zeal. Jefferson took delight in his peas. He enjoyed experimenting with planting dates, sowing different varieties on the same day, or planting the same type successively weeks apart, to compare and record ultimate harvest dates. Jefferson's published "General Gardening Calendar" stated that when Frame peas, Hotspurs, and Leadman's were sowed on the same day, "they will come in succession of a fortnight's interval." Although a close reading of the Kalendar indicates that successive sowings only rarely resulted in earlier peas, Jefferson's puppy love for peas was an enduring theme of his gardening career. In 1824 Jefferson ordered a gallon and a half of Marrowfat seed peas from his Richmond merchant. That's a lot of peas for an eighty-year-old man. Jefferson's love of peas became part of public lore, much like President Ronald Reagan's infatuation with jelly beans. Martha Jefferson Randolph reported how her father's Poplar Forest neighbors would plant special beds of peas in early spring to bring as gifts during Jefferson's visits.[13]

gal, where it was "greatly esteemed . . . for its beautiful sweet-smelling flowers" and used to cover arbors and garden seats. Miller, seemingly with firsthand experience, recommended sowing seeds in hot beds, moving the plants into pots outdoors in early July, and bringing them into the greenhouse for the winter. Caracalla beans are grown today in the Monticello garden; the corkscrew-shaped flowers are a novelty to visitors, and they have become a popular offering at commercial nurseries.[12]

7.11. Early spring peas climb peach-tree cuttings from the orchard

Etienne Lemaire recorded purchasing peas for the President's House only ten times in 1806 for the elaborate state dinners Jefferson hosted, and no record survives of Jefferson or his family members purchasing garden peas from slaves at Monticello. Perhaps if one had never tried Mary Randolph's pea soup recipe, fresh peas blended with mint, onions, and lots of butter, one might speculate that Jefferson enjoyed growing peas more than he liked to eat them. Jefferson's granddaughter Anne compiled a recipe for sautéed fresh peas boiled with onion, egg yolks, cloves, and brown sugar to make a "sweet custardy sauce." Surely, Monticello peas were also simply boiled and served with butter and mint as a side dish. Garden peas need to be distinguished from field peas, a coarser fruit suited to all-season porridges and animal feed. Pea soup, gruel, and porridge were made from the mealy field pea and were subsistence staples in European cooking since the Middle Ages. Garden peas, of course, were also commonly dried for use through the year.[14]

Some have challenged the historical veracity of Jefferson's legendary pea "contests," and their apparent noncompetitive nature suggests more of a "tradition." Although Jefferson seemed to seek out every advantage to get a jump on the season—with early plantings, changing microclimates, and novel varieties—the Monticello harvest usually did not begin until late May. On May 10, 1813, a bit late for his neighbor's first harvest, Jefferson wrote his close friend Elizabeth Trist that he was "hastening" back to Charlottesville from Poplar Forest to partake in Divers's "pea-dinner." Divers wrote to Jefferson on May 6, 1814, "Our peas are very backward this year, we shall expect you will come and partake of the first dish" (fig. 7.12). The following year, however, on April 30, Divers invited Jefferson "to partake of our first dish [of peas] today & that Mr. Maddison would come with you." Jefferson accepted the invitation but confessed how his peas were a month behind: "I dined with them (the Divers) on peas the 29th of April, here our peas were the 29th of May." Ellen Randolph Coolidge summed up her grandfather's competitive wariness when she recalled how "several of his neighbors had better gardens and orchards than his own and with them he was particularly ready to share any prize in the way of roots, seeds or slips sent him from a distance." One can only speculate about the participation of neighbors other than James Madison, such as John Hartwell Cocke and James Monroe. General Cocke's wife, Louisa, confirmed that the tradition was widespread in central Virginia when she recorded in her diary on April 29, 1822, "Our garden had been in so forward a state as to promise us pease today, & in that expectation our friends were invited to partake of them."[15]

Jefferson usually began the methodically choreographed pea season in February with sowings of the Frame, Early Frame, or a superior form he obtained in 1820, the May pea. Frame peas were often sowed in the northwest border beds, possibly in actual frames, and later, beginning in 1819, in the submural beds. The "principal" crops of peas were sowed in squares, beginning at the southwest end of the garden in square I (fig. 7.13). The frantic-growing Hotspurs were planted first, followed throughout March and April by such later varieties as Leadman's Dwarf and Marrowfat, each reserved for at least an entire square. Peas are a cool-season crop and usually burn up in

7.12. Jefferson's neighbors at Poplar Forest near Lynchburg, planted their gardens early in the season in the hope of presenting the ex-president with peas on his arrival

the heat of a Virginia summer. Although there were notable exceptions, peas were successfully harvested through May until late June (fig. 7.14). Jefferson never tried to grow peas through the winter as advocated by British authors, who used hotbeds, and as successfully accomplished by Joseph Prentis in Williamsburg in the open ground. Jefferson's summer plantings in August 1809 for a potential fall pea harvest were killed by freezing temperatures, effectively dooming a legitimate experiment. The 1809 Kalender provides a partial glimpse of how peas were typically set out. The northwest border beds, I–V,

7.15. A rustic fence, an alternative to brushy sticks,
supports twining peas in the 2011 garden

to bed. It is both a passion and a madness." Distinct varieties began to emerge in early eighteenth-century British garden literature. Richard Bradley began his *Compleat Seedsman's Monthly Calendar* (1738) with a "large Catalogue" of thirty-seven pea varieties.[17]

Peas were planted by the crew of Columbus at La Isabela, Hispaniola, in 1493, and according to historian Robert Beverley they were sowed in Sir Walter Raleigh's Lost Colony of Roanoke in North Carolina in 1584. As in England, garden peas became the symbol of a civilized garden. Early eighteenth-century recorders of Virginia's cultural and natural landscape—Mark Catesby, William Hugh Grove, Robert Beverley, and William Byrd—document garden peas in Virginia vegetable gardens. In Jefferson's time, seed merchants such as Minton Collins in Richmond and George French in Fredericksburg sold the legendary and traditional pea varieties imported from London: Early Frame, various Hotspurs, Marrowfats, Leadman's Dwarf, Spanish Morotto, and Blue Prussian. Charles Carroll of Annapolis wrote his son in 1773 and expressed the enthusiasm of local gentlemen for fresh peas, "I send You . . . a larger Dish of Green Peas than the last: I gathered a good Dish on the 24th & a very large Dish on the 25th, 12 dined with me & all eat of them, most were Helped to them twice." Richard

Henry Lee loved peas as much as Jefferson and sowed large squares at Chantilly in 1780 with some thirteen varieties, many named after people, "40 day pea from Mr. Geo. Turberville," or places, "Green Spring early pea." Like Jefferson, Francis Taylor recorded when his peas came to table and when they blossomed, while William Faris documented the sprouting, podding, and flowering of many early gardeners' favorite vegetable (fig. 7.15).[18]

Pea culture was intensively reviewed by American garden writers. Gardiner and Hepburn's *American Gardener* urged readers to take risks with their sowing seasons, planting peas as early as January and as late as November. McMahon seemed more concerned with successive plantings of twenty-two varieties through the season and the necessity of staking plants than with growing peas in hotbeds. Cobbett said that peas were "one of those vegetables which all men most like. Its culture is universal . . . Never were finer peas grown than that are grown in the United-States." Although most peas were English varieties, a distinct American variety, Early Washington, a form of Early Frame, appeared on seedsmen's lists in Lynchburg in the 1820s and was grown by a Jefferson family friend from Charlottesville, John A. G. Davis, in 1828. Philadelphia's renowned nurseryman David Landreth developed a more enduring variety in 1823, Landreth's Early Bush. Still, the golden age of pea breeding in the United States did not occur until later in the nineteenth century.[19]

Jefferson mentioned more than eighteen pea varieties by their bearing season ("latest of all"), the geographic or personal source of the seed ("dwarf peas of Holland" or "Mrs. Coles Forward"), or by a basic physical characteristic ("cluster peas"). He also planted named varieties heralded by garden writers and sold by American seedsmen. Seed of Blue Prussian, named for the intense light blue color of the seeds, were bought from Theophilus Holt in Washington as Jefferson was planning for his retirement to Monticello. Although not a favorite of Jefferson's, Blue Prussian has en-

dured as a parent of Alaska, a very popular twentieth-century pea. Named for their impetuous growth, Hotspur peas were a fabled variety planted in the second round of pea sowings. Frame or Early Frame peas, celebrated for their early bearing, dwarf habit, and suitability in hotbeds, were sowed yearly by Jefferson from 1809 to 1824. Bernard McMahon sent Jefferson eight quarts of Leadman's Dwarf seed peas in 1809. Jefferson praised them as "the very best of all the kinds of latter peas," and planted them annually in the first four squares of the garden until 1820, when they were supplanted by Marrowfat peas, a family of late-season, tall-growing, coarse peas best suited for drying or soups.

"Indian Pea," Cow Peas, Crowder Peas, Black-Eyed Peas: The Perfect Vegetable

The English name for the cool-season European field pea (*Pisum sativum* var. *arvense*) is often confused with names for crowder peas (*Vigna unguiculata*), an African native referred to as "Indian pea" by eighteenth-century Virginians, "cow pea" by Thomas Jefferson, and "field" or "crowder" pea today. In turn, crowder peas, named for the Scotch-Irish word *crowdy*, or porridge, are often confused with black-eyed peas, a subspecies with a distinctive "eye." Crowder and black-eyed peas originated in Africa, were introduced with the slave trade from the Caribbean and South America, and thrive in hot, humid weather; no vegetables grow as vigorously today in the Monticello vegetable garden. Delicious and highly nutritious, crowder and black-eyed peas are the perfect vegetable to bring to one's desert island. Jefferson used the crowder pea as a Monticello field crop but experimented with new varieties in the peripheral sections of the garden. He wrote the agricultural innovator John Taylor in 1797, "I have also received all the *good kinds* of field pea [*P. sativum* var. *arvense*] from England. But I count a great deal more on our Southern cow-

7.16. Crowder, or "Indian," peas were widespread in Virginia around 1800

7.17. Whippoorwill peas became a popular ingredient in hoppin' John

pea [*V. unguiculata*]" (fig. 7.16). He described cow peas in 1798 as a "very productive, excellent food for man and beast, [that] awaits without loss our leisure for gathering, and shades the ground through the hotter months of the year."[21]

Cow or crowder peas were an important agricultural crop in eighteenth-century Virginia but were also integral to large-scale vernacular gardens. John Custis claimed to have shipped hundreds of bushels of peas to the West Indies in a 1736 letter to his gardening mentor, Peter Collinson. William Hugh Grove had never before seen the "Indian pea," which he thought was a kind of kidney bean, "the pod 8 inches Long & rounder." Landon Carter experimented with crowder peas as a soil improver, and they were commonly found in slave gardens in Virginia. Crowder peas continued to be associated with Southern and African American gardens through the next two centuries. The best-known product of the black-eyed pea is hoppin' John, a soft cake of rice, beans, peas, and either pork or bacon, considered a dish with African American origins. Mary Randolph's *Virginia House-wife* provides a similar version for "Field Pea" cakes, the crowder or black-eyed peas harvested when fresh, then boiled, after which they are mashed, fried into crispy cakes, and garnished with bacon. This was another defining break from European cooking tradition (fig. 7.17).[22]

Asparagus Beans: A "Tender and Delicate" Curiosity

The asparagus bean is botanically similar to the crowder pea, but it is not commonly shelled from the pod. Jefferson obtained seed from General Thomas Sumpter of Georgia and sowed a row on April 13, 1809, in square II: "1. row. Long pod soup pea. or Asparagus bean. pods 3.f. long, to run on poles. when green they are dressed as Asparagus, or as snaps, or boiled in soup." He also planted square VII with asparagus beans and noted harvesting the "last dish" on October 15. Jefferson recorded planting them again in 1811, harvesting the pods continually for over three months, and proudly sending George Divers a supply of Monticello seed (fig. 7.18). He wrote his son-in-law John Wayles Eppes after sampling them at the table: "It is a very valuable one [bean], much more tender and delicate than the snap."[23]

Today the asparagus bean is sold as "Yard-long Bean," a name that effectively depicts the elongated, hanging pods. A South American native, asparagus bean was first described by the Swedish botanist Carl Linnaeus in 1763 and was introduced into England in 1781. Boston market gardener Fearing Burr in 1863 concluded that they were "more curious than useful," but ethnobotanist E. L. Sturtevant uncharacteristically proclaimed, "A tender, asparagus-like dish it is."[24]

7.18. The "very valuable" asparagus bean

8.1. "No person has been more zealous to enrich the United States by the
introduction of new and useful vegetables"—Nicholas King, 1806

Beets: Same Time, Same Place

8.2. Harvest of young Early Scarlet Turnip-
rooted beets, December 2011

BEETS (*BETA VULGARIS*) WERE DUTIFULLY PLANTED almost every year from 1809 to 1824, usually with rooty companions like salsify and garlic, and were relegated to the exact same row every year, a dubious horticultural practice but likely one that worked. Beets were readily available for ten months of the year from Washington markets, and Etienne Lemaire recorded purchasing them fifteen times in 1806. Beets were also purchased twice from Squire, who represented the most productive slave garden on the Monticello plantation (fig. 8.2). The quantity of beets (five bushels), that Jefferson felt sufficient for the winter table was less than for other root crops like turnips (twenty bushels) or carrots and salsify (ten bushels). Mary Randolph wrote that beets were "not so much used as they deserve to be," and recommended they be served with salted fish and boiled beef, "when young, large, and juicy . . . [they are] an excellent garnish, and easy converted into a very cheap and pleasant pickle." One wonders if beet greens were commonly prepared in the "Virginia style," boiled or steamed with bacon fat like turnip greens.[1]

The early history of the beet is muddled by its botanical association with chard, also *Beta vulgaris* but eaten only for its leaves. Swiss herbalist Leonhard Fuchs wrote that beet roots were grown in Germany in 1542, but they were slow to become cultivated in England, where John Parkinson discussed six beets, including the "Romane red Beete," "very sweet and good," eaten hot or cold with oil and vinegar. Beets were noted by John Lawson in North Carolina in 1709 and recorded as Virginia fare by William Byrd in 1737, but they were sold commercially only occasionally in Virginia in the late eighteenth century. A few of Jefferson's fellow Virginians, like Francis Taylor and John Hartwell Cocke, grew beets. McMahon provided full directions for growing this "very excellent vegetable," including the essential task of preserving roots through the winter by building beet piles protected with sand, earth, and straw.[2]

Eighteen Bushels of Carrots

Carrots (*Daucus carota*) were an everyday staple in the Monticello vegetable garden, and Jefferson was a determined and dedicated carrot grower, documenting the sowing of seeds some thirty times. Carrot seed was sowed in the retirement garden every spring, sometimes for more than one crop; at least an entire garden square was dedicated solely to carrots in order to fulfill Jefferson's requirement of a ten-bushel yearly harvest (fig. 8.3). In 1814 Jefferson recorded the harvest of eighteen bushels of carrots from two garden squares on November 25, an impressive accomplishment given the garden's heavy clay soil and the long, hot summer the plants were forced to endure. Perhaps Jefferson's success was due to the horticultural expertise of his accomplished neighbor, George Divers. A Garden Book entry from 1809 reads, "G. Divers finds the following sufficient for his family . . . Carrots 320. f = 8. do [rows] 12. I. apart." Available from Washington markets ten months of the year, carrots were served with butter sauce in the President's House. Garden-grown carrots were also incorporated into Monticello soups, beef dishes, and porridge. A Jefferson family recipe for "Chartreuse" creatively showcased the colorful Monticello root crops, particularly carrots. According to Jefferson's granddaughter Virginia Randolph Trist, "At Monticello the vegetables, all roots, no cabbage, were cut in slices & arranged in a fanciful way, alternating carrots with white vegetables, in a straight-sided vessel. It turned out in a beautiful form and made a very pretty dish for a ceremonious dinner. The inside was filled up with forced meat balls." Like all root crops, carrots were especially useful because they could be left in the ground all winter until chefs were ready for them, or they could be easily stored in cellars for months at a time.[3]

Few vegetables have such an ancient lineage as the carrot. Both the Queen Anne's lace type of European white carrot and the yel-

8.3. Purple carrots harvested in October 2010

low and purple forms native to Afghanistan were described by Greek and Roman authors but evolved for centuries into the smooth, bright orange carrot grown by Jefferson and known to us today (fig. 8.4). Although its origin is disputed, most authorities believe that the orange carrot was a sixteenth-century Dutch innovation, created from yellow and purple West Asian carrots. John Gerard only described the yellow and purple forms, and John Parkinson, while he hinted

8.4. Danvers carrot, a nineteenth-century variety, is well suited to Monticello's heavy clay soils

at the emerging "deep gold yellow" carrot, inferred that orange carrots were still unknown in England in 1629. By 1768, however, Philip Miller would prefer the "esteemed" orange carrot, and he gave exacting directions for its cultivation for a succession of harvests throughout the year. In contrast, John Randolph of Williamsburg preferred the white, "much the sweetest kind," while Orange County's Francis Taylor identified only yellow and white kinds in 1796.[4]

Carrots were introduced into the American colonies with the first settlers and were a common colonial garden staple. Seed was sold by Virginia seed dealers, including the standard variety, Long Orange, and carrots were grown by Jefferson contemporaries like Francis Taylor, William Faris, and John Hartwell Cocke. Taylor mentioned how he collected "wild carrot seed," or Queen Anne's lace, for a friend's wife, probably to sow in a flower garden. While Richard

Parkinson described American carrots as "almost tasteless and nothing like those in England," a 1786 edition of *Pennsylvania Mercury* reported that every family in the state grew carrots. Gardeners such as William Faris sowed twenty rows of carrot seed "at end of onion bed" in April and dug his carrots in March for consuming during the traditional "starving" season of early spring. Jefferson was not particular about carrot varieties. He identified them generically and simply as "early," "large," "orange," and "yellow."[5]

Garlic and the "Conspiracy of Bonaparte"

Like many other members of the onion tribe, garlic (*Allium sativum*) received only brief attention in the retirement garden, occupying a single row in square XIV with other root crops in 1812 and 1813. Jefferson also planted garlic from Philip Mazzei in 1774, "Aglio di Toscania." Since Robert Bailey went to the trouble to save garlic cloves for future plantings in 1794 and Jefferson advised novice gardeners to plant garlic in March as part of his published calendar, it seems likely garlic was planted more often than the documentary record indicates (fig. 8.5). Garlic was integral to a recipe Jefferson copied for venison at the President's House, and Jefferson's granddaughters used quantities of garlic in a recipe for pot au feu. Historian Karen Hess was impressed by Mary Randolph's "consummate skill" in the use of garlic as a seasoning, "reflecting an elemental change of palette," a decided break from the English tradition of avoiding such an earthy and potent seasoning. The indomitable Yankee Amelia Simmons perhaps best expressed this English tradition when she declared that garlic, "tho used by the French, [is] better adapted to the use of medicine than cookery." William Cobbett displayed a similar bias, writing that "the French use it, frequently, to an extent that would drive us from the table." Since Jefferson was, according to his granddaughter Cornelia Jefferson Randolph, "under the influence of Bonaparte" in his fondness for French cuisine, surely garlic, now America's favorite *Allium* and a species that thrives at Monticello, might have slipped into the garden under the documentary radar.[6]

Garlic is considered a native of south-central Asia and was widely distributed in the ancient Mediterranean. Romans may have shunned garlic for cooking, but they reputedly fed it to their laborers for strength and to their soldiers for courage. John Parkinson wrote that "this remedy for all diseases" was "exceeding wholesome for them that can take it." The earliest Spanish explorers brought garlic to the New World, but it was sparse in colonial Virginia gardens. William Byrd in 1737 mentioned both white and red garlic, and the Moravians brought garlic cloves to North Carolina from Pennsylvania in 1759. Early Southern garden writers like John Randolph and Robert Squibb wisely advised their readers to plant garlic in the late fall for a spring crop. Landon Carter tried garlic at Sabine Hall, the ever-experimenting William Faris planted a row or "line" of garlic as a border to his city garden, and Joseph Hornsby planted it among herbs at the edge of one of his asparagus squares. Garlic was slow to appear on American seed and nursery lists in the nineteenth century.[7]

Irish Potatoes: Presidential French Fries

Although late in arriving, potatoes (*Solanum tuberosum*) were grown everywhere in Virginia by 1800. Jefferson's use of the universal potato, however, was groundbreaking. In his handwritten list of dishes for the President's House, presumably composed between 1801 and 1809, he wrote, "pommes de terre frites, a cru en petites tranches," or, as translated by food historian Karen Hess, "potatoes deep-fried, raw, having been cut into small slices." According to Hess, "Of all the foods that pop historians credit Thomas Jefferson with having introduced to America, that of French fries is one that just may have some historical foundation, that is, by way of his French entourage

8.5. Garlic was not a common crop in Virginia gardens around 1800

[Etienne Lemaire]." With her characteristic caustic precision, Hess lambastes food historians who trace the American French fry anywhere from their "invention" by a hotel chef in Saratoga Springs, New York, in the early 1850s to their introduction by American soldiers after World War I. Lemaire may have picked up the idea of deep-frying sliced potatoes from French culinary books or from Paris street vendors. Hess also suggests that Lemaire was the source for Mary Randolph's recipe in *The Virginia House-wife,* "To Fry Sliced Potatoes." Her recipe begins, "Peel large potatoes, slice them about a quarter of an inch thick, or cut them in shavings round and round, as you would peal a lemon." We have here not only French fries but potato chips, then known in Paris as potato fritters but still another American innovation of Mary Randolph.[8]

Etienne Lemaire recorded purchasing potatoes, available year-round in the Washington market, some twenty times during 1806, in quantities as large as twenty bushels (fig. 8.6). Jefferson also noted that potatoes were prepared "with all sorts of sauces," and a recipe, "To Dress Potatoes," essentially mashed with abundant butter and cream, survives in his hand in his copy of *The Virginia House-wife.* The importance of the potato in Virginia could be gauged simply by how much attention—two full pages of

8.6. Kennebec potatoes harvested at Monticello in 2009

detailed and specific directives—Randolph devoted to preparing simple boiled potatoes. She also offered numerous savory potato dishes in *The Virginia House-wife*. For example, Randolph recommended that lavishly buttered mashed potatoes be crowned and crisped by placing them "slightly over a slow fire," and her "Potato balls" were fried in egg and bread crumbs.[9]

Potatoes were planted casually in the Monticello vegetable garden, usually below the wall in the south orchard or nursery, and were regarded by Jefferson more as an experimental agricultural crop for both domestic use within the plantation and for livestock feed (fig. 8.7). Jefferson hoped that Irish potatoes might replace soil-depleting, heavy-feeding crops like corn during his outbreak of farming renovations in the 1790s, but he ultimately concluded in 1817 that Jerusalem artichokes served this role more effectively. Potatoes were planted between peaches and apples in the north and south orchards from 1806 to 1809 and in and about the terraced garden five times during the retirement years. In 1809 Jefferson calculated that twenty-five bushels were needed for the winter table at Monticello, the most of any root crop. Potatoes were abundant enough at Monticello that Jefferson could forward excess seed potatoes to George Divers in 1817. Since potatoes were the third

8.7. Irish potatoes in square XXIII, May 2011

most frequently documented vegetable purchased from Monticello's slave community, there were many sources for them other than the Jefferson garden.[10]

The path that brought the potato to the American garden is as disputed as that of the tomato. Native to the Andes in western South America, where the mother lode of potato germplasm is still miraculously rich and varied, potatoes were not encountered by the Spanish until tubers were collected from a storage cache along the headwaters of the Rio Magdalena, now a part of Colombia, in 1537. Jefferson's own history of the potato may well be as credible as any. In a letter to New York geographer Horatio Spafford, Jefferson credits Sir Walter Raleigh with bringing potatoes from Guiana to Ireland, where the roots sprouted and spread throughout the English-speaking world. John Gerard, who first illustrated the Andean potato, insisted that the potatoes in his garden came from Virginia, and *Solanum tuberosum* became known initially in England as the "Virginia" potato. Thomas Harriot, an observant member of the Raleigh expedition in 1588, described the "Openauk, a kind of roots of round forme of the bignes of walnuts, some far greater, . . . growing many together one by another in ropes, or as though were fastened with a string." Although many historians now believe that Harriot's "openauk" was a Jerusalem artichoke, particularly since it was found wild in a marsh, John Gerard and John Parkinson borrowed his imagery for the "Virginia potato" (fig. 8.8). Both English herbalists compared the potato's taste favorably with the more familiar sweet potato. Potato growing became more common over the next century. As Philip Miller reported, potatoes "despised by the Rich and deemed only proper Food for the meaner Sort of Person," in 1754, were "so well known now, as to need no description" by 1768.[11]

Often confused with the sweet potato, Irish potatoes, according to documentary reports, were adopted by the English in Virginia only during Jefferson's lifetime. The chroniclers of the colonial

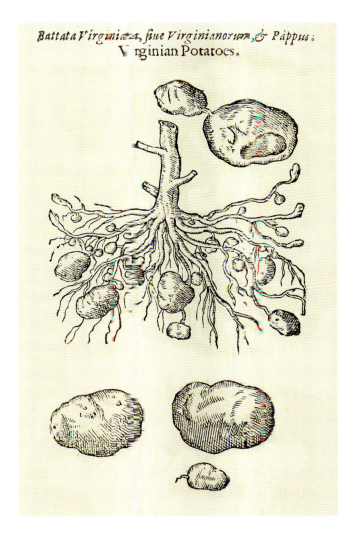

8.8. John Gerard's *Herball*, 1633, includes the earliest European illustration of "Virginian Potatoes"

landscape—John Banister in 1685 and Robert Beverley, who used the term "Irish potato" in 1705—wondered why the "Virginia" potato was not in Virginia, while William Grove observed only the sweet potato, the "Barmudas Kind." William Byrd, however, included "many species of potatoes" on his list of Virginia vegetables in 1737, suggesting at last the presence of *Solanum tuberosum*. John Randolph's *Treatise*, written in the 1760s, reviews potato culture, but it is so slavishly copied from Miller's *Dictionary* that one wonders if he grew them personally. Landon Carter, who like Jefferson and others believed that the potato came from Virginia, began experiments with potatoes in 1770 after concluding that "things raised from roots" survived Virginia summer droughts more effectively than seed-sown crops.[12]

Potatoes were grown by just about all of Jefferson's contemporaries. Richard Henry Lee used infusions of green elder to keep "flies and lice" from his potatoes, and Francis Taylor planted his potatoes in April and harvested them in October every year between 1787 and 1799. Amelia Simmons in 1797 wrote from either Connecticut or New York that "potatoes take rank for universal use, profit, and easy acquirement." At the same time, Richard Parkinson felt that American potatoes were inferior, writing that "there are no Potatoes equal in flavour to the English" and that potatoes are "very bad all over the country." William Cobbett confirmed the integration of the potato into American life in 1821, when he said, "Every body knows how to cultivate this plant."[13]

Although potato varieties failed to proliferate in the United States until the middle of the nineteenth century, the species included some earlier variations. Amelia Simmons recommended the smooth-skinned "How's potate, the most mealy and richest flavor'd," and also the "yellow rusticoat" over the "red" and "red rusticoat," which she considered only "tolerable." Richard Parkinson complained about locally named varieties "from some small cause," such as the "poor-

house potatoes" he saw in Baltimore around 1800. Bernard McMahon listed only the "common" potato in *The American Gardener's Calendar*. References to seed potatoes being passed between neighbors, often in barrels, in the records of Francis Taylor, George Divers, and John Hartwell Cocke, suggest that potatoes were more a "passalong plant" than a commercial nursery item around 1800.[14]

Onions: Mighty Earthen Pearls

In the South, onions (*Allium cepa*) are a specialty item, grown in quantity under specific conditions. Mid-Atlantic home gardens usually contain only "green onions" or scallions (*Allium fistulosum*), especially because large onions are so cheap and abundant in supermarkets. Onions were recorded as being planted in the Monticello garden only nine times. Since onions were a staple in some of Jefferson's favorite dishes and were purchased twenty-one times from the Washington market in 1806, one might conclude that Jefferson found other sources for this age-old but prized culinary treasure of the subterranean world. In 1809 Jefferson wrote in the Garden Book that Thomas Mann Randolph's onion harvest at Edgehill, across the river from Monticello, "yielded at the rate of 240. bushels per acre." This suggests that his son-in-law was growing them commercially as an agricultural crop. Jefferson lined up onions in all the proper planning documents in 1794 ("Objects for the garden") and 1812 ("Arrangement"); he planted the standards of eighteenth-century onion excellence, the White Spanish and Madeira; and he experimented with a new type of onion, the Egyptian or tree onion (*Allium cepa* var. *proliferum*). Despite these records of garden plantings, Jefferson likely was given or bought most of his onions.[15]

Jefferson's 1809 planting of tree, hanging, or Egyptian onions in the asparagus bed "failed," but he set out more in square XVIII in

1811. In 1809 he wrote, "Of these seed bulbs, 111 fill a pint to plant a square of 40. f in drill 12. I. apart & 4. I. in the drill will take 5 1/2 gallons, say 3. pecks" (fig. 8.9). Jefferson also wrote to his daughter Martha from Poplar Forest in 1816, asking for "some of the small bulbs of the hanging onion," so this vegetable curiosity was evidently well established at Monticello and valuable enough to be considered for the table at Jefferson's retreat home. The sharp-flavored tree onion multiplies in two ways: as the bulbs split apart in the ground and as the leaf stalks form bulblets at the top of the stem. Bernard McMahon was a fan of the tree onion and observed how they were good for pickling, "superior in flavour to the common kinds." McMahon's botanical name, *Allium canadense,* reflects the prevailing view that this onion was a North American native, observed by French explorer Jacques Marquette along Lake Michigan as early as 1674. Culinary historian William Woys Weaver believes that the tree onion arose "out of nowhere" and was first observed in Edinburgh and London in the 1790s. William Faris of Baltimore routinely harvested (as much as three bushels) and replanted his Egyptian onions in late summer, Joseph Hornsby planted them with garlic and herbs in 1798, and McMahon offered seed bulbs for sale in 1804.[16]

8.9. The home of the unique top-setting tree. Egyptian, or hanging onion—Jefferson's most commonly planted variety—has never been determined

The Magical Peanut:
From Slave Gardens to "American Icon"

Jefferson's only documented garden trial with the peanut—called "ground-nut" or "peendar," a corruption of the Congolese word *mpinda*—was a pioneering experiment with a magical food plant that was little known among Europeans in North America. In 1794 Jefferson recorded an October 7 harvest: "65 hills of peendars have yielded 16 1/2 lb weighed green out of ground which is 1/4 lb each. It was about 1 1/2 peck." President Jefferson also included peanuts, "a very sweet ground-nut," among shipments of seeds to Madame de Tessé in Paris in 1805 and 1807. Culinary historian Andrew Smith aptly describes the peanut as an "American icon" that has attained "culinary stardom." Of all the economic plants so zealously championed by Jefferson—sesame, upland rice, Gloucester hickory, "sprout kale," rutabaga, asparagus beans—it seems almost unlucky that he failed to promote the one useful plant that would become an essential American food. Though rare in gardens today, perhaps because store-bought peanuts are inexpensive and ubiquitous, the peanut is a delightfully modest, cloverlike plant in the garden (fig. 8.10). The unusual way that the yellow flowers form underground peanuts is one of the great curiosities of the vegetable world.[17]

Although peanuts (*Arachis hypogaea*) are native to South America, probably to the warm river basins of the Guarani region of what is now Paraguay, the first European explorers reported them growing throughout the Caribbean. Spanish physician and botanist Nicolas Monardes was the first European to comment on the "Turmas of the earth" he received from Peru in 1574. He likened their "gooed savour and taste" to almonds and recommended that they be served after the meat course but before the dessert serving of fruit.

Portuguese explorers collected peanuts in Brazil and introduced them in the sixteenth century into western Africa, where they were found comparable, and even superior, to the indigenous Bambosa groundnut. John Parkinson was the first Englishman to describe and illustrate, albeit poorly, "Indian earth-nuts" in *Theatrum Botanicum* (1640). Peanuts are virtually impossible to cultivate in England without artificial warmth, and Parkinson relied only on secondary sources to depict "the face therof above ground." John Ovington brought "Pindars" in 1696 from Guinea to London, where they were planted at Bishop Compton's garden in London, "but whether they will thrive in this climate is uncertain."[18]

Peanuts quickly became a common crop in warm, humid Africa, and the natural historian Sir Hans Sloane in *Catalogus Plantarum* (1696) reported that slaves were fed peanuts on slave ships to the New World. Peanut plants were later cultivated in slave gardens in Jamaica. Philip Miller in 1754 believed that the "earth-pistachio" was an African native brought to the British colonies by slaves: "In South Carolina there is great Plenty of these Nuts; which the Inhabitants roast, and make use of as Chocolate." Peanuts are formed after the seed of the faded flower dips into the soil and miraculously expands underground (fig. 8.11). Miller reported how "the Negroes kept this a secret among themselves, therefore [they] could supply themselves with these nuts unknown to their masters."[19]

Records of peanut growing, preparation, and consumption were rare in the young United States. Peanut oil from Edenton, North Carolina, was pressed and sent in 1769 by George Brownwigg to England's Sir William Watson, who published a paper in the *Philosophical Transactions* of the Royal Society. Watson confirmed that "ground nuts" were commonly roasted and eaten raw in the Southern colonies. He also attributed their introduction to the slave trade and their culture to slave gardens. Englishman Henry Wansey enjoyed roasted

8.10. Peanuts are formed when the small yellow flowers develop threads that dip into the soil and then swell into the edible "nut"

8.11. Peanuts harvested in October 2010

peanuts on his tour of the United States in 1794, and he is credited with first using the word *peanut* in print. The accepted term in the United States until the Civil War was *ground nut,* a term Jefferson used in his *Notes on the State of Virginia* (1781), when he included them among the state's garden fare. According to Andrew Smith, author of *Peanuts: An Illustrious History,* peanuts arrived in Philadelphia in 1791 with French Huguenot immigrants from Haiti. Their slaves, dressed in madras turbans, sold peanut cakes on the streets. Peanut trade from the Carolina Lowcountry to northern cities began in 1787, and George Washington ordered a bushel of "the Ground Pease, or Pindars as they are called" from Philadelphia in 1798. By the early 1800s peanuts were becoming increasingly prevalent as a "snack food" sold by street vendors in large cities, but only in the 1830s did peanuts enter mainstream American cookery. Even Bernard McMahon's simple inclusion of the groundnut, *Arachis hypogaea,* among esculent vegetables in the 1806 *Calendar* was a first for American horticulture. If Thomas Jefferson were to return today, one wonders if the sensational rise of any other "useful plant" would surprise him as much as that of the modest "peendar."[20]

Radish: A Companionable but Supporting Role

The world's easiest vegetable to grow—simply and quickly germinated, speedily harvested—radishes (*Raphanus sativus*) today seem only a diversion for most gardeners; to munch on the sharp, biting, peppery root while hoeing rows in the garden is a working interlude. The radish played an essential but supporting role in the Monticello garden. Radish seed was recorded as sowed more than seventy-three times at Monticello, a testament to Jefferson's admiration for the most refreshing of all root crops. During the intense gardening years between 1809 and 1817, Jefferson sowed a succession of radish seed, often weekly through the early spring, and always mixed with lettuce when planted in rows. Jefferson never planted radishes in large quantities, sowing only a thimbleful at a time in discrete sections of the northwest border for the earliest crops, then later in half-rows in garden squares. Interestingly, Jefferson placed the radish among "leaves" rather than "roots" in his 1812 "Arrangement of the Garden." In 1804 Jefferson's daughter Martha blamed her severe stomach cramps on "eating radishes and milk at the same meal," despite her husband's assertion that the illness was due to "hysterics" (fig. 8.12).[21]

8.12. Early Scarlet Globe radish

8.13. Jefferson was a pioneer cultivator of the rutabaga, a revolutionary crop for its storage capabilities and food value

Although regarded as a native of China, radishes were well represented in the ancient Mediterranean, depicted in Egyptian tombs, and cherished by the Greeks. In offerings to Apollo at Delphi, turnips were presented on lead platters, beets on silver, and radishes on gold. Radishes, still in their primitive black-and-white-skinned form (with white flesh), not only were the most common root crop during the Middle Ages but were grown to prodigious size, as large as forty pounds. John Parkinson knew only black-and-white radishes, long respected for their medicinal value as well as culinary use. Philip Miller listed the "small-topped Deep red," but he regarded the "round" radish as uncommon. The round red radish we see most commonly today was a relative newcomer to the garden stage. Radishes were brought by the first English settlers to Virginia and grown frequently and in greater variety than other root crops. Although Francis Taylor did not bother with radishes, they were avidly grown by gardeners such as Richard Henry Lee at Chantilly, William Faris of Annapolis, and John Hartwell Cocke. Despite experimenting with numerous radish varieties—Black, "leathercoal," "summer," "rose," "white," "salmon," and even "violet"—Jefferson wrote his son-in-law in 1795 that the Scarlet radish, the closest of all to the radish we know today, was "the only kind worth cultivating."[22]

Rutabaga or Swedish Turnips: A Jefferson Introduction?

Although Jefferson grew turnips as an agricultural crop in three-acre plots at Monticello, the Swedish turnip or rutabaga (*Brassica napobrassica*), despite being regarded by him as the latest innovation in livestock fodder, was confined largely to the vegetable garden. Jefferson recorded eleven plantings in the retirement garden, his disappearing seed stock continually requiring periodic replenishing by other progressive farmers like General John Mason, John Ronaldson, and Benjamin Vaughan. Jefferson may have introduced this plant into the United States. Originally sent to Monticello by James Strickland of Yorkshire, the seed was forwarded by Jefferson to James Taylor, the Virginia author of the agricultural treatise *Arator* in 1795, along with a description of how it had become England's "chief turnip" after being brought by the English government from Sweden. The rutabaga was a revolutionary crop—the root round and yellow, hardy to the north of Sweden, and twice as heavy as a turnip (fig. 8.13). As late as 1749 it was unknown to the Swedish immigrant community in Pennsylvania, further suggesting its newcomer status.[23]

Distinguished from the turnip by its secondary roots, the rutabaga, according to most sources, was not introduced into England until 1790. However, it was an established and successful agricultural crop in the northern United States by 1819, when Jefferson sent James Madison "Notes on the Culture of the *Swedish Turnip*," a treatise on rutabaga culture by a Maine farmer. Seeds of "Turnip-rooted cabbage underground" were sold by Bernard McMahon in 1804; Theophilus Holt sold rutabaga in 1805 and William Booth offered Swedish turnip in 1810. John Hartwell Cocke was growing them as early as 1816. In 1806 McMahon wrote dryly, "Some will expect that I should take notice of the Swedish turnip, or Roota Baga." He delegated the rutabaga to the field rather than the kitchen garden but acknowledged "it was by most people preferred" to the turnip. William Cobbett was another rutabaga enthusiast, writing that they "were very good to eat" as roots or as "most excellent greens in Spring."[24]

"Salsifia," the Delectable Oyster Plant

Jefferson sowed his spring salsify (*Tragopogon porrifolius*) enough times that it would qualify as a favorite fixture in the retirement garden. Although the "Monticello salsifia" was confined to one or two rows in square XIV and in the terraces in the western circular beds, Jefferson was surely proud of the eleven bushels harvested in Novem-

8.14. Salsify was a favorite fixture in Jefferson's retirement garden

Salsify was grown by the Greeks and Romans, at least the yellow-flowering type, *Tragopogon pratensis,* the wild goat's beard. John Gerard knew both this kind, "Johnny go to bed at noon" because of its reticent afternoon flowering, and the purple flowering *T. porrifolius,* Jefferson's "salsafia," whose roots were "better than carrots." In 1754 Philip Miller wrote that salsify was "formerly more in Esteem than at present," but by 1768 he retracted his words, hinting at its garden revival. Garden historian Wesley Greene concludes that salsify has been a trendy vegetable, periodically falling out of fashion. Although culinary historian Karen Hess has proclaimed salsify "enormously popular in early Virginia," salsify was only occasionally found in Virginia gardens. Williamsburg garden writers around the American Revolution like John Randolph and Joseph Prentis mention salsify in passing, but its only seed list appearance is in Minton Collins's Richmond list of 1793. Bernard McMahon sold salsify seed in 1804 and discussed its cultivation fairly thoroughly in the 1806 *Calendar:* "By some highly valued, for its white eatable root, which grows a foot or more long. Some have carried their fondness for it so far, as to call it vegetable oyster." Jefferson's neighbors grew oyster plants. George Divers advised Jefferson on how much to plant to feed a family, and John Hartwell Cocke sowed two beds of salsify in 1810 at Bremo.[26]

Sweet Potato: "Over Luscious best in a pye"

The sweet potato, known in Virginia also as "Spanish," "Indian," "Barbadoes," "Bermudian," "long," and "red" potato, was never documented in Jefferson's retirement garden. In 1787 Jefferson wrote from Paris asking for sweet potato seeds, and his son-in-law Thomas Mann Randolph wrote from Monticello to Jefferson in Philadelphia in 1792 that garden-grown sweet potatoes were nipped by an early October frost. Two barrels of sweet potatoes were shipped from Monticello west across the Blue Ridge Mountains to Jefferson's friend Archibald

ber 1814. His consistent planting of salsify in the garden suggests a favoritism also expressed in the family recipes (fig. 8.14). Virginia Randolph Trist left three alternative means of preparing salsify, all of which involved scraping the dark-skinned roots to reveal the white flesh beneath. Sometimes they were boiled, then "mashed well and fried in little cakes the size of sausages." The roots were also diced, boiled, and then stewed in a pan with butter, milk, and bread crumbs. In addition, salsify was cut lengthwise and fried. Salsify, perhaps at Jefferson's urging, was available in Washington markets ten months of the year. Etienne Lemaire purchased as much as a peck of salsify in 1806, and according to Jefferson's "master plan," salsify was "dipped in batter and fried, or with butter sauce" when served at presidential dinners. Mary Randolph, after describing alternative preparations, concluded, "They are delicious in whatever way they are dressed."[25]

Stuart in Staunton in 1794, when "Indian potato" was planned as among the "Objects for the garden" in the Garden Book. Jefferson considered sweet potatoes for crop rotation under the category of "articles for minor husbandry," but it is unclear if they were planted out in fields on the Jefferson farm. Monticello slaves grew sweet potatoes in their gardens and sold them to the Jefferson family. Etienne Lemaire purchased sweet potatoes only twice in 1806, and except for a sweet potato pudding recipe from Virginia Randolph Trist, they seemed underused in both garden and kitchen at Monticello. Perhaps sweet potatoes, surely the sweetest of all cultivated vegetables, were so universal that they went unrecorded (fig. 8.15). Mary Randolph, on the other hand, offered intriguing recipes: sweet potatoes broiled on a griddle and "served with butter on a boat"; a pudding or pie made from sweet potatoes, eggs, butter, sugar, and brandy; and stewed and topped with slices of ham, herb-based chicken, and gravy. Although technically not a North American species, the sweet potato was regarded by the earliest natural historians as an indigenous Virginia product, thriving in all soils during hot, muggy summers. Native Americans cultivated sweet potatoes before the arrival of Europeans to Virginia, and they were quickly embraced in Southern American cuisine.[27]

A tropical plant in the morning glory family, *Ipomoea batatas* originated in South and Central America and was encountered immediately by the Spanish in the Caribbean. Originally called "batatas," they quickly created a sensation in southern Europe and were adapted by growers and cooks at least a hundred years before the Irish potato. Although sweet potatoes are too tender and sun-loving for England, John Gerard described them as "common and ordinarie meate" throughout Spain and Portugal. Gerard also repeated the species' reputed aphrodisiacal qualities, perhaps based on the effects of mobby, a spiritous liquor then commonly distilled from Caribbean sweet potatoes. John Parkinson in 1633 carefully illustrated this recent "dis-

8.15. Sweet potatoes were cherished by people from all walks of life in Virginia around 1800

covery" along with Irish potatoes and Jerusalem artichokes, writing that imported sweet potatoes were roasted in embers, "a dainty and costly dish for the table." Philip Miller gave directions for growing the "Spanish Potatoe" in hotbeds, alluded to the "sprightly" mobby of the West Indies, and wrote that sweet potatoes were regularly imported from the Mediterranean region.[28]

Many of the earlier Virginia natural historians documented and were notably impressed by the sweet potato in American Indian gardens. Robert Beverley in 1705 observed both red and white Spanish potatoes "as long as a Boy's Leg." Mark Catesby in the 1730s was inspired by "the Wholesomeness and Delicacy of its Food," and considered the sweet potato worthy "of a Place at Principal Tables" (fig. 8.16). In 1737 William Hugh Grove described four varieties, "commonly rosted they are Sweet & over Luscious best in a pye." Swed-

8.16. "Bead Snake and Indian Potato" from Mark Catesby's *The Natural History of Carolina, Florida, and the Bahama Islands*, 1754, depicts a typical sweet potato root, but the leaves and flowers appear misrepresented

ish botanist Peter Kalm had never seen or eaten "Bermudian" potatoe ("they almost melt in the mouth") until he visited Pennsylvania in 1748 and saw them in the gardens of "common people and gentry without distinction." Like Robert Beverley in Virginia, Kalm noticed that harvested sweet potatoes were buried indoors next to the hearth; stored potatoes require storage in temperatures between freezing and fifty degrees. The potatoes Philip Fithian observed in the slave gardens at Nomini Hall in 1774 were likely the sweet potato, a universal Virginia staple (fig. 8.17).[29]

Sweet potatoes are not propagated from seed but are preserved asexually from potato cuttings that sprout when given sunlight and warmth; they therefore became a species that was shared between friends and neighbors rather than a nursery item. They were also a "vernacular" crop associated with poorer whites and African Americans, and this perhaps explains why they were neglected in the kitchen garden manuals of the late eighteenth and early nineteenth centuries. William Faris of Annapolis bought rather than grew sweet potatoes, perhaps because of the limited size of his urban garden. Francis Taylor planted sweet potatoes in 400 hills at a time and preserved fall harvests by putting the potatoes in holes beneath farm buildings. He exchanged plants with slaves, gave them days off for planting, and rotated cultivation between his own and his laborers' "patches." Joseph Hornsby of Kentucky planted 237 hills of "Spanish" potatoes in the "pasture" adjacent to his kitchen garden in 1798, and John Hartwell Cocke grew "Pudding Potato," "Pumpkin Spanish," and "Barbadoes" sweet potatoes at Bremo.[30]

Turnips: The Edible Virginia Lawn

Turnips (*Brassica rapa*) were cultivated as an agricultural crop in two- to four-acre plots of Monticello farmland, and occasional experimental varieties were recorded in the garden. Although Jefferson found European turnips superior to those grown in America, the turnip's relative scarcity in the Monticello garden did not mean that Jefferson disliked this most versatile vegetable; he needed twenty bushels a year for the Monticello kitchen, more than any other root crop except potatoes. No other Monticello root crop was so universally used. Jefferson's granddaughter Virginia Randolph Trist wrote, "At Monticello we used to have turnips dressed with cheese and they were very good." She observed that turnips were peeled, boiled, then mashed through a colander, after which they were added to a little butter and milk and stewed until dry. A variation involved cooking turnip pieces with a spoonful of butter and abundant brown sugar. Turnips were an ingredient in numerous recipes for Monti-

8.17. Sweet potatoes, with their lush, almost tropical foliage, thrive in the warm, humid summer of Virginia.

cello soups, they were purchased ten times for President's House meals, and Jefferson's own "Master Plan" documents that turnips were served with butter sauce in the President's House. In his 1814 Calendar he mentions "loppd Turnep" at Lego, the nearby farm across the Rivanna, and this suggests that turnip greens may also have been served at the Monticello table. Among numerous turnip recipes, Mary Randolph included "Virginia style" turnip greens that were boiled for twenty minutes with bacon, possibly a result of the African American influence in Virginia cuisine. Turnips were also purchased by the Jefferson family from Monticello slave gardens (fig. 8.18).[31]

In *Heirloom Vegetable Gardening,* William Woys Weaver states that "at one time, Americans were as enthusiastic about turnips as they now are about tomatoes." An example was at Landon Carter's Sabine Hall, where the parterre flower garden, located next to the house on the uppermost of landscaped terraces leading to the Rappahannock River, was among the most ornate ornamental gardens in eighteenth-century Virginia. In 1777, mourning the demise of his drought-stricken bulbs and crippled by colic, lamenting his inability to walk out and "injoy the pleasure of flowers," Carter inaugurated his "turnip Project." He plowed up the flower beds and planted footwide rows

8.18. Root crops like sweet potato, turnip, and even radish are easy to preserve and so provided essential sustenance when food was scarce during the spring and winter months

of turnips. "It proved a very fine crop, and answered its Proposed end much" by providing him turnip greens in the fall and fodder for his cows that winter. Perhaps in the same spirit, Francis Taylor "plowed Turnip patch before the house" in 1795, and John Hartwell Cocke recorded in his garden diary on July 17, 1817, that he "ploughed the Lawn for turnips." Today, local food advocates urge American suburbanites to plant front-yard food gardens instead of wasteful lawns. Unfortunately, turnips might not do. *The Oxford Dictionary of Food and Drink* derides the place of the turnip, which "remains a barely tolerated visitor to most traditional American tables."[32]

Turnips were brought to Virginia by the first Jamestown settlers in 1609. These hardy and versatile roots were mentioned as a Virginia garden staple by William Byrd and William Hugh Grove in the 1730s, and they became the earthy stars of the underground garden by 1800. Landon Carter not only enjoyed turnip greens in the Virginia style, "an excellent green," but documented six-acre turnip fields that were planted for livestock at Sabine Hall. Turnips there struggled to survive the turnip fly, probably a flea beetle, as well as attacks by hornworms and birds. Carter preserved his summer-sowed turnips in winter by heaping them into pyramidal piles to prevent them from rotting, a technique observed by Swedish botanist Peter Kalm in the landscape of eastern Pennsylvania in 1749 and described in 1798 by Kentuckian Joseph Hornsby, who reserved precious garden beds solely for saving turnip seed. Francis Taylor was a typical turnip gardener who sowed seed thirty-six times between 1787 and 1799, usually in March and July, in fourteen different sites, often in abandoned wheat, corn, and tobacco "patches." Taylor also enjoyed turnip greens and constructed a special "turnip house" for preserving the harvested roots. Turnip growing was an important component of most early American gardening manuals. Robert Squibb insisted that gentleman plantation owners wanted only their "steadiest hand" hoeing between the rows of turnip seedlings. Around 1800 Maryland turnips were sold for a dollar a bushel, the equivalent of twelve dollars in 2007. Urban seed distributors sold scores of turnip varieties in the early 1800s, further confirmation of the popularity of the turnip in the age of Jefferson.[33]

9.1. "We will sow our cabbages together"—Thomas Jefferson to Martha J. Randolph, 1792

9. Leaves

Asparagus: The Green Lords of Spring

OFTEN THE FIRST VEGETABLE harvested in spring, asparagus (*Asparagus officinalis*), with its dramatic thrust of spring's first spear, is a cause for celebration (fig. 9.2). Jefferson ranked asparagus with peas, artichokes, salad greens, and novelties like sea kale and lima beans among his favorite vegetables. His granddaughter Ellen Randolph Coolidge wrote, "He loved farming and gardening, the fields the orchards, and his asparagus beds." Asparagus and artichokes were the first vegetables planted at Monticello, in March 1771, and prime and permanent garden real estate was reserved for this harbinger of spring. The asparagus beds at the western end of the retirement garden were a landmark to identify other garden features and, along with the choice asparagus terraces below the garden wall, contained what were likely the finest soils on the mountain. Asparagus received uncommon attention and was one of the few vegetables for which Jefferson documented performing a cultural technique: asparagus beds were "littered" (mulched) with tobacco leaves and "dressed" (fertilized) with manure. These beds were also diligently revived with fresh plantings throughout Jefferson's gardening career.[1]

Jefferson was an accomplished grower of asparagus. The first Monticello asparagus was often cut before harvests were sold by professional gardeners in the Washington market. A barometer of the season, the arrival of asparagus at the table was noted by Jefferson twenty-two times; the average date was April 8, the earliest March 23, and the latest April 17. Jefferson cultivated two varieties, the white-stemmed Cooper's Pale Green and East India, both state-of-the-art improvements. Surplus seed and plants were sent to Poplar Forest and to John Hartwell Cocke, another sign of success. When Jefferson forwarded prized vegetable seed like sea kale or "long haricots" to friends and neighbors, he commonly instructed them to "dress like asparagus." Few vegetables received such exacting attention in the kitchen. Mary Randolph's direc-

9.2. Gardeners anticipate the first thrust of the year's asparagus

9.3. The asparagus square occupied prime real estate
at the southwest end of the garden

tions for the preparation of fresh asparagus (it was also pickled) were more precise than for any other vegetable: stalks were meticulously scraped, bundled carefully in lots of twenty-five, and immersed in boiling water. The cooking was delicately timed so "their true flavour and colour" was preserved, because "a minute or two more boiling destroys both." Randolph's asparagus was served on buttered toast.[2]

Jefferson fussed over his garden asparagus far more than any other vegetable. Asparagus was grown in carefully amended beds because this long-lived perennial, usually lasting longer than twenty years, was a major investment. The 1812 asparagus square included seven beds, each forty feet long; the Poplar Forest bed was eighty feet long; and the five beds at Jefferson's boyhood home, Shadwell, were four feet wide, each with four rows of asparagus. The standard directions for creating such beds were exhaustive, and Bernard Mc-Mahon's advice in *The American Gardener's Calendar* was typical:

cover the best soil in the garden with one foot of well-rotted manure, trench it two spades deep, add another two or three inches of manure, and dig again. Jefferson was attuned to the advice given in his garden library. His directions to the enslaved gardener Wormley Hughes in 1808 warned against disturbing the asparagus crowns and advised the use of an asparagus fork, a specialized and essential tool in Philip Miller's *Gardener's Dictionary*.[3]

Jefferson's fellow gardeners around 1800 were also particular about their asparagus, and in the garden diaries of Francis Taylor, William Faris, and Joseph Hornsby the asparagus bed or square was often used as a geographical reference ("Sowed peas by asparagus bed") because of its prominent location in the garden (fig. 9.3). As at Monticello, the asparagus square also commonly performed double duty: Taylor and Faris, for example, sowed annual crops like cabbage, lettuce, turnips, and lima beans between the rows of the perennial asparagus. Although John Randolph believed that "nothing more is necessary than to make your beds perfectly rich and light," he recommended soil two feet deep and consisting of rich mold and dung. The gardener at Mount Airy in 1805 diligently "covered" and "forked" asparagus beds twice a year, and Landon Carter was pleased that his asparagus seeds, steeped in saltpeter, produced such an abundance of young plants. Joseph Hornsby was surely proud of the bushel of asparagus delivered by his slave, John, to a neighbor in 1798, and William Faris sent 130 "stocks" of his well-manured asparagus to Annapolis neighbors in 1802. Asparagus was lord of the garden.[4]

Asparagus culture was popular with the ancient Romans, but the wild species had not been altered dramatically by the mid-eighteenth century, when Philip Miller noted that the cultivated forms were larger and later than the wild English asparagus. Asparagus was standard fare in Virginia kitchen gardens. William Hugh Grove observed Virginia asparagus in 1732, William Byrd was impressed by the colony's "very large and long asparagus of splendid flavor" in 1737, and Philip Fithian observed asparagus in the garden at Nomini Hall, side by side with violets and figs. Richard Parkinson wrote that Baltimore's wild asparagus "grows very fine," and William Cobbett declared American asparagus "far superior to that in England . . . though so little care is, in general, taken of it." Amelia Simmons called it an "excellent vegetable" in 1796, but Landon Carter blamed his sleeplessness on eating asparagus. Asparagus was not solely a gentleman's recreation; William Faris cultivated neat, orderly rows in his Annapolis garden.[5]

Timothy Matlack, an accomplished fruit grower and horticulturist from Philadelphia, sent Jefferson a small parcel of seed of Cooper's Pale Green asparagus in February 1807. The seed was sown in nursery beds and resulted in 237 plants in 1808. Matlack wrote that "the head is large in proportion to its stem & very tender." Joseph Cooper of Gloucester County, New Jersey, was, according to historian U. P. Hedrick, "The first man in America to undertake as his life's work the breeding of plants," and Cooper's asparagus was one of the first deliberately bred native vegetable varieties known in American vegetable gardens. Cooper's Pale Green asparagus was a white-stemmed variety, which was traditionally achieved by blanching the shoots as they emerged in spring. White asparagus was deemed an improvement, "more sweet and pleasant," by English herbalist John Parkinson as early as 1629. Francis Taylor of Orange County grew white asparagus in 1790.[6]

A Banner of Broccoli: Purple, White, and Green

Jefferson planted green as well as purple and white sprouting types of broccoli (*Brassica oleracea* var. *acephala*), regarded as more than novelties in the nineteenth century. In 1812 he sowed adjacent rows in square XII, creating a banner of color and enabling him to document the differences scientifically. The crucial issue in growing the long-

9.4. After deer consumed young potted plants of Monticello's fall crop of Green Sprouting broccoli in 2010, gardeners purchased a modern variety, Major, from a local garden center. The size of the heads surprised everyone accustomed to traditional broccoli varieties.

season (ten months from sowing to harvest) nineteenth-century broccoli was sustaining plants through the winter. Jefferson sowed seed from March through May and transplanted the seedlings to rows in June or early July, but heads could still not be expected until the winter or following spring. Although broccoli was sold in the Washington markets during Jefferson's presidency, its short tenure, April 7–24, suggests limited availability (fig. 9.4). Etienne Lemaire purchased broccoli twice for presidential dinners. Mary Randolph mentioned two sorts of broccoli, including a sprouting broccoli harvested as stalks smaller than what is available in markets today. It was scraped, tied in bundles, boiled "like asparagus," and served with melted butter.[7]

Botanically, broccoli is the same as cauliflower, distinctive because the unopened flower buds are harvested with the thick stalks. Broccoli (the word comes from the Italian *brocco*, meaning "little branches") is older than cauliflower and historically associated with Italy. As late as 1727, English author Stephen Switzer described it as a "stranger" in England. Richard Bradley, a year later, called it "sprout Cauliflower," and compared the preparation and taste to asparagus. Jefferson's White or Cauliflower broccoli was also familiarly known as Neapolitan, more common than green broccoli through the nineteenth century in America. Jefferson's "early purple" or "purple" forms were synonymous with Roman, described in 1768 by Philip Miller as "little inferior to asparagus" and, at the time, the sweetest of all broccoli. As with modern varieties of green broccoli, the plants initially set large heads, which were cut and later replaced by numerous branching sprouts for a continual harvest. "Early" broccoli for Jefferson meant that spring-sown plants would produce in the late fall or early winter. "Green" broccoli was documented at Monticello as early as 1795, when Robert Bailey found seeds "wanting." [8]

Broccoli never achieved the stature of cauliflower in America. William Hugh Grove wrote that in Virginia in 1732, the "Gentry . . . have very lately tried the Brochili." White and Purple broccoli were grown at the Governor's Palace garden in 1759, and Virginia seed merchants sold both consistently before 1800. Williamsburg's John Randolph and Joseph Prentis gave specific directions for growing and, surprisingly for them, cooking Roman broccoli: "the stems will eat like asparagus and the heads like cauliflower." Landon Carter was especially challenged by broccoli cultivation. He lamented the winter-kill of garden plants in 1764 and 1770, blaming "my fool" gardener for covering the plants in January with straw rather than protecting them with "bushes on forks" as ordered. In 1771 Carter's fall broccoli became "foods for creatures" like grasshoppers and "flies," or aphids, which destroyed still another crop. Richard Henry Lee grew "Brocoly" in beds during the 1780s, and it was documented in the gardens of such contemporaries as Lady Jean Skipwith and John Hartwell

Cocke. William Cobbett concluded that broccoli "is not much cultivated in America; and indeed, scarcely at all," but that it was worth the trouble to have it in New York markets. [9]

Cabbage: Garden Workhorse
"as beautiful dressed as when growing"

Cabbage (*Brassica oleracea* var. *capitata*) was a garden workhorse at Monticello. A dizzying array of more than thirty types and varieties were recorded, often set in the garden as transplanted seedlings, on some sixty documented occasions in more than twenty sites (fig. 9.5). Thomas Jefferson liked to eat cabbage. In 1806 Etienne Lemaire purchased a total of 159 cabbages on fifty-nine days for presidential dinners; only lettuce and parsley were purchased more often from the farmers' market in Washington. Cabbage was the second most commonly purchased vegetable from slave gardens at Monticello, bought by Jefferson family members in great quantities, as many as a hundred at a time. On Christmas Eve, 1824, sixty-five heads were purchased from the enslaved Gill Gilette, the head of a family of productive gardeners. Jefferson tried new cabbages from around the world, and seed was sent to Monticello from Paris, Leghorn (Livorno), Edinburgh, Mexico City, and Philadelphia. Jefferson consistently planted two choice varieties throughout his retirement years: Savoy, usually the highly blistered Green Curled Savoy, and Early York, among the best known and most cherished cabbages of the day. Jefferson likely shared Mary Randolph's admiration for the nobility of this ancient but most common garden plant. While describing how to boil cabbage, she concluded, "With careful management, they will look as beautiful when dressed as they did when growing." When in 1792 Jefferson wrote his daughter Martha that "the next [year] we will sow our cabbages together," this modest but beautiful vegetable became an image of their familial happiness (fig. 9.6). [10]

Jefferson commonly sowed cabbage seed in February and March for an early summer transplanting into garden rows and an ultimate harvest in the fall or early winter months. Cabbage often occupied squares IX and XII as well as border beds V and VI. Perhaps dissatisfied with the performance of such a cool and moisture-loving crop in a hot, dry garden site, Jefferson experimented after 1813 with a remarkable variety of cabbage habitats. Cabbage was moved out of the terraced garden to the bottomlands along the Rivanna River, the rich asparagus beds, the abandoned Northeast Vineyard, and even the old tobacco "plant beds" at Lego Farm across the river and miles from Monticello. Only occasional references to fall plantings suggest cabbage was grown through the winter months, perhaps because few vegetables are preserved so easily in cellars or sawdust outdoors. In 1821 John Hemmings wrote to Jefferson how a Poplar Forest slave, Nace, was stealing cabbage from what was apparently his master's garden and burying it in the ground, a common method for keeping cabbage fresh for months at a time. Orange County's Francis Taylor also apprehended a cabbage thief among his slave population at Middleton Plantation in 1794.[11]

Jefferson composed a recipe for cabbage pudding, in reality a cabbage stuffed with lean beef, egg yolks, suet, onions, and

9.5. Cabbages, as many as one hundred heads at time, were purchased from slave gardens and consumed by the Jefferson family

9.6. Early Jersey Wakefield, a nineteenth-century cabbage variety

bread crumbs. Otherwise, cabbage heads were simply boiled for thirty to sixty minutes, as directed by Mary Randolph, or included in the "Monticello" vegetable soup. The Monticello Chartreuse was a fanciful means of displaying root crops for a "ceremonious" occasion that, in at least one version, included cabbage. Jefferson's granddaughter Septimia Meikleham compiled recipes for "pickled" red and green cabbage, and perhaps the large quantities of cabbages purchased from Monticello slave gardens were preserved as slaw or pickled in a Virginia rendition of sauerkraut. One wonders if the cabbages purchased from Gillette on Christmas Eve were distributed as presents to the Monticello community.[12]

Few plants exhibit so many forms as the cabbage, and few vegetables have been so universally grown because of their nutritional and storage capabilities. Wild cabbage grows as a colewort, a non-heading primitive type, along the seashore of Europe, and these loose-leafed varieties were cultivated by the ancient Greeks and Romans. Garden forms eventually evolved into heading cabbages around 1600, when John Gerard depicted "the great ordinarie Cabbage knowne everywhere." Although he illustrated numerous nonheading cabbages, John Parkinson in 1629 also described the "ordinary" cabbage that "closeth hard and round." Cabbage was boiled with beef, "much fat put upon them," but Parkinson also alluded to the cultivation of cabbage for "delight," as an ornamental. Eighteenth-century English garden writers gave ample directions on growing abundant varieties of cabbage: flat, round, and cone-shaped; red-, white-, and yellow-leaved; blistered and smooth-leaved; winter and summer; for cattle and for pickles. Writers winnowed down the varieties to a few select types, most grown by Jefferson: Early York, Sugarloaf, Battersea, and the Green and Yellow Savoy (fig. 9.7).[13]

Cabbage seed was brought to Jamestown in 1619, and by 1732 William Hugh Grove observed "plenty" of cabbage, including the blistered Savoys. Five years later William Byrd listed five varieties,

9.7. Savoy was the cabbage of choice among gentlemen gardeners in Virginia in 1800

and Landon Carter often mentioned it as both a garden and an agricultural product. Cabbage seed was regularly sold by merchants and seed dealers in Williamsburg, Richmond, and Petersburg: George French sold sixteen varieties in Fredericksburg in 1800. Early Virginia gardening manuals, such as John Randolph's *Treatise,* mimicked Philip Miller's directions for spring and winter plantings and repeated his threefold command to water, "hill" (earth around the cabbage stems), and weed so that cabbage could be harvested every month of the year. Everyone who gardened in Virginia grew cabbage, including Francis Taylor, who either sowed cabbage seed or set out transplants forty-seven times between 1787 and 1799. Taylor mixed cabbage with other vegetable seed and often sowed it in beds that had been prepared by setting fire to the previous year's debris. He

9.8. Early Jersey Wakefield, a cone-shaped variety with similarities to Jefferson's Oxheart, Battersea, and Early York, in square VI, October 2010

planted as many as two hundred plants at a time, provided gifts of both cabbages and cabbage plants to neighbors, and set his harvested cabbages in trenches in November to preserve them through the winter. William Faris grew many of the established cabbage varieties like Sugarloaf and Early York and sowed seeds early in spring in "boxes," perhaps modified cold frames, for later transplanting into the garden (fig. 9.8). No one documented such extensive plantings or as many varieties as Jefferson, but his contemporaries all grew cabbage in some variety. Cabbage was so much in demand that urban nurseries in Philadelphia (John Lithen) and Washington (Theophilus Holt) sold cabbage transplants in the early 1800s.[14]

Amelia Simmons described the variations in the cabbage family as "multifarious," and Jefferson reveled in this diversity, documenting the names of as many as thirty-two forms and varieties of cabbage. These included Choux de Milan (fig. 9.9), a beautifully variegated Savoy type, and Oxheart, a French variety with a thickset, blunt-pointed cone that Jefferson sent home from Paris around 1786. Battersea, sowed at Monticello in August 1816, is a large, three-foot-wide, cone-shaped variety, the "earliest of all" for John Randolph. Early York was the most frequently planted of the standard white cabbage varieties at Monticello.

9.9. Choux de Milan cabbage

A small, cone-shaped cabbage, rounded at the top, Early York was observed by Amelia Simmons in fall markets in New England. Jefferson planted Green Curled and Yellow Curled Savoy cabbages in adjacent rows of square XII in 1812. Savoy cabbage, distinguished by its bold blistered and crinkled leaves, was planted almost every year in the retirement garden. Named for the duchy of the province of Savoy, this cabbage has a milder flavor and looser head and is less cold hardy than standard types. Savoys were considered high-class cabbages, and serving up a handsome specimen was an affirmation of one's place in the world. Sugarloaf cabbage, sent by McMahon to Monticello in 1809, was the most frequently planted cabbage variety in eighteenth-century Virginia and the standard of excellence. It was Philip Miller's favorite cabbage for its long-lasting, early heads. Sugarloaf was distinctive for its bluish green hue and the spoon-shaped leaves that clasped the head in the manner of a hood.[15]

Herbs: "Stripped" of Their Leaves

The word *herb* comes from *herbaceous* but commonly refers to useful perennial garden plants, especially Mediterranean species, used for culinary flavoring, fragrance, and medicine. The documentary evidence about Jefferson's use of herbs, particularly for medicine, or about the place of herbs in the Monticello garden, is limited. Jefferson's "Objects for the Garden" in 1794 includes a random list of sixteen species of herbs, many from southern Europe, traditionally used for cooking, medicine, or other domestic purposes (fig. 9.10). Leaves from the native yucca (*Yucca filamentosa*), for example, were used at Monticello to fabricate a rope for staking and tying up grapevines. No other documents survive about actually planting herbs, except for Jefferson's favorite, French tarragon (*Artemesia dracunculus* var. *sativa*), from which he used dried leaves in a French-style, *vinaigre d'estragon* dressing. Jefferson sought to establish this species again and again. In 1814 Jefferson responded to a request for "kitchen herbs" from a neighbor, L. H. Girardin, and described his garden as "so bare of kitchen herbs as to have but a single plant of sage, & that stripped of it's leaves." Jefferson was writing on January 9, so winter cold may have "stripped" the foliage from his perennial herbs. He also requested annual culinary herbs—sweet marjoram, basil, and summer savory—from his friend George Divers in February 1820, suggesting some desire to enhance Monticello's kitchen products. Although the garden is admirably sited for cultivating Mediterranean herbs, they were hardly the stars of the show.[16]

Contrary to modern popular opinion and despite their tidy, all-season appeal, herb gardens, except those medicinal gardens associated with a few homes of physicians or in botanical gardens, were rare in colonial America and throughout the nineteenth century. Herb gardens, sometimes designed as formal "knot gardens," are commonly

9.10. Red Acre cabbage, French lavender, and thyme

planted near restored houses throughout the United States, their installation a mythical fabrication of the Colonial Revival movement in the early and mid-twentieth century. An idealized view of a harmonious and orderly past, coupled with an interest in using the English Tudor model in "restored" gardens, incited landscape architects and designers associated with popular historic restorations such as at Colonial Williamsburg, as well as garden clubs throughout the country, to install symmetrical, heavily clipped, sometimes parterred herb gardens. In contrast, the historical record suggests that when kitchen herbs were cultivated in American gardens around 1800 they were distributed informally among the vegetables, in rows, sometimes in a border or in a garden corner, perhaps occasionally set against fences or walls of outbuildings and porches. Jefferson's herbs were probably distributed casually along the northwest border or used as informal edgings to garden squares.[17]

The saga of Jefferson and his favorite herb, tarragon, is a typically exasperating story of failure and futility. Jefferson likely encountered tarragon, or estragon, while in Paris as minister to France. After returning home in 1793 he wrote his French neighbor Peter Derieux that it "is little known in America." Perhaps because of tarragon's noticeable absence from the French cuisine at the President's House, Jefferson in 1805 asked J. P. Reibelt, a Swiss book dealer in New Orleans, to procure him seed. The genuine tarragon used for cooking and vinegar rarely produces seed but is easily propagated from root divisions. Jefferson never realized this, and his fervent search for the seeds is a key reason tarragon may never have been established in the garden. By 1813, after various plantings of roots, plants, and seeds, Jefferson reported tarragon in both square XVII and in the submural beds below the garden wall (fig. 9.11). These were seed-propagated plants from steamy New Orleans and were more likely what is today called Russian tarragon, an inferior sort that mimics but fails to match the sweet, liquorice-like flavor of the genuine article.[18]

9.11. Jefferson tried again and again to grow tarragon

A few of the culinary herbs documented as planned for the 1794 garden appear in the Jefferson family recipes. Thyme was included in recipes attributed to Martha Randolph for okra soup and vegetable porridge; mint was used to help get down the family rhubarb root remedy; and venison was cooked with basil in the President's House, where French chef, Honoré Julien, included artichokes smothered with "fines herbes" (tarragon and perhaps sweet marjoram) butter. The recipes in Mary Randolph's *Virginia House-wife* suggest how herbs were used to enhance the cooking of meat and fish. Many define familiar and enduring associations, such as sage with sausage and goose, thyme in beef soup, and fennel-wrapped fish. Mary Randolph's vinaigre d'estragon was made by pouring three pints of vinegar onto one quart of partially dried tarragon leaves; after standing a week, it was strained, bottled, and corked. Tansy pudding, a traditional omelet dating from the fourteenth century, was enhanced with

9.12. Rosemary thrives in the warm, sunny Monticello garden

"a little juice of tansy [leaves]," according to Randolph. Lavender was made into soaps, and both rosemary (fig. 9.12) and lavender oil were bathing fragrances added to water. Randolph's "Vinegar of the Four Thieves," made from lavender (fig. 9.13), rosemary, sage, wormwood, rue, and mint, was "very refreshing in crowded rooms, in the apartments of the sick, . . . sprinkled about the house in damp weather."[19]

The purely medicinal herbs on the Monticello lists—rue, wormwood, southernwood, chamomile, hyssop, periwinkle, marsh-mallow—were surely intended for use by the Jefferson family. Jefferson owned reference works on the use of herbs, but his list of Virginia medicinal plants in *Notes on the State of Virginia* included only native or naturalized species. In fact, wild North American plants may have contributed significantly more to the practice of medicine than Mediterranean garden herbs. In eighteenth-century Virginia, doctors were apothecaries, and apothecaries were often aspiring botanists. Plantation owners such as Landon Carter and their wives, including George Washington's Martha, were responsible for treating the maladies of their African American population. From the founding of Jamestown, non-European pharmacopoeia relied on the indigenous plants used for healing by American Indians: Virginians "find a World of Medicinal Plants," according to eighteenth-century historian Robert Beverley. The redemptive powers wrought by such wild species as Seneca snake root, *Lobelia siphilitica,* and ginseng were extolled by the earliest natural historians.[20]

Mediterranean garden herbs were secondary resources in early American medicine. The physician Benjamin Rush recommended mint tea for Jefferson's complaints of diarrhea. From the Monticello garden were potential cures for Jefferson's personal ailments: thyme for toothaches, lemon balm for fevers, lavender for Jefferson's potent headaches, tansy as a laxative, rue for bee stings, and wormwood and southernwood as purgatives. The *Hortus Medicus,* a colonial herb garden near Salem, North Carolina, planted in 1761, contained traditional healing herbs ranging from chamomile and marshmallow to rue and southernwood (fig. 9.14). Swedish botanist Peter Kalm reported a first-person account in New York in 1750 of how a rampantly infectious fever was quelled with oil of sage. John de Sequeyra, the Portuguese-born Williamsburg physician who championed the tomato, used wormwood (fig. 9.15) as an antidote for high fevers. Landon Carter, in doctoring his slaves, treated Windsor with "a bitter blyster of common decoction" that included the "bitter" herbs wormwood, tansy, southernwood, and chamomile. Other

9.13. Lavender was among Jefferson's "Objects for the garden" in 1794

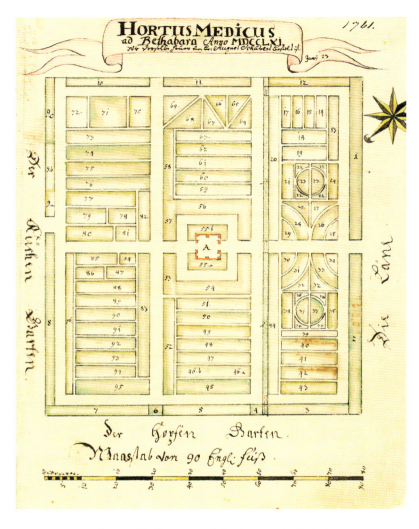

9.14. *Hortus Medicus,* a medicinal garden in Bethabara,
near Salem, North Carolina, is an example of an eighteenth-century
garden devoted solely to herbs

Sabine Hall slaves were treated by a local physician, Dr. Flood, with lavender water to "help in Expectoration."[21]

"Field and Pot Herbs" were well established in Virginia by 1737, according to William Byrd, who listed dozens of European garden plants used in cooking and medicine. Historian U. P. Hedrick considered sage to be the most common herb in American gardens before 1820. It was perhaps rivaled by mint, emphasized in unusual detail in Robert Squibb's *Gardener's Calendar* (1787), distilled by William Faris in 1802, and so essential to both alcoholic and nonalcoholic refreshment in the South. John Randolph's pre-Revolutionary *Treatise* advocated mint "to strengthen the mind" but also described how to grow eleven other species mentioned by Jefferson, including chamomile, a medicinal plant also useful for "making green walks and edging." Orange County's Francis Taylor was probably typical in the way he set out herb plants casually in landscape niches: "mixed lavender, wormwood & sage in bed next the gate toward the meat house." William Faris received a gift of a catnip plant and wrote how he planted it in an out-of-the-way site, the "alley between the new stable & the Fence." Faris also recorded how he "trimed the line of sage," planted out rosemary cuttings "to fill the line," and replanted his "Hedge of time," suggesting that he was using perennial herbs as ornamental hedges and borders in his garden. Joseph Hornsby of Kentucky planted an herb border to his asparagus beds that included rows of thyme and sage as well as mixed plantings of lemon balm, winter savory, southernwood, fennel, chives, and garlic.[22]

Herbs were likely such familiar plants, and so suited as "passalong" specimens relayed from one neighbor to another, that they were absent from eighteenth-century Virginia seed offerings. In contrast, urban American seedsmen began listing seeds of "Sweet and Pot Herbs," "Physical Herbs," and "Medicinal Plants" in Philadelphia and Baltimore in the early 1800s. Although John Randolph made a concerted effort to promote European herbs in the Virginia

9.15. Wormwood and flowering sea kale

kitchen garden, often commenting on their value as ornamental edging species, Bernard McMahon took a step further to endorse American herb growing in his *Gardener's Calendar*. The *Calendar* contains detailed advice on locating herbs in three-and-a-half-foot-wide beds or "as edging along beds and borders." William Cobbett's *American Gardener* (1821) also includes descriptions of, and directions for, growing twenty of the herbs mentioned by Jefferson. Tarragon was also a favorite of Cobbett's, who relayed a tale of English friends who said "beef-steaks were never so eaten" as those cooked with tarragon and shallots. Cobbett also liked mint boiled with peas, as was done at Monticello.[23]

Lettuce: Monday Morning Madness

Thomas Jefferson, horticultural authority and stern garden taskmaster, advised the readers of his "General Gardening Calendar" that

"a thimbleful of Lettuce should be sowed every Monday morning, from Feb. 1st to Sept. 1." Rivaling the garden pea, lettuce (*Lactuca sativa*) was by far the most avidly planted vegetable in the Monticello garden (fig. 9.16). There were more than 125 sowings between 1809 and 1824—including twenty-five plantings in 1809 and twenty-four in 1811—in fourteen sites, an unusual diversity of garden homeland compared to other crops. Jefferson loved lettuce and wanted it all the time, whether the ground was frozen in January or dried up in July. His chart of the Washington farmers' market documents the availability of lettuce throughout the year, and Etienne Lemaire purchased lettuce more than ninety times for presidential meals in 1806. Over the course of his gardening career, Jefferson harvested lettuce every month at Monticello. Although he was not as strict with his Poplar Forest overseer, Jeremiah Goodman, who, at least in 1812, was allowed to sow lettuce seed "every other Monday," Jefferson made an effort to plant lettuce every Monday during the growing season. In 1813, sixteen of Jefferson's nineteen lettuce sowings were on Monday. Altogether, half of the lettuce sowings between 1811 and 1824 took place on Monday. Experienced gardeners plant according to the condition of the soil and are attuned to incipient rainfall and frost, so it is gratifying to realize that Jefferson's Monday morning routine was a stated goal rather than a rigid practice. Jefferson sowed lettuce at Monticello almost every two weeks during the tough growing seasons of 1809, 1811, and 1812. By 1814 he had apparently learned that summer lettuce in Virginia is altogether too bitter and tough, so he moved the earliest sowing dates into February and avoided planting between mid-April and August to escape the summer heat.[24]

Boiled lettuce, "much superior to spinach," according to Bernard McMahon, was popular in the age of Jefferson. Writers recommended coarse and milky-sapped summer leaves or overgrown cabbage-type heads for boiling or soups. It seems possible that Jefferson's insistence from 1809 to 1813 on sowing lettuces in May, June,

9.16. Tennis-ball lettuce, with its pale, loose heads, is the predecessor of the Boston types so popular today

and July was to "dress" or cook his summer lettuce rather than to eat it "raw." Jefferson preferred lettuces that "loafed" or headed, perhaps in a more casual manner than iceberg lettuces form heads today, to lettuce "greens," which formed the majority of the lettuce purchased from the Washington markets. Whatever their final shape, lettuce's usual destination was the salad bowl, sometimes mixed with a bouquet of greens including spinach, orach, corn salad, endive, pepper grass, French sorrel, and sprouts. According to Mary Randolph, lettuce was gathered with other greens early in the morning, laid in cold water, sometimes including ice, and only removed hours later at dinner. Randolph's salad dressing included oil, common and tarragon vinegar, hard-boiled egg yolks, mustard, sugar, and salt. Salads were garnished with sliced egg whites and scallions. The goal advocated by eighteenth-century English author Richard Bradley was to blend "hot" or bitter greens like cress, mustard, celery, and tarragon with "cool and insipid" lettuce, spinach, corn salad, and turnips. The ancient Romans used a dressing of hot oil and vinegar, and Landon Carter adapted this by mixing his "salad" with melted butter and vinegar. Food historian Karen Hess concludes that green salads were eaten before the main meal in nondrinking cultures but after the meal when wine was served, perhaps providing a hint as to the schedule of the salad course at Monticello, where wine was, according to Jefferson, "an indispensable to my health."[25]

Although the year's lettuce crop was regularly sown in February and March, Jefferson rarely recorded harvesting "loaves" or "heads" until June or July. Most years Jefferson planted lettuce for fall and, if the season was mild, winter and early spring harvests; in 1823 a September 2 planting of Brown Dutch lettuce resulted in an "abundance for winter & spring" (fig. 9.17). Fall lettuce was sometimes planted in warm pockets below the stone house (now the Weaver's Cottage) and in submural beds, while the February sowings or earliest spring plantings often took place in northwest border beds. In

9.17. Brown Dutch lettuce was usually sowed by Jefferson in the late summer for winter harvests

1817 Jefferson noted that "the whole of our winter lettuce & endive [was] killed, tho' well covered." McMahon recommended protecting winter lettuce "by sticking in small branches of pine or cedar between the rows, which will yield them considerable protection, especially if some long dry straw be laid over them in frosty or cutting weather."[26]

Jefferson's garden calendars reveal a meticulous and deliberate lettuce planter at work. Each date's sowing took place along an individual row numbered from west to east in the prime garden space of squares IX or XII. Rows were divided into halves—"N," or north side, and "S," or south side—each end planted successively every week. Radish seed and, more rarely, companion species like endive, spinach, and corn salad were sowed in the rows with the lettuce. Jefferson occasionally transplanted his choicest lettuces—Marseilles, Tennis-ball, Ice, White Leaf—from the northwest border or beds

9.18. Rows of beets, spinach, lettuce, and kale, 2011

below the stone house into rows in the principal squares. Garden writers endorsed this practice because they felt that it encouraged "cabbaging," or heading: plants that are carefully spaced ten inches to a foot apart can more effectively achieve their dominion unbothered by competing neighbors (fig. 9.18). In 1809, 245 Marseilles lettuce plants were transplanted on May 19. Although lettuce was most commonly set out in rows in the Monticello garden squares, Jefferson instructed his Poplar Forest overseer, Jeremiah Goodman, to prepare "a bed of 4. f. wide & 6. or 8. feet long" to provide the vacationing ex-president with lettuce "fit for use when I come."[27]

Lettuce has an ancient lineage, traced to the Egyptians, Greeks, and Romans as a salad dressed raw with oil and vinegar but also commonly parched, steamed, or boiled. This crown jewel of the salad tribe was universally acknowledged as the choicest of greens, and it inspired richly tapestried literary associations, from sleep inducement to impotence. In the early seventeenth century, John Gerard described the recent forms of cabbage lettuce, "formed into that glove or round head," so common "the simplest is not ignorant [of it]." John Parkinson mentioned the "great diversitie" of lettuces for all seasons and suggested the superiority of Romaine types, the oldest of all lettuces, with "long leaves like a Teasell" that were "bound and whited" or blanched. A bread-and-butter English kitchen garden crop, lettuce was introduced into North America with the first settlers. Naturalist Mark Catesby was surprised that Americans banished salads from their diet, but Francis Michel, who visited Williamsburg in 1700 and 1701, noted how the colonists "pay little attention to garden plants except lettuce." Lettuce was often overlooked by eighteenth-century narrators of the Virginia landscape, perhaps because it was taken for granted. Nevertheless, lettuce was ubiquitous, in many varieties, on late eighteenth-century Virginia seed lists. John Randolph, an especially discriminating grower of lettuce, provided a minority opinion on the merits of "cutting" lettuce over "heading" types," "the

worst of all the kinds" owing to their "watery and flashy" heads. His disappointment in the "cabbaging" lettuce was caused by trying to grow this cool-weather crop during a Virginia summer.[28]

At least in New England, Amelia Simmons suggested that lettuce was so common that "your taste must guide your market" in selecting among the variety of types. Jefferson's gentlemen contemporaries such as Richard Harry Lee, George Washington, and Francis Taylor included lettuce in their spring and, for Taylor, fall planting rotations. Lettuce was a staple for middle-class craftsman William Faris in Annapolis, who sowed lettuce seed between his rows of peas in March, and for Kentuckian Joseph Hornsby, who like Jefferson carefully transplanted seedling plants of Ice and Cabbage lettuce into his garden in spring and early summer. The omnipresence of lettuce in the Washington markets also dispels any suggestion that lettuce was an overlooked staple in the age of Jefferson. William Cobbett, always successful at summarizing a plant's American role, said that lettuce was "pleasanter to a majority of tastes than any other plant," but complained that "I never saw a really fine Lettuce in America" owing to both cold winters and summer heat, which caused premature bolting. Cobbett preferred the Romaine types, which, after one unfolds the outside leaves, present a lump of white enough for a salad for ten people, unless they be French, and, then you have a lettuce to every person" (fig. 9.19).[29]

Lettuce varieties are conveniently, if imprecisely, divided into Cos (Roman or Romaine), with tall, narrow heads, and cabbaging (heading or "loafing" to Jefferson) varieties. Although more bean varieties were likely grown at the time and both pea and cabbage varieties were abundant, more lettuce varieties appeared in Virginia and American seed offerings before 1820 than any other species of vegetable. At one time or another, as many as twenty lettuce types or varieties were documented as planted at Monticello. However, four lettuce varieties—White Loaf, Brown Dutch, Ice, and

9.19. Spotted Aleppo, an eighteenth-century Romaine lettuce

Tennis-ball—stand out in the retirement garden as Jefferson favorites. Brown Dutch lettuce was planted thirty-one times between 1809 and 1824, often in warm, protected sites like the northwest border. The August- and September-sowed plants were harvested all winter and into the spring. Brown Dutch is a lovely lettuce, with shiny, reddish brown, marbled, and floppy leaves that form a loosely folded head: a jeweled and luscious basket. In 1821 Dr. Phillip Barraud bragged to his son-in-law, Jefferson's friend John Hartwell Cocke, "I never fail in this climate. I have more than 1000 head of Dutch brown bigger than your breakfast cup in Cabbaging order and as fine as possible." Ice lettuce was the third most commonly planted lettuce variety, sowed eighteen times, often with spinach or radishes. Jefferson confessed to his brother, Randolph, that "the ice lettuce does not do well in a dry season." Jefferson's "Ice" is possibly similar to today's Iceberg lettuce, but it may have been a Romaine-type that was referred to by at least one nineteenth-century seedsman as Ice Cos. Jefferson wanted to reserve Tennis-ball for the garden at Poplar Forest because "it does not require so much attention as the kind I have here [at Monticello]." A small and pale-leaved predecessor to the Boston lettuces so revered today, Tennis-ball seed was sowed thirteen times between 1809 and 1824 (fig. 9.20). Best as an early spring lettuce, it was planted by Jefferson too late for producing the most succulent harvest. When properly grown, its soft, tender, melting leaves form a delicious pale green head, a delicate, buttery bowl of moist, vegetable bliss. Jefferson's favorite and most commonly planted lettuce variety was the White Loaf (or "loaf" or "white"), sowed forty-seven times between 1809 and 1824. This was likely the same as the Common Cabbage lettuce universally discussed and grown in Virginia kitchen gardens, the type that John Randolph had trouble with because he tried to grow it in the summer.[30]

9.20. Jefferson forwarded seed of Tennis-ball lettuce to Poplar Forest because "it does not require so much attention"

PI. CCXVIII.

RHEUM *folus cordatis glabris, marginibus sinuatis spicis densis.*

P. Lunardi delin. *Published according to Act of Parliament by Ph. Miller, March 21, 1758.* *J. Mila Sculp.*

9.21. A medicinal species of rhubarb from Philip Miller,
*Figures of the Most Beautiful, Useful, and Uncommon Plants
Described in the Gardener's Dictionary,* 1755–60

The Puzzle of Monticello Rhubarb

One of the most puzzling of all Garden Book references is Jefferson's notation about planting one "row of rheum undulatum, esculent rhubarb, the leaves excellent as Spinach," in square II on May 13, 1809. Jefferson's rhubarb was probably *Rheum rhabarbarum* (known by some as *Rheum undulatum*), the treasured "pie plant" grown for the tart internal leaf stalks that are harvested when one to two feet long. Today, conventional wisdom warns against eating rhubarb leaves, which contain oxalic acid, which can be toxic if consumed, like spinach, in large quantities. What was Jefferson thinking and where did he get his information? Bernard McMahon, who succinctly ordered and described the confused tribe of rhubarbs in his 1806 *Calendar,* alluded to the "acidic taste" of the leaves of the pie rhubarb, suggesting personal experience. Jefferson's regard for rhubarb leaves as a boiled green is puzzling, but like McMahon he survived to write about it.[31]

Jefferson, by using the adjective "esculent," was definitively contrasting his *Rheum undulatum* with the medicinal rhubarb that was more common in the eighteenth century, *Rheum officinale,* a native of western China grown for its purgative dried root (fig. 9.21). Although Benjamin Franklin has been credited with introducing rhubarb into the United States, seeds from London's Peter Collinson of both the edible and medicinal species were grown in the 1730s by John Bartram in Philadelphia. Landon Carter used rhubarb root regularly from 1757 to 1777, probably improperly, as a laxative (rather than an astringent) to treat both himself and his slaves. Carter occasionally mixed it with calamus, made from the swamp-loving sweet rush (*Acorus calamus*) and noted for its ability to relieve stomach cramps and flatulent colic. On an undated list of herbs from around 1825, perhaps in Martha Randolph's handwriting, "rhubarb" is listed adjacent to "calamus," suggesting the tandem medicinal usage of both plants among the Jefferson family. Jefferson himself apparently used rhubarb to treat spastic bowels later in his life.[32]

In 1629 John Parkinson grew and illustrated the edible *Rhaponticum verum,* with two-foot stalks the "size of a man's thumb between root and leaf" and "first grown with me before it was ever seen or known elsewhere in England." John Bartram wrote the major facilitator for international plant exchange, London's Peter Collinson, in 1739: "Siberian Rhubarb . . . the true sort . . . or the Rhapontick make excellent tarts . . . Eats best Cold, it is much admired here, and none of the Effects that the Root Have. It eats most like Goose-berry Pye." Bernard McMahon was not only confident and concise in describing the two rhubarbs but also championed both the medicinal and pie rhubarb and provided extravagantly detailed directions for their cultivation. The medicinal rhubarb, "of national importance," had palmate leaves among other distinguishing features, whereas the "esculent rhubarb" was "frequently used, and much esteemed for tarts and pies." Despite McMahon's nod to the pie plant's frequency in American gardens, rhubarb remained a novelty in both gardens and cookbooks in the first two decades of the nineteenth century. In 1820 William Cobbett wrote, "This is one of the capital articles of the garden, though I have never seen it in America." Maria Eliza Rundell's *New System of Domestic Cookery,* published in both London and the United States in 1807, included a recipe for "Rhubarb Tart." The popularity of rhubarb was surely slower to rise in the southern United States because few cultivated plants suffer in heat like rhubarb, with its large and luxuriant leaves.[33]

Sea Kale: Friends to the Rescue

Jefferson was undoubtedly inspired to grow sea kale (*Crambe maritima*) by Bernard McMahon, who praised this rare vegetable as "highly deserving of cultivation" and sent him seeds in 1809. Following an unsuccessful sowing, Jefferson set aside a choice garden spot in the mysterious circular terraces at the southwestern end of the garden for another sowing of McMahon seeds in 1812. The Garden Book was ominously silent on sea kale until 1819, when Jefferson wrote with characteristic detail: "Oct. 9. planted Seakale 6. rows 100. f. long, 16. I. apart, and the seeds 6. I. distd. in y rows making 6. rows of 75. holes each = 600 holes or plants. 6 seeds in each hole." McMahon devoted five pages to sea kale cultivation, and his planting methods, including the sowing of six seeds to a hole, were obviously being copied at Monticello. The following May, in 1820, Jefferson obtained four hundred sea kale seedlings from the skillful George Divers, who had cautioned Jefferson that the plants "were too small to transplant." Jefferson also obtained seed from Bremo's John Hartwell Cocke the following April. Although it is unclear whose supply of plants or seeds finally produced, Jefferson's Garden Book chart of the harvest dates for perennial vegetables reveals that sea kale came to the table yearly from 1822 to 1825. Perseverance and the gifts from friends' gardens finally paid off.[34]

Sea kale is a perennial, cabbagelike plant that grows wild along Britain's seashore beaches. As the plant sends forth leaf stalks in the spring, usually in March, the unfolding leaves are covered by shifting, wind-driven beach sand, effectively blanching the shoots, preventing the production of chlorophyll, and thereby enhancing the delicacy of the plant's flavor (fig. 9.22). Although harvested in the wild for centuries, sea kale appeared in London markets only late in the 1700s, when gardeners used artificial means—clay pots, heavy mulches of leaves, sand, or wooden boards—to blanch the emerging leaf stalks. According to McMahon, "the neatest and cleanest mode" of blanching sea kale was by using clay pots. Following McMahon's directive, Jefferson ordered fifty pots from his Richmond agent Bernard Peyton in 1821 and again from pot wholesaler Richard Randolph in 1822. The pots are left atop the dormant plants all winter and lifted

9.22. Blanching sea kale shoots by covering them with pots mellows the natural flavor of the vegetable

as the stalks are harvested in April, when they reach six to fifteen inches. Archaeological investigations of the garden in 1980 unveiled shards of these pots, which were reproduced for the restored garden in 1995. *The Virginia House-wife* recommended that sea kale be "tied up in bundles, and dressed in the same way as asparagus," while the enthusiastic McMahon, who said most people preferred this "delicious esculent" to asparagus, recommended twenty minutes of boiling, adding, "The goodness of the article depends on it."[35]

Sea kale is a distinctly British vegetable, relatively unknown on the Continent and cherished because it can be harvested so early in the spring. In 1768 Philip Miller suggested that the harvesting of wild sea kale in Sussex and Dorset, "the residents preferring it to any of the Cabbage kind," was an activity just as prominent as the species' cultivation in gardens, where "it will soon overspread a large spot of ground." Miller advised that sea kale be planted in sandy soil and covered with a five-inch mulch of sand or gravel in early winter. Miller also admired "the fine regular heads of white flowers, which appear very handsome," and gardeners have always been taken by the robust, bluish green, glaucous leaves of a full-grown sea kale plant in summer. Sea kale was virtually unknown in the United States until Bernard McMahon popularized it by selling the seed around 1804 and discussing it in his book two years later. John Hartwell Cocke's garden at Bremo was renowned for its abundant sea kale, and he became a source of seed not just for Jefferson but for other Virginia friends and relatives. William Cobbett, despite never seeing sea kale in an American garden, was also an enthusiastic promoter who described it as "unquestionably (after the Asparagus) the very best garden vegetable that grows." According to food historian William Woys Weaver, sea kale became "a culinary trophy" later in the 1800s, particularly for wealthy patrons who employed professional gardeners.[36]

9.23. Corn salad

Small-Sallading:
The Greens of Spring

Jefferson, at one time or another, grew an uncommon variety of "small-sallading," winter and spring greens, that provided a flavorful punch to fresh Monticello salads. "A mess of salad" and "greens" were also commonly purchased from Monticello slaves, as were "sprouts," which were more likely members of the cabbage family, commonly "dressed" like spinach rather than eaten fresh like lettuce. Bernard McMahon recommended planting a succession of mustard, orach, cress, pepper grass, corn salad, and rape throughout the coolest months of the year in a warm, slanting border bed or, if the labor and space were available, in frames. William Faris harvested his "greens" in March, while Francis Taylor pulled up plants from his garden in November to set in trenches so that they could be more conveniently

harvested throughout the winter. Richard Parkinson, who lived outside Baltimore in 1800, described how "vegetables are so much used in America, that young clover is very frequently eaten for greens in the spring . . . Indeed, in the spring, they boil everything that is green, for use at the table." William Cobbett was astounded by the spring mania for anything green, "for, at that very season, the people of New York, are carrying home *wild dock leaves* from the *market*, bought at three or four cents a handful."

Listed among the "raw sallads" section of the garden in 1812, Jefferson grew celery (*Apium graveolens* var *dulce*) with determined resolution, sowing seed and transplanting seedlings as often as any other crop in the preretirement years and ever searching for the perfect garden spot for this cool-temperature, moisture-loving vegetable. Celery was purchased twenty-nine times for President's House meals in 1806, the fifth most frequently purchased vegetable. Although it was grown by Jefferson's neighbors John Hartwell Cocke and George Divers, most contemporary gardeners did not bother with such a specialty crop that required so much attention: trench making, constant hoeing to blanch the stems, and watering during the dry months.[38]

Corn salad (*Valerianella locusta*), now fashionable as the French mache, traditionally known as "lamb's lettuce" to the English, was grown at Monticello from 1809 to 1813 (fig. 9.23). Named for its weedy ubiquity in European "corn" (actually wheat) fields, the cold-hardy but petite leaves of corn salad suffer under the slightest touch of heat. William Cobbett dismissed corn salad as a "mere weed." Corn salad seed was sold only rarely in Virginia but became more common in urban seed houses in the early 1800s.[39]

Seeds of both pepper grass (*Lepidum sativm*) and "Cresses," likely the same species but with a more refreshing flavor, were planted in 1774 and 1777. Cresses were more esteemed and popular in English North America than most other "small sallading," and they were sold in the Washington market from December 16 through May. Cobbett

9.24. Red orach was eaten raw or cooked and grown in both green and red forms.

wrote that the curled is the "prettiest, but the plain is the best," and both cress and pepper grass were common in early nineteenth-century seed offerings.[40]

In 1802 Jefferson wrote to his former Monticello gardener Robert Bailey and asked him to provide the President's House with plants of endive (*Cichorium endivia*), which could be heeled into a nursery bed for harvesting through the winter months. Jefferson's enthusiasm for this winter vegetable, grown for both its leaves and crisp white heart, waned during his retirement years.[41]

Jefferson only occasionally grew typical brassica family greens like kale (*Brassica oleracea*) and coleworts (*Brassica oleracea*), open-headed cabbages cultivated in the winter and spring for their young, green sprouts. Coleworts possessed the smooth leaves we now associate in the southern United States with collards, a phonetic corruption of *colewort*. Most of Jefferson's contemporaries grew some form of kale or collard for harvesting during the cold depths of winter. "Sprouts," probably a reference to these members of the cabbage family—distinct from "greens," "a mess of greens," or "cresses"—were available at Washington markets from February 22 to May 20. Etienne Lemaire recorded twenty-one purchases in 1806, and "sprouts" were also bought from Monticello slaves. In *The Virginia House-wife,* Mary Randolph conveniently lumped "sprouts" with "young greens," boiled like cabbage for fifteen minutes.[42]

Orach (*Atriplex hortensis*) is an ancient salad green resembling lamb's quarters in appearance but milder than other greens and tasting like spinach or chard (fig. 9.24). Jefferson adopted orach as a pet vegetable in his later years, when seeds were sowed in 1813 in both spring and fall, then annually, usually in March for spring greens. John Parkinson mentioned the "divers kindes" of "Arrack," especially the highly ornamental variety with "dusty, purplish" foliage. Leaves of the "white [actually, pale green] garden" sort were "boyled and buttered." Although mentioned as early as 1714 by John Lawson in North Carolina, orach was rare in American gardens. William Faris sowed orach, "English Lamb q[u]arter," in his garden in Annapolis in 1793.[43]

Mustard was listed in the 1812 "Arrangement of the Garden" as a "dressed salad," and the variety, Durham, was sowed the same year in square XII. Seeds of white mustard (*Brassica hirta*), the common species used for growing as a "small sallading" when the leaves are young or as a boiling green when more mature, were saved by Robert Bailey from the 1794 garden and also planted in 1815 (fig. 9.25). Red or black mustard (*Brassica nigra*), which sets the black seeds from which the condiment is produced, was planted with other salad plants in April 1774. Jefferson imported mustard from France and would have given his plantings more space if his goal had been to create a domestically grown condiment. Francis Taylor sowed it annually in Orange County between 1786 and 1799. The condiment mustard was rarely grown in the colonies and young United States, but seeds were offered commercially by larger seed houses in the early 1800s. William Cobbett ranted about the "poisonous stuff" sold in the United States as English mustard: "Why should any man that has a garden *buy* mustard?"[44]

Sorrel, either French (*Rumex scutatus*) or common (*R. acetosa*), possibly both, was a perennial herb included by Jefferson among "dressed" leaves in 1812. French sorrel was listed under the "Objects for the garden" in 1794, and the seed was saved by Robert Bailey. Both sorts provide a deliciously sour lemon-flavored herb, the French being less acidic. Philip Miller noted that the more desirable, round-leafed French sorrel, as common as any esculent vegetable in Paris markets, was becoming more popular in London with the importation of French taste in cooking. Although William Byrd noted sorrel in Virginia in 1737, it was rare in American gardens before 1800. Cranky William Cobbett wrote that, though the French "make large messes of it," only a square foot of sorrel "may suffice for an American garden." Mary Randolph recommended that sorrel be "dressed as spinach," possibly mixing the two kinds to "improve each other."[45]

Spinach (*Spinacia oleracea*), or "spinage," was an essential "dressed" salad green planted four or five times a year in the Monticello retirement garden for spring, fall, and winter consumption. Mary Randolph's recipe for boiling the leaves only "a few minutes," then sautéing them lightly in a stew pan with butter, salt, and pepper, was, for food historian Karen Hess, an example of how Virginia vegetables were not necessarily overcooked in the English tradition. "Spinage" was grown only occasionally by Jefferson's contemporaries. Like Jefferson, Landon Carter learned to plant spinach in September, including "a large patch for the deer," after his yearly November plantings were destroyed by cold weather. The exceptional William Faris sowed spring "spinage" yearly in the walkways between the rows of his asparagus beds or between his peas, and his smallish garden included seventy rows in 1799. When confronting Prickly–seeded winter spinach (fig. 9.26) and Round summer spinach, the two varieties grown at Monticello and standard five through the nineteenth century, many expressed preference for the larger, thicker, and more robust leaves of the round variety.[46]

9.25. Mustard greens in square XXXIII, November 2010

9.26. Prickly-seeded spinach is featured in the restored garden

Sprout Kale:
Monticello Mystery Plant, *"fine, tender, sweet"*

"Sprout" kale was one of Thomas Jefferson's magnificent horticultural obsessions. Sent to Monticello by André Thöuin in 1809, sprout kale appeared in the retirement garden for thirteen consecutive years. Jefferson forwarded seeds to virtually every gardening correspondent he could find and roared enthusiastically about its value. He wrote to Bernard McMahon that the winter sprouts of this hardy kale were "among the most valuable garden plants," to John Hartwell Cocke that the harvests were "tender and delicious," and to Randolph Jefferson that it was "the finest winter vegetable we have." To former Virginia governor James Barbour he described it as "a very delicate green," to his son-in-law John Wayles Eppes, "a fine, tender, sweet winter vegetable," and to L. H. Girardin, "the most precious winter vegetable he [Jefferson] knows." Few Monticello garden plants received such repeated accolades. Jefferson cherished "sprout" kale for its continual harvest—"a few plants will give a dish every day"—for its "tender and delicious" flavor, and for its rarity. He reminded McMahon that "sprout kale" was missing from his catalogue and boasted to Barbour that "no body in the U. S. has [it] but those to whom I have given it."[47]

Although Jefferson considered "sprout kale" his "discovery," the plant itself is unidentifiable today. Jefferson provided a botanical name familiar only to himself or André Thöuin, *Brassica sempervirens,* but virtually all kales are green throughout the winter (hence the name *sempervirens*). In all the descriptive praise Jefferson offered to "sprout" kale, no quality distinguishes it from any other kale. Colonial Williamsburg's Wesley Greene has suggested that it might be dwarf German kale, while William Woys Weaver has a "gut feeling" that it is broccoli raab (or rabe) or a type of baby kale. The inability of Jefferson to more specifically describe "sprout kale" boosts its allure as a Monticello mystery plant.

Appendix 1
Vegetables Mentioned in Thomas Jefferson's Garden Book, Correspondence, and Memoranda

Dates represent the first year of mention. Varieties in quotation marks represent Jefferson's personal name; others are recognized names.

Artichoke, Globe, *Cynara scolymus* (1770)
  Green (1808), Red (1808)

Artichoke, Jerusalem ("Topinambours"), *Helianthus tuberosus* (1794)

Asparagus, *Asparagus officinalis* (1767)
  Cooper's Pale Green (1807), "East India" (1804)

Bean (1772)
  Asparagus Bean, *Vigna unguiculata* ssp. *sesquipedalis* (1809)
    "long pod soup pea" (1804)
  Broad Bean, *Vicia faba* (1774)
    "brown Windsor" (1794), Early Mazagan ("Mazareen," 1794), Horse (1794), Windsor (1774)
  Caracalla, *Vigna caracalla* (1792)
  Garbanzo ("garavance"), *Cicer arietinum* (1814)
  Green or Kidney, *Phaseolus vulgaris* (1774)
    "Snaps" ("Snapbeans," 1774)
      "Alexandrian" (1820), Arikara ("Ricara," 1807), "Bess" (1813), "Blue speckled snap" (1794), "dwarf" (1809), "dwarf beans of Holland" (ca. 1786), "E[arly] dwarf" (1809), "Fagiuoli bianchi di Parigi" (1774), "Fagiuoli bianchi di Toscana" (1774), Fagiuoli coll'occhio di Provenza"(1774), "Fagiuoli d'Augusta" (1774), "Fagiuoli verdi coll'occhio bianco" (1774), "Feve de Marais" (ca. 1786), "forward" (1809), "French kidney" (1815), "Golden Dwarf" (1794), "grey beans of Switzerland" (ca. 1786), "grey snaps" (1809), "ground snap" (1794), "hominy" (1812), "Italian" (1820), "little" (ca. 1786), "Mazzei" (1774), "Purple" (1774), "red snaps" (1809), "Reid [Red] speckled snap"

(1794), "Roman" (1820), "Tuscan" (1820), "White snap" (1794"), "yellow snaps" (1809)
  "Haricots" (1810)
    "Alleghany" (1794), "gray haricot" (1820), "Early Sesbon" (1794), Flageolet (ca. 1786), "Fresh dry haricot" (1814) Friholio ("the red bean called Friholio," 1832), "haricots roussatres" (1810), "Julian" (ca. 1786), "long haricot" (1820), "nain d'hollande" (ca. 1786), "red haricots" (1809), "white haricot" (1819), Wild Goose ("red blossomed kidney bean," 1819)
  Lima Bean, *Phaseolus lunatus* (1777)
    Carolina White (1794), Honey (1824), "large lima" (1815), Sugar or Bushel (1794)
  Scarlet runner ("Arbor"), *Phaseolus coccineus* (1791)

Beet, *Beta vulgaris* (1774)
  "Red" (1774), "Scarlet" (1774), "white" (1774)

Black Salsify, *Scorzonera hispanica* (1812)

Broccoli, *Brassica oleracea* (1767)
  Black (1824), "Cavol broccolo Francese di Pisa" (1774), "Cavolo Romano a broccolini" (1777), "Cavolo Romano Paonazzo" (1777), Cauliflower or White (1809), "December" (1824), "Florence" (1824), "Green" (1795), "Leghorn" (1811), "Malta" (1824), "March" (1824), "October" (1824), "Palermo" (cauliflower? 1824), Purple Early Purple (1809), Roman (1809), "white" (1794)

Brussels Sprouts, *Brassica oleracea* var. *gemmifera* (1812)

Burnet, *Sanguisorba minor* ("Pimpinastella di Pisa," 1774–1778)

Cabbage, *Brassica oleracea* var. *capitata* (1771)
  "Aberdeen" (1812), Battersea (1816), "Cattle" (1812), "Cavol Capuccio Spagnolo di Pisa" (1774), "Cavolo Romano a broccolini" (1777), "Cavolo

Romano Paonazzo" (1777), "Choux pommé" (ca. 1786), Dwarf Early (1813), "early" (1807), Early York (1809), "Giant" (1809"), "Large Cattle" (1812), "Large White" (1824), "many head" (1811), "May" (1812), "Neapolitan" (1777), Oxheart (ca. 1786), "paisinette" (ca. 1824), Red (1774)

Savoy (1774)
 Choux de Milan (ca. 1786), "Curled Cabbage of Paisinetta" (1824), "Curled Savoy" (1811), "Curled Schiane" (1824), Green-curled (1809), "Savoy Green" (1812), "schiane" (ca. 1824), Yellow Savoy (1812)

Scotch (1794), Sugarloaf (1809), "Tall" (1810), "Winter" (1817), York (1809)

Carrot, *Daucus carota* (1774)
 "Carote di Pisa" (1774), "early" (1812), "large" (1812), "orange" (1809), "yellow" (1811)

Castor Bean, *Ricinus communis* ("Palm of Christi," 1794; "Palma Christi," 1811)

Cauliflower, *Brassica oleracea* (1767)
 "bon Choux-fleur marcher" (ca. 1786), "Choux-fleurs de la Meilleure espece" (ca. 1786), "December" (ca. 1824), "Dutch Hard" (ca. 1786), Early (1809), "English Hard" (ca. 1786), "February" (ca. 1824), "March" (ca. 1824)

Celery, *Apium graveolens* var. *dulce* (1767)
 Red (1809), Solid (1774)

Chicory, *Cichorium intybus* (1805)

Chives, *Allium schoenoprasum* (1812)

Collards, *Brassica oleracea* var. *acephala* ("Coleworts," 1774)
 "Cavolo nero" (1777)

Corn Salad, *Valerianella locusta* (1794)
 "Candia" (1810)

Cress, *Lepidum sativum, Barbarea* sp. (1774)
 "English" (1794), "Italian" (1774), "mountain" (1794)

Cucumber, *Cucumis sativus* (1767)
 "early" (1794), Early Frame ("frame," 1818), "early green" (1812), Early White (1812), "forward" (1794), Gherkin, *Cucumis anguria* (1812), Long Green (1811), serpentine ("mammoth"), *Cucumis flexuosus* (1825)

Eggplant ("Melonzoni," "melongena"), *Solanum melongena* (1793)
 "Prickly" (1812), Purple (1812), White (1812)

Endive, *Cichorium endivia* (1777)
 Broad-leaved ("broad," 1794), "Chicore de Meaux" (ca. 1786), "Chicore frize" (ca. 1786), Green Curled (1809), "smooth" (1809), "winter" (1794)

Garlic, *Allium sativum* (1774)
 "Aglio di Toscania" (1774)

Gourd (1809)
 Long (*Lagenaria siceraria*, 1809), Orange (*Cucurbita pepo*, 1809)

Hops, *Humulus lupulus* (1794)

Horseradish, *Armoracia rusticana* (1794)

Indian Corn, *Zea mays* (1774)
 Broom (1786), "Derieux's" white (1794), "drying corn from Cherokee country" (1787), "Erie" (1809), "forward" (1794), "forward corn from Claxton" (1810), "Guinea" (1791), "Homony" (1787), Mandan (1807), "Mazzei's" (1794), "Missouri hominy corn" (1807), "Pani" (Pawnee, 1807), Quarantine (1806), "soft" (1807), "sweet or shriveled" (1810)

Kale, *Brassica oleracea* (1809)
 "Buda" (1809), Delaware (1809), Malta (1809), "Russian" (1777, 1812), Scotch (1809), "Sprout Kale" ("*Brassica sempervirens,*" 1812)

Kohlrabi ("Turnip Cabbage"), *Brassica oleracea* (1801)

Leek, *Allium ampeloprasum* (1794)
 "common" (1812), "flag" (1812)

Lentils, *Lens culinaris* (1774)
 "green" (1774), "large" (1814), "small" (1774)

Lettuce, *Lactuca sativa* (1767)
 "Berlin" (ca. 1786), "brown" (1809), Brown Dutch ("Dutch brown," 1809), "cabbage" (1794), Cos (1794), "endive-leaved" (ca. 1786), "forward" (ca. 1786), "Ice" (1774), "Loaf," "White loaf" (1809), "longleaved" (1794), Marseilles (1809), Roman (1804), "shell-winter" (ca. 1786), Silesia (1819), "summer" (ca. 1786), Tennis-ball (1809), "white" (1812)

Melon, *Cucumis melo* (1774)
 Cantaloupe (1774), "Cette" (ca. 1812), "Chinese" (1809), citron (*Citrullus lanatus* var. *citroides,* 1794), "Egyptian" (ca. 1812), "green" (1794), "Miami" (1811), Nutmeg (1811), Persian (1812), Pineapple (1794), "Popone Arancini di Pistoia" (1774), "Venice" (1794), winter (*Cucumis melo inodorus,* 1805), "Zatte di Massa" (1774)

Mustard, *Brassica* sp. (1774)
 "Durham" (1812), red (*Brassica nigra,* 1774), white (*B. hirta, B. juncea,* 1794)

Nasturtium, *Tropaeolum majus* (1774)

Okra, *Abelmoschus esculentus* (1809)

Onion, *Allium cepa* (1774)
 Madeira (1778), scallions (*A. fistulosum,* 1812), shallots (*A. cepa* var. *aggregatum,* 1794), Spanish (1767), tree or "hanging" (*A. cepa* var. *proliferum,* 1809), White Spanish ("Spanish onion of Miller," 1774)

Orach, *Atriplex hortensis* (1813)

Parsley, *Petroselinum crispum* (1774)
  Curled ("double," 1774), Plain-leaved (1809)

Parsnip, *Pastinaca sativa* (1774)

Pea, Chick ("Garavance"), *Cicer arietinum* (1777)

Pea, Garden, *Pisum sativum* (1767)
  Blue Prussian ("Prussian blue," 1809), Charlton (Hotspur) (1768), "cluster or bunch" (1774), "dwarf peas of Holland. for frames" (ca. 1786), "earliest of all" (1767), "early" (1773), "early dwarf" (1794), Early Pearl (Nonesuch, 1778), "forward" (1774), "Forwardest" (1767), "forward peas of Marly" (ca. 1786), Frame, Early Frame (1809), Hotspur (1774), "Hunter's" (1818), "latest of all," "latter," "latest" (1767, 1774), Leadman's Dwarf (1809), "Leitch's frame" (1820), "Leitch's latter" (1821), "Leitch's pea" (1820), Marrowfat (1773), "May" (1820), "Middling" (1767), Spanish Morotto (1768)

Pea, Field, *Pisum sativum* var. *arvense* (1774)
  "Albany" (1808)

Pea, Field, Crowder, Cow, *Vigna unguiculata* (1774)
  "African early" (1809), Black-eyed (1774), "Black Indian" (1794), "early" (1809), "French" (1794), "gray" (1809), "Indian" (1794), "Mazzei" (1814), "pearl-eye" (1794), "Ravenscroft" (1807), "Ravensworth" (1808), "White-eyed" (1794)

Peanut ("Peendars"), *Arachis hypogaea* (1794)

Pepper, Bell, *Capsicum annuum* (1774)
  Bullnose (1812), "Large" (1824), "Major" (1812)

Pepper, Cayenne, *Capsicum annuum* (1767)
  Texas bird, *Capsicum annuum* var. *glabriusculum* ("Capsicum Techas," "minutissimum," 1814)

Pepper Grass, *Lepidium sativum* (1774)

Potato, Irish, *Solanum tuberosum* (1772)
  "early" (1812), "forward" (1813)

Pumpkin, *Cucurbita pepo* var. *pepo* and *C. maxima* (1774)
  "black" (1774), "Chilikiote" (1824), "long pumpkin from Malta" (1809), potato (*C. moschata,* 1794), "solid pumpkin from S. America" (1809), "white" (1774), "Zucche bianche" (1774), "Zucche da Pescatori" (1774), "Zucche di Monacho" (1774), "Zucche Lauri" (1774), "Zucche nere" (1774)

Radicchio, *Cichorium intybus* ("Radicchio di Pistoia," 1774)

Radish, *Raphanus sativus* (1767)
  "black" (1812), English Scarlet (1794), "leather coat" (1824), Oil (1809), "Rose" (ca. 1786), "Salmon" (1794), Scarlet, Early Scarlet (1774), "summer" (1809), "violet N.Y." (1817), "White" (ca. 1786)

Rape, *Brassica napus* (1774)
  "green" (1794)

Rhubarb ("esculent rhubarb"), *Rheum rhabarbarum* (1809)

Rhubarb, Medicinal, *Rheum officinale* (ca. 1824)

Rutabaga ("Swedish turnip"), *Brassica napus* (1795)

Salsify, *Tragopogon porrifolius* (1774)
  "Columbian" (1812), "Missouri" (1807)

Scurvy Grass, *Cochlearia officinalis* ("di Pisa," 1774)

Sea Kale, *Crambe maritima* (1809)

Sesame, *Sesamum indicum* (1808)

Sorrel, French, *Rumex scutatus* (1794), and Common, *R. acetosa* (1774, 1809)
  "Acetosa di Pisa" (1774)

Spinach, *Spinachia oleracea* (1771)
  Prickly-seeded ("winter." "prickly," 1809), Smooth-seeded ("Summer," "Round-leaved," 1809, 1811)

Squash, *Cucurbita pepo* vars. *pepo* and *melopepo* (1782)
  "Cape du Verd" (ca. 1812), "Cape of Good Hope" (ca. 1812)
  Cymling ("simelines," 1784)
    "soft" (1809), "warted" (1807)
  "long crooked & warted" (1807), "Squash from [Thomas] Maine [Main]" (1809), "Summer" (ca. 1809), "Warted" (1809), "Winter" (1815), "Winter Crooked Neck" (ca. 1812)

Sweet Potato ("Indian Potato"), *Ipomoea batatas* (1796)

Tomato ("tomatas"), *Lycopersicon lycopersicum* (1809)
  "dwarf" (1817), "Spanish tomato (very much larger than the common kinds)" (1811)

Turnip, *Brassica rapa* (1774)
  Early Dutch (1812), "English" (1794), "forward" ("Raves natives," ca. 1786), "Frazer's new" (1808), Hanover (1794), Long French (1809), "rose" ("Raves conteur de rose," ca. 1794), "Summer" (1811)

Watermelon, *Citrullus lanatus* (1774)
  "Cocomere di Pistoia" (1774), "Cocomere di seme Neapolitane" (1774), "Mexican" (1824), Roman (1811), Savannah (ca. 1812)

Herbs

Anise, *Pimpinella anisum* (ca. 1824)

Basil, *Ocimum basilicum* (ca. 1824)

Caraway, *Carum carvi* (ca. 1824)

Catnip, *Nepeta cataria* (ca. 1824)

Chamomile, *Chamaemelum nobile* (1794)

Coriander, *Coriandrum sativum* (ca. 1824)

Fennel, *Foeniculum vulgare* (ca. 1824)

Hyssop, *Hyssopus officinalis* (1794)

Lavender, *Lavandula angustifolia* (1794)

Lemon Balm, *Melissa officinalis* (1794)

Madder, *Rubia tinctorum* (ca. 1824)

Marjoram, Pot, *Origanum vulgare* (ca. 1824)

Marjoram, Sweet, *Origanum majorana* (1794)

Marshmallow, *Althaea officinalis* (1794)

Mint, *Mentha* sp. (1794)

Periwinkle, *Vinca minor* (1794)

Rosemary, *Rosmarinus officinalis* (1794)

Rue, *Ruta graveolens* (1794)

Sage, *Salvia officinalis* (1794)

Savory, *Satureja* sp.
    Summer, *S. hortensis* (1809)
    Winter, *S. montana* (1809)

Southernwood, *Artemisia abrotanum* (1794)

Tansy, *Tanacetum vulgare* (1794)

Tarragon, French, *Artemisia dracunculus* var. *sativa* (1806)

Thyme, *Thymus vulgaris* (1794)

Wormwood, *Artemisia absinthium* (1794)

Yucca ("beargrass"), *Yucca filamentosa* (1794)

Appendix 2
Sources for Historic and Heirloom Vegetables

Baker Creek Heirloom Seed Company
2278 Baker Creek Rd, Mansfield, MO 65704
Phone: 417-924-8917
Fax: 417-924-8887
Website: www.rareseeds.com

D. Landreth Seed Company
60 East High St, Bldg #4, New Freedom, PA 17349
Phone: 800-654-2407
Fax: 717-227-1112
Website: www.landrethseeds.com

Fedco Seeds
PO Box 520, Waterville, ME 04903
Phone: 207-873-7333 or 270-430-1106
Website: www.fedcoseeds.com

Heirloom Seed Project, Landis Valley Museum
2451 Kissel Hill Rd, Lancaster, PA 17601
Phone: 717-569-0401
Fax: 717-560-2147
Website: www.landisvalleymuseum.org

Heritage Harvest Seed
PO Box 40, RR#3, Carman, MB R0G 0J0, Canada
Phone: 1-204-745-6489
Fax: 1-204-745-6723
Website: www.heritageharvestseed.com

Sand Hill Preservation Center
1878 230th St, Calamus, IA 52729
Phone: 563-246-2299
Website: www.sandhillpreservation.com

Seed Savers Exchange
3094 North Winn Rd, Decorah, IA 52101
Phone: 563-382-5990
Fax: 564-382-6511
Website: www.seedsavers.org

Seeds from Italy
PO Box 149, Winchester, MA 01890
Phone: 781-721-5904
Fax: 612-435-4020
Website: www.growitalian.com

Seeds of Change
PO Box 4908, Rancho Dominguez, CA 90020
Phone: 800-762-7333
Website: www.seedsofchange.com

Southern Exposure Seed Exchange
PO Box 460, Mineral, VA 23117
Phone: 540-894-9480
Fax: 540-894-9481
Website: www.southernexposure.com

Thomas Etty, Esq.
Seedsman's Cottage, Puddlebridge, Horton,
Ilminster, Somerset, TA19 9RL United Kingdom
Phone: +44 (0) 01460-298249
Website: www.thomasetty.co.uk

Thomas Jefferson Center for Historic Plants
PO Box 316, Charlottesville, VA 22902
Phone: 800-243-1743
Website: www.monticello
.org/site/house-and-gardens/
thomas-jefferson-center-historic-plants
Seed orders: www.monticellocatalog.org/
outdoor---garden-plants--- seeds.html

ABBREVIATIONS

AF   *American Farmer,* Baltimore, 1819–34

APS   American Philosophical Society, Philadelphia (Thomas Jefferson Papers, Mss. B J35, unless otherwise noted)

HL   Huntington Library, San Marino, CA (Thomas Jefferson Papers, 1764–1826, unless otherwise noted)

JL   Jefferson Library, Thomas Jefferson Foundation, Charlottesville, VA

LOC   Library of Congress, Washington, DC (Thomas Jefferson Papers, 1606–1827, unless otherwise noted)

MHS   Massachusetts Historical Society, Boston (Thomas Jefferson Papers, unless otherwise noted)

NJHS   New Jersey Historical Society, Newark

PTJ   Julian P. Boyd et al., eds., *The Papers of Thomas Jefferson,* 1950–, 36 vols. to date

PTJRS   J. Jefferson Looney et al., eds., *The Papers of Thomas Jefferson: Retirement Series,* 2004–, 7 vols. to date

SA   *Southern Agriculturist and Register of Rural Affairs,* Charleston, SC, 1828–39

VHS   Virginia Historical Society, Richmond

UNC   University of North Carolina, Chapel Hill (Southern Historical Collection, Nicholas Philip Trist Papers, 1765–1903, unless otherwise noted)

UVA   Small Special Collections Library, University of Virginia Libraries, Charlottesville (The Thomas Jefferson Papers, unless otherwise noted)

VMHB   *Virginia Magazine of History and Biography*

A NOTE ON SOURCES

This book benefitted from the work of Edwin Morris Betts, the first scholar to transcribe Jefferson's sixty-six-page garden diary and place it in the context of the time, with references to correspondence and drawings. Jefferson's original "Garden Book" is held by the Massachusetts Historical Society (MHS), and a virtual facsimile, part of The Thomas Jefferson Papers: An Electronic Archive, can be viewed on the MHS website at http://www.masshist.org/thomasjeffersonpapers/. All citations of "Jefferson, Garden Book" refer to this digital edition. The MHS website also offers a digital version of Jefferson's Farm Book and an extensive collection of his architectural drawings, which are identified online by the "N" numbers provided in the citations.

Thomas Jefferson correspondence held by the Library of Congress (LOC) can be viewed in its original manuscript form online at http://memory.loc .gov/ammem/collections/jefferson_papers/, the website for The Thomas Jefferson Papers, part of the library's American Memory Project. Jefferson's Weather Book is also located at this website as the "Thomas Jefferson Weather Memorandum Book," in *The Thomas Jefferson Papers,* Ser. 7, Misc. Bound Volumes, Vol. 2, Weather Record, 1776–1818.

The majority of correspondence cited throughout is from the *The Papers of Thomas Jefferson* and *The Papers of Thomas Jefferson Retirement Series,* published by Princeton University Press. These letters are accessible online through The Papers of Thomas Jefferson Digital Edition (University of Virginia Press, 2009), a subscription website located at http://rotunda.upress.virginia .edu/founders/TSJN.html.

The Family Letters Project features correspondence between Jefferson's immediate and extended family. This collection is continually growing as additional letters and documents are transcribed. See http://retirementseries .dataformat.com.

The botanical names used throughout this book are from L. H. Bailey, *Hortus Third: A Concise Dictionary of Plants Cultivated in the United States and Canada* (New York: Macmillan, 1976).

NOTES

Chapter 1. "A Rich Spot of Earth"

1. Jefferson to Charles Willson Peale, August 20, 1811, *PTJRS* 4:93.

2. European travelers in Dankaerts, *Journal,* 80; Grove, "Virginia in 1732," 44; "customary products" from Schoepf, *Travels in the Confederation,* 192–93.

3. Jefferson, "Summary of Public Service" [after September 2, 1800], *PTJ* 32:124; Jefferson to Samuel Vaughan Jr., November 27, 1790, *PTJ* 18:98.

4. Thweatt, "Visit to Monticello," 154; "observatory" in Elizabeth Trist to Jefferson, July 29, 1814, *PTJRS* 7:501; Jefferson to Maria Cosway, October 12, 1786, *PTJ* 10:447.

5. Jefferson to Dr. Vine Utley, March 21, 1819, in Peterson, *Thomas Jefferson: Writings,* 1416; Hess, "Mr. Jefferson's Table," Intro.:2; Fowler, *Dining at Monticello,* 106; Hess, "Mr. Jefferson's Table," Intro.:4.

6. See Campbell, *History of Kitchen Gardening.*

7. Julien Niemcewitz's observation of Mount Vernon in Griswold, *Washington's Gardens at Mount Vernon,* 121; Fitz, *Southern Apple and Peach,* 65.

8. Malone, *Jefferson the Virginian,* 101–2; Prentis, *Monthly Kalendar,* 31; Taylor, "Diary," June 30, 1791.

9. Jefferson, Garden Book, March 20, 1766, September 25, 1824, 1, 66.

10. Jefferson to James Barbour, March 5, 1816, in Betts, *Garden Book,* 556; Jefferson to Martha J. Randolph, March 22, 1792, in S. Randolph, *Domestic Life of Thomas Jefferson,* 209.

11. Reference to "long haricots" in Jefferson to L. H. Girardin, March 31, 1813, *PTJRS* 6:45–46; "sesame" in Jefferson to John Taylor, January 6, 1808, in Betts, *Garden Book,* 362; "cymlin" in Jefferson to Madame de Tessé, October 26, 1805, in W. Ford, *Thomas Jefferson Correspondence,* 119.

12. Jefferson to Tessé, October 26, 1805, in W. Ford, *Thomas Jefferson Correspondence,* 119; Isaac Jefferson in Bear, *Jefferson at Monticello,* 38, 18; seed rack in M. Smith, "Recollections."

13. Jefferson to André Thöuin, April 29, 1808, in W. Ford, *Thomas Jefferson Correspondence,* 162–63; Jefferson to Martha J. Randolph, December 23, 1790, *PTJ* 18:350.

14. Nicholas King to Jefferson, September 11, 1805, LOC.

Chapter 2. Building the Garden

1. Jefferson, Garden Book, 2.

2. Jefferson, Garden Book, 5, 8.

3. Jefferson, Garden Book, 14. For information on Jefferson's surveying and mathematical interests, see Bedini, *Jefferson and Science* 18–20, 27–28. See also "Plan of the Monticello house and rectangular flower beds, prior to 1772," N-57, MHS; and "General plan of Monticello," Betts, *Garden Book,* pl. IX.

4. Jefferson, Garden Book, 19–21. In a conversation with the author on January 10, 2011, Monticello archaeologist Derek Wheeler described how he excavated the garden wall in 2004 and found evidence that this early garden was partially leveled; see Jefferson's plan for the vegetable garden, ca. 1774, N-87, MHS; Jefferson's plan of the vegetable garden, ca. 1800, N-127, MHS; and Jefferson, "Garden as laid off for leveling 1806, May 26, 27, 28, 29," collection of Carolyn and David S. Thaler, Baltimore.

5. Jefferson to Patrick Henry, March 27, 1779, *PTJ* 2:242.

6. Jefferson, "Notes of a Tour in the Southern Parts of France, March 3–June 10," 1787, *PTJ* 11:415–64; Jefferson to Marquis de Chastellux, in Adams, *Paris Years,* 114; Jefferson to George Wythe, September 16, 1787, *PTJ* 12:127. For more on Jefferson's adventures with rice, see Stanton, "Cultivating Missionaries."

7. Adams, *Paris Years,* 18–22, 244; Jefferson to Madame de Tott, April 5, 1787, *PTJ* 11:271; Jefferson's English travel journal in *PTJ* 9:69–75.

8. Betts, *Garden Book,* 1–14; Jefferson to John Page, May 4, 1786, *PTJ* 9:445; Jefferson to Ferdinand Grand, December 28, 1785, *PTJ* 10:641; Cobbett, *American Gardener,* no. 3.

9. Malone, *Jefferson and the Rights of Man,* 3–237; Stanton, "Nourishing

the Congress," 11; Damon L. Fowler, "Thomas Jefferson's Place in American Food History," in Fowler, *Dining at Monticello,* 3.

10. Adams, *Paris Years,* 18, 56; Jefferson to Nicholas Lewis, September 17, 1787, *PTJ* 12:568, 135.

11. Jefferson to Martha J. Randolph, March 24, February 9, 1791, *PTJ* 19:604, 264; Jefferson to Maria Jefferson, June 13, 1790, *PTJ* 16:491–92; Jefferson to Maria Jefferson Randolph, April 24, 1791, *PTJ* 20:250.

12. Thomas M. Randolph to Jefferson, April 16, 1792, *PTJ* 23:429, Martha J. Randolph to Jefferson, May 7, 1792, *PTJ* 23:486; Thomas M. Randolph to Jefferson, June 13, 1793, *PTJ* 26:278; Martha J. Randolph to Jefferson, July 2, 1792, *PTJ* 24:147.

13. Bear and Stanton, *Jefferson's Memorandum Books,* February 2, 11, 1794, 2:913; Jefferson, Garden Book, 28–29.

14. R. Bailey, "Seeds"; Jefferson to Bernard McMahon, January 13, 1810, *PTJRS* 2:140.

15. Jefferson to John Freeman, February 26, 1806, in Betts, *Garden Book,* 316–17; Jefferson to Maria Jefferson, February 26, 1804, in Randall, *Life of Thomas Jefferson,* 3:98.

16. Jefferson to Robert Bailey, March 21, 1802, *PTJ* 37:100; Jefferson, "Statement of the vegetable market"; M. Smith, "President's House," 216; Lemaire, "Market Accounts."

17. Jefferson to John W. Eppes, June 4, 1804, in Randall, *Life of Thomas Jefferson,* 3:99; Jefferson, "General ideas for the improvement of Monticello," N-171-1, MHS (the first of two pages of undated entries dealing with the Monticello landscape and part of a larger fourteen-page notebook with the earliest dated entry, September 4, 1804, on p. 4). See also Beiswanger, "Report on Monticello Vegetable Garden," 1 n. 5.

18. Hatch, "'Public Treasures'"; Ambrose, *Undaunted Courage,* 181–82; Jefferson, Garden Book, 35, 39, 36; Jefferson to McMahon, March 27, 1807, LOC; Jefferson to Benjamin S. Barton, October 16, 1810, LOC. For more on Northern Plains Indian agriculture, see Buchanan, *Brother Crow, Sister Corn;* and G. Wilson, *Buffalo Bird Woman's Garden.*

19. Jefferson to John Freeman, February 26, 1806, in Betts, *Garden Book,* 316; Jefferson sketch of the top of Monticello mountain, 1806, N-156, Benjamin Franklin Papers, Beinecke Rare Book and Manuscript Library, Yale University.

20. Jefferson, "Garden, as laid off for leveling, May 26, 27, 28," and "Notes on the Layout of the Garden, May, 1806."

21. Jefferson to Lewis W. Dangerfield, September 5, 1806, MHS; Jefferson to Edmund Bacon, December 28, 1806, LOC, and May 13, 1807, in Betts, *Garden Book,* 348.

22. Bacon to Jefferson, January 29, 1808, MHS; Jefferson to Bacon, February 23, 1808, in Betts, *Garden Book,* 364; Bacon to Jefferson, February 26, 1808, UVA.

23. Jefferson to Bacon, February 23, 1808, in Betts, *Garden Book,* 364; Jefferson to Thomas M. Randolph, February 23, 1808, in Betts, *Garden Book,* 364; Bacon to Jefferson, April 15, 1808, UVA.

24. Jefferson to Bacon, June 7, 1808, in Betts, *Garden Book,* 371; Bacon to Jefferson, June 17, 1808, MHS; Bacon to Jefferson, June 30, 1808, UVA; Jefferson to Bacon, October 17, 1808, in Betts, *Garden Book,* 378; Bacon to Jefferson, December 1, 1808, MHS.

25. Jefferson to Bacon, December 19, 1808, in Betts, *Garden Book,* 382; Jefferson to Mr. Watkins, September 27, 1808, in Betts, *Garden Book,* 377; Isaac Jefferson as quoted in Bear, *Jefferson at Monticello,* 12.

26. Jefferson to Bacon, December 26, 1808, in Betts, *Garden Book,* 383; Bacon to Jefferson, January 12, 1809, UVA; Jefferson to Bacon, January 24, 1809, NJHS.

27. Jefferson to Pierre Samuel Dupont de Nemours, March 2, 1809, LOC; Jefferson to James Madison, March 17, 1809, in Bergh, *Writings of Thomas Jefferson,* 11–12:266; Jefferson, Garden Book, 35; M. Smith, *Washington Society,* 68.

28. Bear and Stanton, *Jefferson's Memorandum Books,* February 6, 1809, 2:1239; Jefferson to Etienne Lemaire, April 25, 1809, *PTJRS* 1:157.

29. Jefferson to Mary Lewis, November 28, 1809, *PTJRS* 2:38.

30. Jefferson to William Thornton, October 11, 1809, *PTJRS* 1:599–600; Jefferson to William Short, November 9, 1813, *PTJRS* 6:605; Jefferson to James Monroe, June 19, 1813, *PTJRS* 6:210; M. Smith, *First Forty Years,* 68; Jefferson to Benjamin Henry Latrobe, October 10, 1809, *PTJRS* 1:595.

31. Thomas Jefferson Documents, 1808–24, #11164, Special Collections, UVA; Jefferson, Weather Book, February 24–March 1, 1810; Jefferson, Garden Book, 41.

32. Jefferson, "General ideas for the improvement of Monticello"; Jefferson, "A Pavilion for the center of the long walk of the garden," 1810, N-182, MHS; Henry D. Gilpin, "A Tour of Virginia in 1827," in M. Peterson, *Visitors to Monticello,* 112; Thweatt, "Visit to Monticello," 154; see also Beiswanger, "Temple in the Garden," 170–88; and Elizabeth Trist to Jefferson, July 29, 1814, *PTJRS* 5:501.

33. Pages 37 and 38 are missing from the original Garden Book. May 7 is the first Kalendar entry in 1810. Jefferson, Garden Book, 42–44.

34. Jefferson, Garden Book, 45, 48; Jefferson, "General Gardening Calendar," May 21, 1824.

35. Jefferson, Garden Book, 46–47; Thomas Jefferson Documents, 1808–24, #11164.

36. Jefferson, Garden Book, 54; Jefferson to Madison, July 13, 1813, *PTJRS* 6:290; Jefferson to Trist, May 10, 1813, *PTJRS* 6:110; Samuel Brown to Jefferson, May 25, 1813, *PTJRS* 6:128.

37. Jefferson, Garden Book, 54, 56; Jefferson to Martha J. Randolph, June 6, 1814, *PTJRS* 7:400; Jefferson to Brown, April 17, 1813, *PTJRS* 5:67.

38. Jefferson to L. H. Girardin, March 31, 1813, *PTJRS* 6:44; Jefferson to Randolph Jefferson, February 16, 1815, in Betts, *Garden Book,* 541; Jefferson to Charles Thomson, January 9, 1816, in Bergh, *Writings of Thomas Jefferson,* 13–14:386.

39. Jefferson, Garden Book, 58–66; Jefferson to Edward Livingston, March 25, 1825, LOC; Jefferson to Thomas Worthington, November 29, 1825, in W. Ford, *Thomas Jefferson Correspondence,* 298; Jefferson to Charles Willson Peale, August 20, 1811, *PTJRS* 2:93.

Chapter 3. The Garden and Its People

1. G. Tucker, *Life,* 1:530; M. Smith, "Recollections," 4.

2. Martin, *Pleasure Gardens of Virginia,* 102–25 (Chastellux quotation, 102; John Adams quotation, 117); for more about Chesapeake plantation landscapes, see Brown, "Eighteenth-Century Virginia Plantation Gardens," 125–62.

3. Bear, *Jefferson at Monticello,* 47.

4. Malone, *Jefferson the Virginian,* 108; wine quotations in Jefferson to Baron Hyde de Neuville, December 13, 1818, in Bergh, *Writings of Thomas Jefferson,* 15:178, and in Jefferson to John Oliveira Fernandes, December 16, 1815, LOC; "good taste and abundance" from Daniel Webster, December 1824, in Wiltse, *Papers of Daniel Webster,* 1:371.

5. M. Randolph, *Virginia House-wife,* 4, 1. Culinary historian Karen Hess describes Jefferson's President's House recipes as a "Master Plan." The recipes are located in the Coolidge Collection, MHS; see Hess, "Mr. Jefferson's Table," 1:10–51; see also Hess, "Thomas Jefferson's Table" and Damon L. Fowler, "Thomas Jefferson's Place in American Food History," in *Dining at Monticello,* 65–69, 1–9.

6. Ellen R. Coolidge to Henry S. Randall, in Randall, *Life of Thomas Jefferson,* 111:675; Cornelia J. Randolph to Coolidge, November 12, 1826, Correspondence of Ellen Wayles Randolph Coolidge, UVA; Lemaire, "Market Accounts"; Beth L. Cheuk, "Who Dined at Monticello?," in Fowler, *Dining at Monticello,* 73.

7. For more information on family recipes, see Hess, "Mr. Jefferson's Table"; and Jefferson to J. P. P. Derieux, July 4 [?], 1796, *PTJ* 29:141.

8. Bowman, "Research File"; Jefferson to James Madison, February 20, December 8, 1794, *PTJ* 6:550, 7:559; Jefferson to Tadeusz Kosciuszko, February 26, 1810, *PTJRS* 2:259.

9. For a synopsis of pea contests, including Jefferson's reference to Divers, see Betts, *Garden Book,* 558–59; "Ellen Wayles Coolidge: The House at Monticello, and the Garden," Ellen Coolidge Letter Book 38, #9090, Coolidge Collection, UVA.

10. George Divers to Jefferson, April 20, 1809, *PTJRS* 1:157; Divers to Jefferson, May 3, 1820, in Betts, *Garden Book,* 592.

11. Rives, "Autobiography," 42; Jefferson to Divers, May 24, 1807, LOC; Judith Page Walker Rives in Chamberlain, "Farmington," 44.

12. Hatch, *Fruits and Fruit Trees,* 132–33.

13. Jefferson to Madison, March 16, 1784, *PTJ* 7:30; Betts, *Garden Book,* 56–57. See Jefferson's description of "vines . . . planted by some Tuscan Vignerons who came over with mr. Mazzei," Jefferson, Garden Book, 15.

14. John Hartwell Cocke, Diary, March 27–28, 1817; Jefferson to John Hartwell Cocke, March 27, 1817, Cocke Papers (640/23), UVA; L. Cocke, Diary, April 29, 1822 (640/192).

15. Jefferson to Peter Derieux, July 4, 1796, *PTJ* 29:14; Jefferson to Mary Lewis, November 28, 1809, *PTJRS* 2:38; Jefferson to John Taylor, July 21, 1816, LOC.

16. Taylor, "Diary," August 25, 26, 28, 1787.

17. Bear and Stanton, *Jefferson's Memorandum Books,* September 7, 1771, 1:260; Martha J. Randolph to Jefferson, July 2, 1792, *PTJ* 24:147.

18. Coolidge to Randall in Randall, *Life of Thomas Jefferson,* 346–67.

19. Cobbett, *American Gardener,* no. 10; Isaac (Granger) Jefferson in Bear, *Jefferson at Monticello,* 87–88; M. Smith, "Recollections;" for reference to "veteran aids," see Jefferson to Maria J. Eppes, April 21, 1802, in Betts and Bear, *Family Letters,* 201; "senile crops" in Jefferson to Thomas M. Randolph, January 29, 1801, LOC; "old people" in Jefferson's instructions to Richard Richardson, ca. December 24, 1799, reprinted in *New York Times,* April 15, 1923; the dropping of manure is described in Jefferson to Edmund Bacon, December 26, 1808, in Betts, *Garden Book,* 453; Jefferson to Randolph Jefferson, March 2, 1813, *PTJRS* 5:658.

20. Jefferson to John W. Eppes, May 10, 1810, *PTJRS* 2:378; Jefferson to Bacon, November 24, 1807, in Betts, *Garden Book,* 355; Jefferson to Bacon, April 21, 1806, MHS; Wormley Hughes digging grave in Randall, *Life of Thomas Jefferson,* 3:346.

21. Jane Hollins Randolph to Peggy Nicholas, March 14, 1829, #1397, UVA; George Wythe Randolph to Mary B. Randolph, February 3, 1866, #1397, UVA; Stanton and Swann-Wright, "Getting Word," 10–13.

22. Jefferson to Martha J. Randolph, April 6, 1792, *PTJ* 23:382; Martha J. Randolph to Jefferson, May 2, July 2, 1792, *PTJ* 23:486, 24:147; Jefferson to

Henry Remsen, ca. May 15, 1799, in Betts, *Farm Book*, 271; Stanton, *Free Some Day*, 38–39.

23. Jefferson to Thomas M. Randolph, February 4, 1800, in Betts, *Farm Book*, 17; Jefferson to Richard Richardson, ca. December 24, 1799; Jefferson to Thomas M. Randolph, March 22, 1798, LOC; Jefferson to Randolph, January 29, 1801, in Betts, *Garden Book*, 261–62, 274; "Jefferson's instructions to Richard Richardson," ca. December 14, 1799, reprinted in *New York Times*, April 15, 1923; Jefferson to Maria J. Eppes, April 11, 1802, in Betts and Bear, *Family Letters*, 201.

24. Jefferson to Giovanni Fabbroni, June 8, 1778, *PTJ* 2:196.

25. Jefferson to Antonio Giannini, February 5, 1786, in Betts, *Garden Book*, 632; Jefferson to Charles Bellini, April 24, 1799, *PTJ* 31:99; see Bear and Stanton, *Jefferson's Memorandum Books*, January 14, 1781–October 11, 1782, for records of Giannini's wages; Jefferson to Thomas M. Randolph, September 2, 1793, *PTJ* 27:21; Jefferson to Carlo Bellini, April 24, 1799, *PTJ* 31:99; Bear and Stanton, *Jefferson's Memorandum Books*, March 17, 1812, 2:1275.

26. Jefferson to Thomas M. Randolph, September 2, 1793, *PTJ* 27:1; R. Bailey, "Seeds"; Jefferson to Robert Bailey, September 9, 1804, in Betts, *Garden Book*, 297; Etienne Lemaire to Jefferson, September 17, 1804, MHS.

27. Griswold, *Washington's Gardens at Mount Vernon*, 103; Lund Washington to George Washington, October 1, 1783, in Norton and Schrage-Norton, "Upper Garden at Mount Vernon," 132; "Weekly Reports"; Tayloe, "Gardener's Work," 1805.

28. Taylor, "Diary," April 15, 1788, October 25, 1799; Ann B. Cocke to Ann B. Barraud, March 12, 1815, Cocke Papers; John H. Cocke, "Inventory of Garden Seeds Made out by Blair at his departure 1st Jany 1818," Cocke Papers (640/26).

29. Jefferson Survey of Tufton fields, February 27, 1796, November 7, 1794, N-522, MHS.

30. Bear and Stanton, *Jefferson's Memorandum Books*, July 2, 1825, 2:1412; Randolph Household Account Book, September 26, 1825, 35; Bear and Stanton, *Jefferson's Memorandum Books*; Anne Cary Randolph, Account Book, July 31 [?], 1806; Kelso, *Archaeology at Monticello*, 35, 58–60, 62, 67–68; Bear and Stanton, *Jefferson's Memorandum Books*, inventory of cellar holdings, February 1, 1826, 2:1415.

31. Griswold, *Washington's Gardens*, 121; Grove, "Virginia in 1732," 9; Kimber quotation in Heath and Bennett, "Little Spots," 4; John Custis to Peter Collinson, May 28, 1737, in Swem, *Brothers of the Spade*, 44; Fithian, *Journal*, April 10, 1774, 96; Feltman quotation in Morgan, *Slave Counterpoint*, 193; Taylor, "Diary," October 25, 1799.

32. Morgan, *Slave Counterpoint*, 140, 193–94; Penningroth, *Claims of Kinfolk*, 47–51, 89.

33. Stampp, *Peculiar Institution*, 165; Phillips, *American Negro Slavery*, 238, 268; Giannini to Jefferson, June 9, 1786, *PTJ* 9:624; John Hemmings to Jefferson, November 29, 1821, MHS; Jefferson to Thomas M. Randolph, June 14, 1798, *PTJ* 30:410.

34. Bear and Stanton, *Jefferson's Memorandum Books*, December 11, 1824, 2:1408; Anne Cary Randolph, Account Book, May 25, 1806; Bear and Stanton, *Jefferson's Memorandum Books*, January 12, 1773, 1:353.

35. Bear and Stanton, *Jefferson's Memorandum Books*, October 28, 1818, 2:1348; Randolph Household Account Book, February 1825; Stanton, *Free Some Day*, 44–45, 87–90; Bear and Stanton, *Jefferson's Memorandum Books*, November 10, 1822, 2:1391; Randolph Household Account Book, July 1823; Anne Cary Randolph, Account Book, May 24, 1808.

36. Jefferson to Samuel Vaughan, November 27, 1790, LOC; Bear and Stanton, *Jefferson's Memorandum Books*, October 11, 1794, 1:920; M. Randolph, *Virginia House-wife*, 132; Jefferson to Giannini, February 5, 1786, *PTJ* 9:255; A. Smith, *Tomato in America*, 8.

37. Nicholas P. Trist to Virginia R. Trist, October 1829, UNC; Morgan, *Slave Counterpoint*, 139; Genovese, *Roll, Jordan, Roll*, 535; Olmsted references in Heath and Bennett, "Little Spots," 41.

38. Jefferson to William Drayton, January 1788, *PTJ* 12:507.

CHAPTER 4. THE CULTURE OF THE GARDEN

1. Jefferson to Philip Tabb, June 1, 1809, *PTJRS* 1:252.

2. Sowerby, *Catalogue of Library*, 4:364–65; Miller, *Gardener's Dictionary* [1768], "Kitchen Garden"; Kalm in Henrey, *British Botanical Literature*, 1:217; see Swem, *Brothers of the Spade*, 164n, for a list of colonial Virginians owning a copy of Miller's *Gardener's Dictionary*.

3. Miller, *Gardener's Dictionary* [1768], "Hot Beds"; Tayloe, "Gardener's Work," March 16, 1805; Sowerby, *Catalogue of Library*, 4:366–67; Henrey, *British Botanical Literature*, 358, 353. Other English gardening guides at Monticello included two popular works by British nurseryman John Abercrombie, the 998-page, three-volume *Gardener's Pocket Dictionary* (1786) and the fifteenth edition of *Every Man His Own Gardener* (1794).

4. Nicholas P. Trist to Virginia J. Trist, March 1, 1829, UNC; Stetson, "American Garden Books," 356–57; see J. Randolph, *Treatise*.

5. Jefferson to Martha J. Randolph, January 7, 1805, in Betts, *Garden Book*, 299; Jefferson to Randolph Jefferson, June 20, 1812, UVA; Gardiner and Hepburn, *American Gardener*, preface, 8, 11, 79, 38, 27, 50, 77, 37.

6. Bernard McMahon to Jefferson, April 17, 1806, MHS; Jefferson to Mc-

Mahon, April 25, 1806, LOC; McMahon, *American Gardener's Calendar,* iii; Loudon, *Encyclopaedia of Gardening,* 104.

7. McMahon, *American Gardener's Calendar,* 72, 38–40, 193; Jefferson, Garden Book, 56.

8. Martin, *Pleasure Gardens,* 131.

9. McMahon, *American Gardener's Calendar,* 104; Taylor, "Diary," July 13, 1789, April 28, 1796, May 16, 1789, June 1, 1796, March 21, July 16, 1789; Hornsby, "Diary," April 21, 26, 28, July 26, 1798.

10. McMahon, *American Gardener's Calendar,* 105; Miller, "Kitchen Garden"; Robert F. Becker, preface to Prentis, *Monthly Kalendar,* 3; J. Randolph, *Treatise,* 7; Hume, *Colonial Gardener,* 21–29; Griswold, *Washington's Gardens,* 123; Kelso, "Summary Report," 1.

11. Faris, *Diary,* August 20, 1792, April 11, 1793, 128, 149; Kelso, "Summary Report," 10.

12. Jefferson to John Dortie, October 1, 1811, LOC; McMahon, *American Gardener's Calendar,* 102.

13. Jefferson to Martha J. Randolph, July 21, 1793, *PTJ* 26:546; Jefferson to Edmund Bacon, December 26, 1808, in Betts, *Garden Book,* 383.

14. Jefferson to Anne C. Randolph, March 22, 1808, in Betts, *Garden Book,* 368; Miller, "Kitchen Garden"; Jefferson, Garden Book, 28, 48.

15. J. Randolph, *Treatise,* 6; Prentis, *Monthly Kalendar,* 36–37; Miller, "Kitchen Garden."

16. Tayloe, "Gardener's Work," February 9, 28, 1805; Griswold, *Washington's Gardens,* 115; "Weekly Reports," January 5, 12, 19, 1799; Faris, *Diary,* March 14, July 24, 1792, March 11, 1793, 110, 126, 146; Taylor, "Diary," March 18, 1794, March 6, 1795; J. Cocke, *Diary,* March 8, 1819 (640/112).

17. Jefferson, Garden Book, 46, 42.

18. "The portable Frame for Ridges," Jefferson Papers, Special Collections, UVA.

19. Miller, "Kitchen Garden."

20. McMahon to Jefferson, December 26, 1806, LOC; Taylor, "Diary," April 30, 1794.

21. Jefferson to James Barbour, March 5, 1816, MHS; McMahon, *American Gardener's Calendar,* 178, 311, 356; Faris, *Diary,* April 16, 1792, April 3, 1794, 115, 180; Tayloe, "Gardener's Work," February 2, 1805.

22. Jefferson to L. H. Girardin, March 31, 1812, APS; Jefferson to Ran-dolph Jefferson, March 2, 1813, UVA; Gardiner and Hepburn, *American Gardener,* 85.

23. M. Smith, "Recollections"; M. Smith, *First Forty Years,* 72; Jefferson to Randolph Jefferson, May 6, 1809, in Betts, *Garden Book,* 411; Cornett, "Seeds at Monticello," 10–17.

24. Carter, *Diary,* February 9, 1757, 1:140; Lee, Memorandum Book, April 5, 1794; "Weekly Reports," August 4, 1798; Hornsby, "Diary," January 1, 1798.

25. Appendix 2, "The Water Supply at Monticello," in Betts, *Garden Book,* 629.

26. Betts, *Garden Book,* 330; Bear and Stanton, *Jefferson's Memorandum Books,* December 21, 1771, 1:245–48.

27. Betts, *Garden Book,* 630–31.

28. Anne C. Randolph to Jefferson, March 18, 1808, in Betts, *Garden Book,* 367.

29. Carter, *Diary,* July 25, 1777, 2:1116; George Washington, *Diary,* August 11, 1785, in Norton and Salinge-Norton, "Upper Garden at Mount Vernon"; John Custis to Peter Collinson, July 18, 1738, in Swem, *Brothers of the Spade,* 55; Cobbett, *American Gardener,* no. 187; Faris, *Diary,* March 26, 1792, 113; John Hartwell Cocke was instructed on how to build a cistern by a Richmond friend, J. Gibbons, in response to a "most distressing" drought in the summer of 1822, suggesting that even this more progressive farmer was slow in developing an irrigation plan for his garden (Cocke had been gardening at Bremo for ten years); J. Gibbons to Cocke, September 12, 1822, Cocke Papers (640/37), UVA.

30. Jefferson to Martha J. Randolph, July 21, 1793, *PTJ* 26:546; Thomas M. Randolph Jr. to Jefferson, June 13, 1793, *PTJ* 26:278; Jefferson, Garden Book, April 13, 1809, 35.

31. Cobbett, *American Gardener,* no. 318.

32. Crèvecoeur, *Letters from an American Farmer,* 269; Clinton, "Extracts"; Worth, "Observations on Insects," 394–95; White, *Gardening for the South,* 93.

33. "Orchards," *AF;* Carter, *Diary,* April 25, 1770, 1:393; Beverley, *History of Virginia,* 73.

34. Hornsby, "Diary," April 23, 1798; Carter, *Diary,* April 25, 1770, 1:393; Lee, Memorandum Book, April 1780; Taylor, "Diary," May 23, 1788, April 12, 1795.

35. McMahon, *American Gardener's Calendar,* 401; Marshall, "Destruction of the Cutworm," 125; Jeffers, "Papers for the Farmer," 15; Worth, "An Account of the Insect," 335.

36. "Melons, How to Protect Them from the Depredations of the Bugs," *AF;* Worth, "Observations on Insects," 95; Gardiner and Hepburn, *American Gardener,* 64–67.

37. Carter, *Diary,* July 5, 1757, 1:261; Smith in Crosby, *Ecological Imperialism,* 155; Kalm, *Travels,* 1:5; John Bartram to Philip Miller, June 16, 1758, in Darlington, *Memorials,* 383–85; R. Parkinson, *Tour in America,* 159–60.

38. Faris, *Diary,* March 31, 1792, 113; Byars, "To Destroy Dockweed," 347;

"To Kill Blue Thistle," *AF*; letter to editor, *AF*; "Blue Thistle," *AF*; Cobbett, *American Gardener*, no. 219.

39. Cobbett, *American Gardener*, no. 219; Simple, Letter to editor, *AF*; Bishko, "Agricultural Society of Albemarle," 92.

40. Jefferson to John W. Eppes, June 19, 1808, UVA.

41. Barton, "Usefulness of Birds," 157–63; Worth, "Observations on Insects," 394; Kalm, *Travels*, 1:152–53.

42. Prentis, *Monthly Kalendar*, 59; Carter, *Diary*, July 8, 1757, 1:261; T. M. Randolph, "Speech," 97.

43. Lee, Memorandum Book, April 1780; Cobbett, "Fruit Tree Cultivation," 399.

CHAPTER 5. THE GARDEN RESTORED, THE GARDEN TODAY

1. Beiswanger, "Report," 10:1, 4; Beiswanger, "Proposal," 2; Hatch, "Fruits and Vegetables at Monticello."

2. Kelso, "Summary Report," 1; Beiswanger, Journal, June 17, 1979.

3. Kelso, "Summary Report," 10, 4, 5, 7–9, 11.

4. Kelso, "Summary Report," 11–13, 17.

5. Beiswanger, Journal, April 30, August 1, 1980; James Deetz, introduction to Kelso, *Archaeology at Monticello*, 2; Beiswanger, Journal, April 24, 1981; Beiswanger, "A Proposal," 1.

6. W. Cullen Sherwood, "Rock Materials used in the garden and exit walls at Monticello," app. 1:11, to Beiswanger, "Proposal"; Beiswanger, Journal, July 26, August 3–4, September 11, 14, 1981.

7. Beiswanger, "Proposal," 1; Beiswanger, Journal, February 8, April 31, February 28, May 27, April 8, October 18, March 8, November 30, 1982.

8. Beiswanger, Journal, November 1981–September 1983; Jefferson, "A pavilion for the center of the long walk of the garden," N-182, MHS; Beiswanger, Journal, October 16, 1981.

9. Beiswanger, Journal, September 1981–November 1983; Jefferson, Garden Book, 48; Jefferson, "General ideas for the improvement of Monticello," N-171-1, MHS.

10. Beiswanger, "Proposal," 10; Kelso, "Summary Report," 17.

11. Michelle Obama quoted at http://obamafoodorama.blogspot.com/2009/09/not-so-much-yay-for-vegetables-as-yay.html.

12. For more on the White House kitchen garden, see Kohan, "Obama Foodorama"; "crust master" from http://obamafoodorama.blogspot.com/2011/01/no-state-dinner-guest-chef-comerford.html#more; Yosses quoted at "Monticello Seeds Sprout"; Strzemien, "Michelle Obama."

13. Kristen Hinman, "Thomas Jefferson Founding Foodie," *American History* (April 2011): 42–49, http://www.monticello.org/sites/default/files/media/temp/jeffersonfoundingfoodie.pdf.

14. Charles Willson Peale to Jefferson, March 2, 1812, *PTJRS* 4:532.

15. For more on the Thomas Jefferson Center for Historic Plants, see http://www.monticello.org/site/house-and-gardensthomas-jefferson-center-historic-plants.

16. Philip Mazzei to Jefferson, September 12, 1805, in Marchione, *Philip Mazzei*, 398; Bernard McMahon to Jefferson, January 13, 1810, *PTJRS* 2:140; Jefferson to James Barbour, March 5, 1816, Betts, *Garden Book*, 556; Jefferson to Benjamin S. Barton, October 6, 1810, *PTJRS* 3:150.

17. See Seed Savers Exchange, *Harvest Edition* and *Yearbook*, for yearly collections of essays dealing with the issues of genetic diversity and seed modification; see also Whealy and Adelman, *Seed Savers Exchange*; and Wilkes, "World's Crop Plant Germplasm," 8–16, 33–81.

18. John McPhee quoted in Nicholas von Hoffman, "Afternoon of a Faun," October 28, 1998, http://www.slate.com/id/2000038/entry/1001494.

19. Jefferson to Peale, August 20, 1811, *PTJRS* 4:93.

PART 2. PROLOGUE

1. Bear and Stanton, *Jefferson's Memorandum Books*, February 6, 1809, 2:1239.

CHAPTER 6. FRUITS: ARTICHOKES TO TOMATOES

1. All botanical names are from L. H. Bailey, *Hortus Third*; Jefferson to Thomas M. Randolph, December 26, 1794, *PTJ* 28:225; Jefferson to Jean Baptiste Say, March 2, 1815, LOC.

2. Cobbett, *American Gardener*, no. 152; Bernard McMahon to Jefferson, February 25, 1807, LOC; Jefferson, Weather Book, May 31, 1808, March 22, 1810, May 15, 1811; Jefferson to McMahon, July 6, 1808, LOC; M. Randolph, *Virginia House-wife*, xxi, 127.

3. Miller, *Gardener's Dictionary* [1768], "Cynara"; Randolph Harrison to John Hartwell Cocke, March 29, 1822, Cocke Papers (640/36), UVA; Carter, *Diary*, May 8, 1772, 2:678.

4. J. Parkinson, *Paradisi*, 520; Grove, "Virginia in 1732," 34; Byrd, *Natural History*, 22; Fithian, *Journal*, July 2, 1773, 128.

5. Weaver, *Heirloom Vegetable Gardening*, 139, 140; McMahon, *American Gardener's Calendar*, 362; Jefferson, "General Gardening Calendar."

6. Jefferson to George Washington, June 28, 1793, *PTJ* 26:397; Bear and Stanton, *Jefferson's Memorandum Books,* May 15, 1768, 1:76; Jefferson to Thomas M. Randolph, February 7, 1796, *PTJ* 28:608; Jefferson to John Taylor, December 29, 1794, in Betts, *Garden Book,* 222.

7. M. Randolph, *Virginia House-wife,* 57, 152–53, 172; Jefferson to Nicholas Lewis, September 17, 1787, *PTJ* 12:135.

8. Cutright, *Lewis and Clark,* 110–12; Ambrose, *Undaunted Courage,* 178, 181–82, 200.

9. Jefferson to Christian Mayer, June 20, 1806, in Betts, *Garden Book,* 320; McMahon to Jefferson, July 12, 1806, LOC; Jefferson to Edmund Bacon, April 21, 1806, in Betts, *Garden Book,* 318; Jefferson, Weather Book, August 8, 1807, in Betts, *Garden Book,* 336; Jefferson to John W. Eppes, March 24, 1811, *PTJRS* 3:501; Jefferson, Garden Book, 41, 44, 46.

10. Hulton, *America 1585,* 69 (pl. 20); Weaver, *Heirloom Vegetable Gardening,* 140; Grove, "Virginia in 1732," 34; Anburey quoted in Moore, "'Established and Well Cultivated,'" 78; R. Parkinson, *Experienced Farmer's Tour,* 332.

11. Taylor, "Diary," July 16, 1789, April 22, 1790; Faris, *Diary,* May 7, 1802, 382; Sarudy, *Gardens and Gardening,* 119; Hedrick, *History of Horticulture,* 461–62.

12. Jefferson to Thomas Worthington, November 25, 1825, in Betts, *Garden Book,* 616; Isaetta Randolph Hubard to Sallie Carter Randolph, June 3, 1866, Randolph-Hubard Papers, UVA; Jonathan Boucher to George Washington, September 5, 1768, W. Ford, *Letters of Jonathan Boucher,* 11; Carter, *Diary,* July 24, 1776, 1:321.

13. A. C. Randolph, Account Book, 1805–8, 13; Randolph Household Account Book, September 26, 1825, 35; Hess, "Mr. Jefferson's Table," 5:71, 4:10; Lemaire, "Market Accounts," October 26, 1806.

14. Jefferson, Garden Book, 42, 46, 15, 18.

15. Jefferson to Thomas Worthington, November 29, 1825, in W. Ford, *Thomas Jefferson Correspondence,* 298; Worthington to Jefferson, January 7, 1826, in W. Ford, *Thomas Jefferson Correspondence,* 299–300; Jefferson to George Divers, April 22, 1826, in Betts, *Garden Book,* 619; Bishko, "Agricultural Society of Albemarle," 97.

16. Peter Collinson to John Custis, August 28, 1737, in Swem, *Brothers of the Spade,* 46, 163n; *Virginia Gazette,* August 12–19, 1737, 3, August 25–September 1, 1738, 4; J. Randolph, *Treatise,* 19.

17. Sturtevant, *Edible Plants,* 208; Gerard, *Herball,* 910; Hedrick, *History of Horticulture,* 16; Taylor, "Diary," 1778–99.

18. Taylor, "Diary," April 11, 1788, May 18, 1789; J. Randolph, *Treatise,* 19–23; Gardiner and Hepburn, *American Gardener,* 77, 48, 50; Hedrick, *History of Horticulture,* 465.

19. Jefferson to Randolph Jefferson, June 20, 1813, *PTJRS* 6:214; Tapley et al., *Vegetables of New York,* 4:1, 107; McMahon, *American Gardener's Calendar,* 581.

20. Jefferson to Peter Derieux, March 10, 1798, *PTJ* 25:347; Martha J. Randolph to Jefferson, June 26, 1793, *PTJ* 26:380; Jefferson to Derieux, July 4, 1796, *PTJ* 29:141; Jefferson to McMahon, February 16, 1812, *PTJRS* 4:497–98.

21. M. Randolph, *Virginia House-wife,* 131.

22. Fuchs, *De Historia Stirpium,* 518; Gerard, *Herball,* 345; Milton, *Paradise Lost,* 10:560–67; Miller, *Gardener's Dictionary* [1768], "Melongena."

23. M. Randolph, *Virginia House-wife,* 272; Byrd, *Natural History,* 23; Skipwith in Greene, "Paper"; "Solanaceae"; Faris, *Diary,* April 16, 1793, 150; McMahon, *American Gardener's Calendar,* 319.

24. Lucas, "Philosophy of Making Beer," 1–13; A. Randolph, Account Book, May 13, 1808; Bear and Stanton, *Jefferson's Memorandum Books,* March 2, 1771, November 22, 1800, December 24, 1819, 1:251, 330, 2:1358; Jefferson, Garden Book, 24, 48, 52.

25. Lucas, "Philosophy of Making Beer," 1–13.

26. Sturtevant, *Edible Plants,* 308–9; Byrum, "Cultivated Plants of the Wachovia Tract," 9; Cobbett, *American Gardener,* 224.

27. Jefferson to Richard Cary, August 12, 1786, *PTJ* 10:228; Jefferson to Lewis, September 17, 1787, *PTJ* 12:135; Jefferson to Benjamin Rush, December 14, 1800, *PTJ* 32:305; Jefferson to William Johnson, March 17, 1810, *PTJRS* 2:302; Jefferson to John C. White, August 14, 1816, in Betts, *Garden Book,* 561.

28. J. Parkinson, *Paradisi,* 465, 525.

29. Sturtevant, *Edible Plants,* 206; Grove, "Virginia in 1732," 34; R. Parkinson, *Tour in America,* 168; Carter, *Diary,* August 17, 1772, 2:712; Taylor, "Diary," May 23, 1788; Cobbett, *American Gardener,* no. 158.

30. Miller, *Gardener's Dictionary* [1754], 8; M. Randolph, *Virginia House-wife,* 204–5; Cobbett, *American Gardener,* no. 254; Jefferson to Johnson, March 17, 1809, LOC; Jefferson to Eppes, March 24, 1816, HL.

31. Jefferson to Bernard Peyton, May 6, 1824, in Betts, *Garden Book,* 614; M. Randolph, *Virginia House-wife,* 207; McMahon, *American Gardener's Calendar,* 318.

32. J. Parkinson, *Paradisi,* 281; Miller, *Gardener's Dictionary* [1768], "Tropaeolum"; Betts, *Garden Book,* 49; Hamilton, "Letter from William Hamilton," 149; McMahon, *American Gardener's Calendar,* 318.

33. Hess, "Mr. Jefferson's Table," 4:4, 5:10; M. Randolph, *Virginia House-wife,* 95–96, 376 [Hess note].

34. A. Smith, *Food and Drink in America,* 2:211; Sturtevant, *Edible Plants,*

303; M. Wilson, "Peaceful Integration," 118; Miller, *Gardener's Dictionary* [1768], "Hibiscus"; Kalm, *Travels,* September 18, 1748, 1:42; Squibb, *Gardener's Calendar,* 61, 79; Faris, *Diary,* April 5, 1802, December 26, 1803, 380, 413; McMahon, *American Gardener's Calendar,* 318.

35. Samuel Brown to Jefferson, October 1, 1812, May 25, 1813, *PTJRS* 5:364–65, 6:127–28; Jefferson to Brown, April 17, 1813, *PTJRS* 6:66–67; Jefferson to McMahon, June 15, 1813, *PTJRS* 6:195–96; Hess, "Mr. Jefferson's Table," 5:10, 19, 35.

36. From Greene, "Papers," "Solanaceae"; Miller, *Gardener's Dictionary* [1754], 255; Miller, *Gardener's Dictionary* [1768], "Capsicum"; Andrews, *Domesticated Capsicums,* 30–31.

37. Kalm, *Travels,* November 1, 1749, September 9, 1748, 1:610–11, 42; McMahon, *American Gardener's Calendar,* 582, 200, 319.

38. Andrews, *Domesticated Capsicums,* 119; Weaver, *Heirloom Vegetable Gardening,* 265–66.

39. Brown to Jefferson, May 25, June 13, 1813, *PTJRS* 6:127, 187; Jefferson to Brown, April 17,1813, *PTJRS* 6:66–67; Jefferson to McMahon, June 15, 1813, *PTJRS* 6:195–96.

40. William Few to Jefferson, September 26, 1807, LOC; Jefferson to A. C. Randolph, March 22, 1808, in Betts, *Garden Book,* 368; Jefferson, Garden Book, 66, 44.

41. Jefferson to Few, January 3, 1808, LOC; Jefferson to Anne C. Randolph, March 22, 1808, in Betts, *Garden Book,* 368.

42. Jefferson to John Milledge, June 5, 1811, *PTJRS* 3:636–37; Milledge to Jefferson, July 12, 1811, *PTJRS* 4:39.

43. Sturtevant, *Edible Plants,* 531–32; Few to Jefferson, January 11, 1808, LOC.

44. Sloane, *Voyage to the Islands,* 91; Lowndes reference from Kiple and Ornelas, *Cambridge World History of Food,* 418; Bassett, *Writings of Colonel William Byrd,* 209; Miller, *Gardener's Dictionary* [1754], 1284–85; McMahon, *American Gardener's Calendar,* 611; M. Wilson, "Peaceful Integration," 18, 125–26.

45. Jefferson to Madame de Tessé, October 26, 1805, in W. Ford, *Thomas Jefferson Correspondence,* 119.

46. Jefferson to Phillip Mazzei, March 17, 1801, *PTJ* 33:328; McMahon to Jefferson, December 26, 1806, LOC; Miller, *Gardener's Dictionary* [1768], "Cucurbita."

47. Jefferson, "Memorandum to Jeremiah A Goodman," September 8, 1813, *PTJRS* 6:487; Timothy Matlack to Jefferson, February 25, 1807, LOC.

48. A. Smith, *Food and Drink in America,* 2:495; Tapley, Enzie, and Van Eseltine, *Vegetables of New York,* 3–4; Lawson, *History of Carolina,* 132; Beverley, *History of Virginia,* 143; Grove, "Virginia in 1732," 48.

49. Miller, "Cucurbita"; Kalm, *Travels,* November 23, 1748, November 5, 11, 24, 1749, 1:183, 2:609, 617, 640; Sarudy, *Gardens and Gardening,* 168; Burr, *Field and Garden Vegetables,* 206–28.

50. M. Randolph, *Virginia House-wife,* 95, 97, 107, 201–2, 241, 237, 295 [Hess note]; Lemaire, "Market Accounts."

51. Thomas M. Randolph, "Speech," 97; A. Smith, *Tomato in America,* 24; McMahon, *American Gardener's Calendar,* 319.

52. John Mason to Jefferson, January 22, 1809, in Betts, *Garden Book,* 403; Jefferson, "Planting Memorandum for Poplar Forest," February 27, 1811, in Betts, *Garden Book,* 465.

53. Christian, *Lynchburg and Its People,* 84; J. Parkinson, *Paradisi,* 379; Jefferson, *Notes,* 43.

54. A. Smith, *Food and Drink in America,* 2:545; Sturtevant, *Edible Plants,* 343–44; A. Smith, *Tomato in America,* 12–14.

55. Gerard, *Herball,* 346; J. Parkinson, *Paradisi,* 380; Miller, *Gardener's Dictionary* [1754], 821.

56. A. Smith, *Tomato in America,* 6, 26; Swem, *Brothers of the Spade,* 175–76; John Augustine Smith in Sewall, *Lecture Delivered* [Swem note].

57. A. Smith, *Tomato in America,* 26–27; Gardiner and Hepburn, *American Gardener,* 27, 51; McMahon, *American Gardener's Calendar,* 319; Willich and Cooper, *Domestic Encyclopedia,* 2:484–85.

CHAPTER 7. FRUITS: BEANS AND PEAS

1. Jefferson, "General Gardening Calendar"; Jefferson, Garden Book, 64, 45; Jefferson, "Statement of the vegetable market."

2. Jefferson to James Barbour, March 5, 1816, in Betts, *Garden Book,* 556; Gardiner and Hepburn, *American Gardener,* 52.

3. Simmons, *First American Cookbook,* 46; M. Randolph, *Virginia House-wife,* 126; Jefferson to Barbour, March 5, 1816, in Betts, *Garden Book,* 556; Hess, "Mr. Jefferson's Table," 1:72, 78, 5:103, 107; M. Randolph, *Virginia House-wife,* 129; Lemaire, "Market Accounts."

4. Greene, "Papers"; Cobbett, *American Gardener,* no. 107; Miller, *Gardener's Dictionary* [1754], 1060: Jefferson to Benjamin S. Barton, October 6, 1810, *PTJRS* 3:150.

5. R. Bailey, "Seeds"; Simmons, *First American Cookbook,* 15; Jefferson to Francis Eppes, "A List of Plants Sent by Jefferson from Paris about 1786 to Francis Eppes," in Betts, *Garden Book,* 634–35; Jefferson, Garden Book, 61.

6. J. Parkinson, *Paradisi,* 521; Sturtevant, *Edible Plants,* 423; Catesby, *Natural History,* 2:xxiv; Grove, "Virginia in 1732," 34; Simmons, *First American*

Cookbook, 14–15; Taylor, "Diary," April 16, 1799, June 9, 1794; Hornsby, "Diary," June 26, 1798.

7. Greene, "Papers"; Collins, Seed catalog; French, Seed list, January 21, 1800.

8. Jefferson, Garden Book, 48, 60.

9. Gerard, *Herball*, 1215; Miller, *Gardener's Dictionary* [1754], 1061; Miller, *Gardener's Dictionary* [1768], "Phaseolus"; McMahon, *American Gardener's Calendar*, 368.

10. Jefferson, "General Gardening Calendar"; Jefferson to Madame de Tessé, February 21, 1807, in Betts, *Garden Book*, 339; Lemaire, "Market Accounts"; Jefferson, Garden Book, 63; M. Randolph, *Virginia House-wife*, 130–31; Hess, "Mr. Jefferson's Table," 4:4, 7.

11. Lawson, *History of Carolina*, 76; J. Randolph, *Treatise*, 6; McMahon, *American Gardener's Calendar*, 368; Cobbett, *American Gardener*, no. 197.

12. Jefferson to Benjamin Hawkins, April 1, 1792, *PTJ* 20:89–90; Miller, "Phaseolus."

13. Jefferson, "General Gardening Calendar"; Martha J. Randolph to Ann Cary Morris, May 7, 1822, Ellen Wayles Coolidge Correspondence, UVA.

14. Lemaire, "Market Accounts"; M. Randolph, *Virginia House-wife*, 34; Hess, "Mr. Jefferson's Table," 3:36; Hess, *Martha Washington's Booke of Cookery*, 68; Harbury, *Colonial Virginia's Cooking Dynasty*, 157–58, 251, 154; Simmons, *First American Cookbook*, 46.

15. Hess, "Mr. Jefferson's Table," 1:7, 8; Jefferson to Elizabeth Trist, May 10, 1813, *PTJRS* 6:110; George Divers to Jefferson, May 6, 1814, *PTJRS*, and April 30, 1815, in Betts, *Garden Book*, 544; Jefferson to Trist, June 1, 1815, MHS; "Ellen Wayles Coolidge: The House at Monticello, and the Garden," Ellen Coolidge Letter Book, 38, #9090, Coolidge Collection, UVA; L. Cocke, Diary, April 29, 1822 (640/36).

16. Prentis, *Monthly Kalendar*, 58; Jefferson, Garden Book, 35–36; McMahon, *American Gardener's Calendar*, 26; Miller, *Gardener's Dictionary* [1768], "Pisum."

17. Sturtevant, *Edible Plants*, 442, 443; Gerard, *Herball*, 1221; Maintenon in Hedrick, *Peas of New York*, 7; J. Parkinson, *Paradisi*, 502; Bradley, *Compleat Seedsman's Monthly Calendar*, 5.

18. Sturtevant, *Edible Plants*, 432; Charles Carroll in Sarudy, *Gardens and Gardening*, 117–18; Lee, Memorandum Book, February 29, March 16, 1780.

19. Cobbett, *American Gardener*, no. 241; Owens and Leckie, "Garden and Flower Seeds"; John A. G. Davis, diary entries in *Franklin Almanac*, March 18, 1828, Terrell-Carr Papers, #4757, UVA; Hedrick, *History of Horticulture*, 464; Weaver, *Heirloom Vegetable Gardening*, 238.

20. Jefferson, Garden Book, 12, 22, 35; Burr, *Field and Garden Vegetables*, 525; Weaver, *Heirloom Vegetable Gardening*, 296; Hedrick, *Peas of New York*, 39; Jefferson to Bernard McMahon, February 8, 1809, and McMahon to Jefferson, February 28, 1809, LOC.

21. A. Smith, *Food and Drink in America*, 1:351; Weaver, *Heirloom Vegetable Gardening*, 151; Jefferson to John Taylor, October 8, 1797, *PTJ* 29:546; Jefferson to William Strickland, March 23, 1798, *PTJ* 30:210.

22. John Custis to Peter Collinson, July 29, 1736, in Swem, *Brothers of the Spade*, 33; A. Peterson, "Commerce of Virginia," 302; Grove, "Virginia in 1732," 34; Carter, *Diary*, October 2, 1756, 1:130; Taylor, "Diary," May 1, 1794, May 2, 1795; A. Smith, *Food and Drink in America*, 1:351; M. Randolph, *Virginia House-wife*, 135–36.

23. Jefferson, Garden Book, 31, 39, 42; Jefferson to Divers, March 16, 1811, *PTJRS* 3:454; Jefferson to John W. Eppes, March 24, 1811, *PTJRS* 3:501–2.

24. Vilmorin-Andrieux, *Vegetable Garden*, 16; Burr, *Field and Garden Vegetables*, 494; Sturtevant, *Edible Plants*, 246.

Chapter 8. Roots

1. Lemaire, "Market Accounts"; A. Randolph, Account Book, August 9, 1807; Jefferson to Mary Lewis, November 28, 1809, "Notes on Winter Vegetable Needs," *PTJRS* 2:37–38; M. Randolph, *Virginia House-wife*, 123.

2. Sturtevant, *Edible Plants*, 89; Weaver, *Heirloom Vegetable Gardening*, 83; J. Parkinson, *Paradisi*, 15; Miller, *Gardener's Dictionary*, "Beta" [1768]; McMahon, *American Gardener's Calendar*, 125.

3. Jefferson to Lewis, November 28, 1809, *PTJRS* 2:37–38; Jefferson, "Statement of the vegetable market"; Hess, "Mr. Jefferson's Table," 1:38, 5:110–14, 6:7, 38; "Chartreuse," "Manuscript in the hand of Virginia Jefferson Trist," Trist and Burke Family Papers, UVA; see Hess, "Mr. Jefferson's Table," 6:99, for more on the term *Chartreuse*.

4. Sturtevant, *Edible Plants*, 232; Weaver, *Heirloom Vegetable Gardening*, 120–21; J. Parkinson, *Paradisi*, 508; Miller, *Gardener's Dictionary* [1768], "Daucus"; J. Randolph, *Treatise*, 15; Taylor, "Diary," March 24, 1796.

5. Taylor, "Diary," March 31, 1788; R. Parkinson, *Experienced Farmer's Tour*, 338; Sarudy, *Gardens and Gardening*, 121; Faris, *Diary*, March 5, 1793, 45.

6. R. Bailey, "Seeds"; Jefferson, "General Gardening Calendar"; Hess, "Mr. Jefferson's Table," 1:36, 37; M. Randolph, *Virginia House-wife*, xxvi; Simmons, *First American Cookbook*, 12; Cobbett, *American Gardener*, no. 222.

7. Sturtevant, *Edible Plants*, 38–39; J. Parkinson, *Paradisi*, 514; Faris, *Diary*, April 6, 1796.

8. Hess, "Mr. Jefferson's Table," 1:39–42; Fowler, *Dining at Monticello*, 148; A. Smith, *Food and Drink in America*, 1:511–12 (Hess entry on French fries); M. Randolph, *Virginia House-wife*, 118.

9. Lemaire, "Market Accounts"; Hess, "Mr. Jefferson's Table," 1:38, 76; M. Randolph, *Virginia House-wife*, 116–18, 120, 172; Hess, "Mr. Jefferson's Table," 6:41.

10. Jefferson to Tristram Dalton, May 2, 1817, LOC; George Divers to Jefferson, March 27, 1817, in Betts, *Garden Book*, 569, 570; Jefferson to Lewis, November 28, 1809, *PTJRS* 2:37–38.

11. Greene, "Papers"; Sturtevant, *Edible Plants*, 545–46; Jefferson to Horatio G. Spafford, May 14, 1809, *PTJRS* 1:196–97; Gerard, *Herball*, 925–27; Harriot in M. Randolph, *Virginia House-wife*, 286 (Hess historical glossary); Miller, *Gardener's Dictionary* [1754], 822; Miller, *Gardener's Dictionary* [1768], "Lycopersicon."

12. Banister, *Natural History*, 369; Beverley, *History of Virginia*, 30; Grove, "Virginia in 1732," 34; Byrd, *Natural History*, 22; J. Randolph, *Treatise*, 45, 46; Carter, *Diary*, September 2, 1772, 1:721.

13. Lee, Memorandum Book, April 1780; Simmons, *First American Cookbook*, 10–11; R. Parkinson, *Experienced Farmer's Tour*, 19, 125; Cobbett, *American Gardener*, no. 245.

14. Simmons, *First American Cookbook*, 10; Sarudy, *Gardens and Gardening*, 120.

15. Lemaire, "Market Accounts"; Jefferson, Garden Book, 28, 32, 45, 48, 53.

16. Jefferson, Garden Book, 35, 42; Jefferson to Martha J. Randolph, October 10, 1816, MHS; McMahon, *American Gardener's Calendar*, 189; Weaver, *Heirloom Vegetable Gardening*, 231.

17. Jefferson, Garden Book, 29; Jefferson Madame de Tessé, October 26, 1805, in W. Ford, *Thomas Jefferson Correspondence*, 118–20; A. Smith, *Peanuts*, 14, XV.

18. A. Smith, *Food and Drink in America*, 2:248; Monardes, *Historia medicinal*, 104; J. Parkinson, *Theatrum Botanicum*, 1069–70; Ovington, *Voyage to Suratt*, 77.

19. M. Wilson, "Peaceful Integration," 118; A. Smith, *Food and Drink in America*, 2:248; A. Smith, *Peanuts*, 14; Miller, *Gardener's Dictionary* [1754], 116; Miller, *Gardener's Dictionary* [1768], "Arachis."

20. Watson, "Some account," 59:379–83; A. Smith, *Peanuts*, 14–15; Jefferson, *Notes*, 43; "Shipping List of George Washington to Clement Biddle," February 27, 1798, in Fitzpatrick, *Writings of George Washington*, 35:174–75.

21. Lemaire, "Market Accounts"; Martha R. Jefferson to Jefferson, May 31, 1804, in Betts and Bear, *Family Letters*, 261.

22. Sturtevant, *Edible Plants*, 484; Greene, "Papers"; Jefferson to Thomas M. Randolph, March 5, 1795, *PTJ* 28:293.

23. Jefferson to James Taylor, June 8, 1795, *PTJ* 28:383; Kalm, *Travels*, March 27, 1749, 1:268.

24. Sturtevant, *Edible Plants*, 105; A. Smith, *Food and Drink in America*, 2:565; Jefferson to James Madison, March 29, 1819, LOC; McMahon, *American Gardener's Calendar*, 427; Cobbett, *American Gardener*, no. 271.

25. "Salsify," "Manuscript in the hand of Virginia Jefferson Trist"; Jefferson, "Statement of the vegetable market"; Lemaire, "Market Accounts"; Hess, "Mr. Jefferson's Table," 1:36; M. Randolph, *Virginia House-wife*, 136–37.

26. Sturtevant, *Edible Plants*, 572; Weaver, *Heirloom Vegetable Gardening*, 368; Miller, *Gardener's Dictionary* [1754], 1401; Miller, *Gardener's Dictionary* [1768], "Tragopogon"; Greene, "Papers"; Hess, "Mr. Jefferson's Table," I:39; McMahon, *American Gardener's Calendar*, 315; Divers to Jefferson, April 22, 1809, *PTJRS* 1:157; Cocke Gardening Memoranda, March 20, 1810, Cocke Papers (5685/21), UVA.

27. Jefferson to Nicholas Lewis, September 17, 1787, *PTJ* 12:135; Thomas M. Randolph to Jefferson, October 7, 1792, *PTJ* 24:448; Lemaire, "Market Accounts," September 10, 23, 1806; Hess, "Mr. Jefferson's Table," 6:190; M. Randolph, *Virginia House-wife*, 133, 172, 261.

28. Sturtevant, *Edible Plants*, 315; A. Smith, *Food and Drink in America*, 2:520; Weaver, *Heirloom Vegetable Gardening*, 332–33; Gerard, *Herball*, 925–26; J. Parkinson, *Paradisi*, 516–18; Miller, *Gardener's Dictionary* [1768], "Convolvulus."

29. Beverley, *History of Virginia*, 144–45; Catesby, *Natural History*, 1:xiv; Grove, "Virginia in 1732," 34; Kalm, *Travels*, October 10, 1748, 1:95–96; Fithian, *Journal*, April 10, 1774, 96.

30. Sarudy, *Gardens and Gardening*, 168; Hornsby, "Diary," April 28, 1798; Whiting, "Cocke's Legacy."

31. Jefferson to Mary Lewis, November 28, 1809, *PTJRS* 2:37–38; "Turnips," "Manuscript in the hand of Virginia Jefferson Trist"; Hess, "Mr. Jefferson's Table," 6:7, 9, 38, 5:111, 4:7, 1:38; Lemaire, "Market Accounts," November 22, 1806; M. Randolph, *Virginia House-wife*, 124–25.

32. Weaver, *Heirloom Vegetable Gardening*, 355; Carter, *Diary*, April 20, 1775, 2:1095; Taylor, "Diary," August 1, 1795; John Hartwell Cocke, Diary, July 17, 1817 (640/23), UVA; A. Smith, *Food and Drink in America*, 2:565.

33. Sturtevant, *Edible Plants*, 101; Taylor, "Diary," January 18, 1796, December 20, 1797; Squibb, *Gardener's Calendar*, 136; Sarudy, *Gardens and Gardening*, 119–20.

CHAPTER 9. LEAVES

1. "Extract of a letter written to Henry S. Randall by . . . Ellen Randolph Coolidge," in Randall, *Life of Thomas Jefferson,* 3:346; Jefferson, "General Gardening Calendar."

2. "Jefferson's Summary of his Meteorological Journal," in Betts, *Garden Book,* 627; Jefferson, "Statement of the vegetable market"; Jefferson, Weather Book, April 18, 1807; M. Randolph, *Virginia House-wife,* 121–22.

3. "Planting Memorandum for Poplar Forest," February 27, 1811, UVA; McMahon, *American Gardener's Calendar,* 185–86; Miller, *Gardener's Dictionary* [1768], "Asparagus."

4. J. Randolph, *Treatise,* 5–7; Tayloe, "Gardener's Work," March 16, October 10, 1805; Faris, *Diary,* April 28, 1802, 381.

5. Sturtevant, *Edible Plants,* 72; Byrd, *Natural History,* 22–23; R. Parkinson. *Experienced Farmer's Tour,* 198; Cobbett, *American Gardener,* no. 193; Simmons, *First American Cookbook,* 12.

6. Timothy Matlack to Jefferson, February 25, 1807, LOC; Hedrick, *History of Horticulture,* 432; J. Parkinson, *Paradisi,* 503; Taylor, "Diary," January 10, 1790.

7. Jefferson, Garden Book, 45; Jefferson, "Statement of the vegetable market"; Lemaire, "Market Accounts," April 23, 24, 1806; M. Randolph, *Virginia House-wife,* 127.

8. A. Smith, *Food and Drink in America,* 1:135; Switzer and Bradley references from Greene, "Papers"; Miller, *Gardener's Dictionary* [1768], "Brassica"; R. Bailey, "Seeds."

9. Grove, "Virginia in 1732," 34; J. Randolph, *Treatise,* 8–9; Prentis, *Monthly Kalendar,* 41–42; Carter, *Diary,* January 24, 1764, February 18, 1770, September 2, 1772, 1:261, 361, 2:721; Lee, Memorandum Book, February 16, 1787; Cobbett, *American Gardener,* no, 199.

10. Lemaire, "Market Accounts"; Bear and Stanton, *Jefferson's Memorandum Books,* December 11, 1824, 2:1408; M. Randolph, *Virginia House-wife,* 121; Jefferson to Martha J. Randolph, March 22, 1792, in S. Randolph, *Domestic Life of Thomas Jefferson,* 209.

11. John Hemings to Jefferson, November 29, 1821, MHS; Taylor, "Diary," March 4, 1794.

12. Hess, "Mr. Jefferson's Table," 1:78; M. Randolph, *Virginia House-wife,* 121; Hess, "Mr. Jefferson's Table," 6:98, 5:110, 67, 88.

13. Sturtevant, *Edible Plants,* 113–14; Gerard, *Herball,* 313; J. Parkinson, *Paradisi,* 503–5.

14. Sturtevant, *Edible Plants,* 113–14; Grove, "Virginia in 1732," 10; J. Randolph, *Treatise,* 9–10; Prentis, *Monthly Kalendar,* 41–54; Faris, *Diary,* February 26, 1800, 332; Lithen, Nursery broadside; Holt, Catalogue of garden seeds.

15. Simmons, *First American Cookbook,* 14; Jefferson to Robert Bailey, November 10, 1810, MHS; James Ronaldson to Jefferson, March 4, 1810, *PTJRS* 2:272; "A List of Plants Sent by Jefferson From Paris about 1786 to Francis Eppes," in Betts, *Garden Book,* 634–; J. Randolph, *Treatise,* 10; Bernard McMahon to Jefferson, February 28, 1809, LOC; Greene, "Papers"; "Brassicas"; Miller, *Gardener's Dictionary* [1768], "Brassica."

16. Jefferson, Garden Book, 28, 16; Jefferson to L. H. Girardin, January 9, 1814, *PTJRS* 7:116; George Divers to Jefferson, February 28, 1820, in Betts, *Garden Book,* 591. Two other lists of herbs reside in the Jefferson Papers at the University of Virginia; one is a page in an undated red notebook, possibly in the hand of Martha J. Randolph, Jefferson's daughter. The other memorandum of herbs dates to the same period and is annotated with the method of propagation, whether "slips," "cuttings," or "seeds." Martha J. Randolph, "List of herbs," UVA; memorandum, "list of herbs," Jefferson Papers. Main Series, UVA.

17. A. Tucker, "Colonial Herb Garden"; Favretti "Landscape 'Mythtakes.' "

18. Jefferson to J. P. P. Derieux, March 10, 1793, *PTJ* 25:347; Jefferson to J. P. Reibelt, October 12, 1805, December 22, 1807, LOC; Jefferson to Peter Derieux, June 1, 1812, *PTJRS* 5:8. For more on Jefferson's struggles with tarragon, see Jefferson to McMahon, April 25, 1806, and McMahon to Jefferson, April 30, 1806, in Betts, *Garden Book,* 8–19, 313; and Jefferson to William Thornton, October 11, 1809, *PTJRS* 1:600.

19. Hess, "Mr. Jefferson's Table," 4:4, 6:38, 5:95, 1:56, 38; M. Randolph, *Virginia House-wife,* 67, 29, 114, 203, 151, 220–21.

20. Jefferson, *Notes,* 38; Leighton, *Early American Gardens,* 154–59; Hedrick, *History of Horticulture,* 20; Beverley, *History of Virginia,* 141.

21. Holmes, *Thomas Jefferson Treats Himself* 55–57; Bynum, "Cultivated Plants of the Wachovia Tract, 6–7; Kalm, *Travels,* November 1, 1748, 1:128; Gill, "Doctoring the Diseases of Virginia," 47; Carter, *Diary,* March 17, April 12, 1758, 1:205, 215.

22. Byrd, *Natural History,* 23; Hedrick, *History of Horticulture,* 201; J. Randolph, *Treatise,* 34, 24; Taylor, "Diary," April 9. 1790. Faris, *Diary,* March 4, 1794, April 20, 1799, April 5, May 13, 1802, 232, 304, 380, 403; Hornsby, "Diary," March 20, 1798.

23. Cobbett, *American Gardener,* nos. 268, 235, 321.

24. Jefferson, "General Gardening Calendar"; Jefferson, "Statement of the vegetable market"; Lemaire, "Market Accounts"; Jefferson to Jeremiah Goodman, December 13, 1812, *PTJRS* 5:490.

25. McMahon, *American Gardener's Calendar,* 545. M. Randolph, *Vir-*

ginia House-wife, 115–16; Bradley, New Improvements, 296; Weaver, Heirloom Vegetable Gardening, 172; Carter, Diary, November 25, 1770, 1:527; Hess, Martha Washington's Booke of Cookery, 99; Jefferson to John Oliveira Fernandes, December 16, 1815, LOC.

26. Jefferson, Garden Book, 64, 61, 58; McMahon, American Gardener's Calendar, 504.

27. Miller, Gardener's Dictionary [1768], "Lactuca"; Jefferson to Jeremiah Goodman, December 13, 1812, PTJRS 5:490.

28. Sturtevant, Edible Plants, 322–23; Weaver, Heirloom Vegetable Gardening, 170–72; Gerard, Herball, 307–8; J. Parkinson, Paradisi, 298–99; Michel reference from Greene, "Papers"; J. Randolph, Treatise, 27.

29. Simmons, First American Cookbook, 13–14; Cobbett, American Gardener, no, 230.

30. Crouwells, Peter Crouwells and Co. seed offerings; McMahon broadside seedlist, ca. 1804; Dr. Phillip Barraud to John H. Cocke, February 25, 1821, Cocke Papers (640/33), UVA; Jefferson to Randolph Jefferson, February 16, 1815, UVA; Tennis-ball lettuce described in Jefferson to Jeremiah Goodman, August 9, 1812, PTJRS 5:307.

31. Jefferson, Garden Book, 31; Jefferson also noted in 1811 the planting of esculent rhubarb in the submural beds, the hottest compartment in the Monticello garden, Jefferson, Garden Book, 42; McGee, On Food and Cooking, 367; McMahon, American Gardener's Calendar, 205.

32. Hedrick, History of Horticulture, 83; Sturtevant, Edible Plants, 490–92; John Bartram to Peter Collinson, September 22, 1739, in J. Bartram, Correspondence, 125; Carter, Diary, February 20, 1757, July 14, 1774, 1:44, 2:1111; M. Randolph, "List of herbs"; Holmes, Thomas Jefferson Treats Himself, 44.

33. J. Parkinson, Paradisi, 483; John Bartram to Peter Collinson, September 22, 1739, J. Bartram, Correspondence, 125; McMahon, American Gardener's Calendar, 203–5; Cobbett, American Gardener, no. 252; Hess, "Mr. Jefferson's Table," 1:103.

34. McMahon to Jefferson, February 13, 1809, Betts, Garden Book, 407;

McMahon, American Gardener's Calendar, 191; Jefferson, Garden Book, 35, 42, 46, 56, 55; Divers to Jefferson, May 3, 1820, in Betts, Garden Book, 592.

35. Weaver, Heirloom Vegetable Gardening, 117; McMahon, American Gardener's Calendar, 194–95; Jefferson to Bernard Peyton, February 20, 1821, and Jefferson to Richard Randolph, May 13, 1822, in Betts, Garden Book, 596, 603; M. Randolph, Virginia House-wife, 123.

36. Miller, Gardener's Dictionary [1768], "Crambe"; Cobbett, American Gardener, no. 203; Weaver, Heirloom Vegetable Gardening, 117.

37. A. Randolph, Account Book, June 11, 18, 1806, April 20, 1807; R. Parkinson, Experienced Farmer's Tour, 198; Cobbett, American Gardener, no. 199.

38. Lemaire, "Market Accounts," 1806;

39. Cobbett, American Gardener, no. 215.

40. Jefferson, "Statement of the vegetable market"; Cobbett, American Gardener, no. 216.

41. Jefferson to Bailey, March 21, 1802, in Betts, Garden Book, 279.

42. Jefferson, Garden Book, 17, 20, 35; R. Bailey, "Seeds"; Greene, "Papers"; Jefferson, "Statement of the vegetable market"; M. Randolph, Virginia House-wife, 121.

43. J. Parkinson, Paradisi, 488; Faris, Diary, April 8, 1793, 149.

44. R. Bailey, "Seeds"; Cobbett, American Gardener, no. 236.

45. R. Bailey, "Seeds"; Cobbett, American Gardener, no. 265; M. Randolph, Virginia House-wife, 131.

46. Jefferson, Garden Book, 43, 36, 64, 58; M. Randolph, Virginia House-wife, 135, xxv (Hess commentary); Carter, Diary, September 9, 1770, 1:494; Faris, Diary, April 15, 1799, March 12, 27, 1800, February 17, 1802, 308, 332, 334, 376.

47. Jefferson to McMahon, February 16, 1812, PTJRS 4:497; Jefferson to John H. Cocke, March 12, 1813, PTJRS 6:7; Jefferson to Randolph Jefferson, February 16, 1815, Carr-Cary Papers, UVA; Jefferson to James Barbour, March 5, 1816, and Jefferson to John W. Eppes, March 6, 1817, in Betts, Garden Book, 556, 569; Jefferson to L. H. Girardin, March 31, 1813, PTJRS 6:44.

BIBLIOGRAPHY

Abercrombie, John [Thomas Mawe]. *Every Man His Own Gardener.* London: W. Griffin, 1767.

———. *The Gardener's Pocket Dictionary.* London: Lockyer Davis, 1768.

Adams, William Howard. *The Paris Years of Thomas Jefferson.* New Haven: Yale University Press, 1997.

Ambrose, Stephen. *Undaunted Courage: Meriwether Lewis, Thomas Jefferson, and the Opening of the American West.* New York: Simon and Schuster, 1997.

Andrews, Jean. *The Domesticated Capsicums.* Austin: University of Texas Press, 1984.

Bailey, L. H. *Hortus Third: A Concise Dictionary of Plants Cultivated in the United States and Canada.* New York: Wiley, John and Sons, 1976.

Bailey, Robert. "Seeds Saved from 1794." Memorandum from Robert Bailey [January 1795]. *PTJ* 28:256–57.

Banister, John. *The Natural History of Virginia, 1678–1692.* Edited by Joseph Ewan and Nesta Ewan. Urbana: University of Illinois Press, 1970.

Barton, Benjamin S. "Of the Usefulness of Birds." In "An American Farmer," *An Epitome of Mr. Forsyth's Treatise on the Culture and Management of Fruit Trees.* Philadelphia: T. L. Plowman, 1803.

Bartram, John. *The Correspondence of John Bartram.* Edited by Edmund Berkeley and Dorothy Smith Berkeley. Gainesville: University of Florida Press, 1992.

Bartram, William. *The Travels of William Bartram.* Edited by Francis Harper. New Haven: Yale University Press, 1958.

Bassett, John Spencer. *The Writings of Colonel William Byrd of Westover in Virginia, Esr.* New York: Doubleday, 1901.

Bear, James A., Jr., ed. *Jefferson at Monticello.* 1967. Reprint, Charlottesville: University of Virginia Press, 1995.

Bear, James A., Jr., and Lucia C. Stanton, eds. *Jefferson's Memorandum Books: Accounts, with Legal Records and Miscellany, 1767–1826. The Papers of Thomas Jefferson,* 2nd ser. Princeton, NJ: Princeton University Press, 1997.

Bedini, Silvio A. *Jefferson and Science,* Charlottesville, VA: Thomas Jefferson Foundation, 2002.

Beiswanger, William L. Journal [Daily Record of Transactions.] Thomas Jefferson Foundation. JL.

———. "A Proposal for the Recreation of the Vegetable Garden, Orchard and Vineyards." Research report for the Thomas Jefferson Memorial Foundation, Charlottesville, VA, April 1981. JL.

———. "Report on Research and a Program for the Restoration of the Monticello Vegetable Garden Terrace, Orchard, Vineyard, Berry Squares and Nursery." November 1978. JL.

———. "The Temple in the Garden: Thomas Jefferson's Vision of the Monticello Landscape." *British and American Gardens in the Eighteenth Century.* Williamsburg, VA: Colonial Williamsburg Foundation, 1984.

Bergh, Albert, ed. *The Writings of Thomas Jefferson.* Washington, DC: Thomas Jefferson Memorial Foundation, 1907.

Betts, Edwin Morris, ed. *Thomas Jefferson's Farm Book.* Charlottesville, VA: Thomas Jefferson Memorial Foundation, 1999.

———. *Thomas Jefferson's Garden Book, 1766–1824.* Philadelphia: APS, 1944. Reprint, Charlottesville, VA: Thomas Jefferson Foundation, 2008.

Betts, Edwin Morris, and James A. Bear, eds. *The Family Letters of Thomas Jefferson.* Columbia: University of Missouri Press, 1966.

Beverley, Robert. *The History and Present State of Virginia.* 1705. Reprint, edited by Louis B. Wright. Chapel Hill, NC: Published for the Institute of Early American History and Culture by University of North Carolina Press, 1947.

Bishko, Lucretia Ramsey. "The Agricultural Society of Albemarle and John S. Skinner." *Magazine of Albemarle County History* (1973): 76–113.

"Blue Thistle." *AF*, October 21, 1820, 237.

Booth, William. "A Catalog of Kitchen Garden Seeds and Plants." Baltimore: Dobbin and Murphy, 1810. LOC.

Bordley, John B. *Essays and Notes on Husbandry and Rural Affairs.* Philadelphia: Budd and Bartram, 1799.

Bowman, Rebecca. "The Research File: Fashioning Rational Society." *Monticello Newsletter* 8 (Winter 1997–1998): 125–67.

Boyd, Julian P., et al., eds. *The Papers of Thomas Jefferson.* 34 vols. to date. Princeton, NJ: Princeton University Press, 1950–.

Bradley, Richard. *Compleat Seedsman's Monthly Calendar.* London: W. Mears, 1738.

———. *Dictionarium Botanicum.* London: T. Woodward, 1728.

———. *A General Treatise of Husbandry and Gardening.* London: T. Woodward and J. Peale, 1727.

———. *New Improvements of Planting and Gardening.* London: T. Woodward, 1728.

Bridgeman, Thomas. *The Young Gardener's Assistant.* Brooklyn: Nichols and Matthews, 1829.

Brown, C. Allan. "Eighteenth-Century Virginia Plantation Gardens: Translating an Ancient Idyll." In *Regional Garden Design in the United States,* edited by Theresa O'Malley and Marc Trieb. Washington, DC: Dumbarton Oaks, 1995.

Buchanan, Carol. *Brother Crow, Sister Corn.* Berkeley, CA: Ten Speed Press, 1997.

Burr, Fearing, Jr. *The Field and Garden Vegetables of America.* Boston: J. E. Tilton, 1865.

Byars, William. "To Destroy Dockweed." *AF*, June 3, 1825, 84.

Bynum, Flora Ann. "Cultivated Plants of the Wachovia Tract in North Carolina, 1759–1764." [Brochure for Old Salem Inc., Winston-Salem, NC, 1979.]

Byrd, William. *William Byrd's Natural History of Virginia.* Edited by Richmond C. Beatty and William T. Mulloy. Richmond, VA: Dietz, 1940.

Campbell, Susan. *A History of Kitchen Gardening.* London: Ebury, 1996.

Carter, Landon. *The Diary of Landon Carter of Sabine Hall, 1752–1766.* 2 vols. Edited by Jack P. Greene. Charlottesville: University Press of Virginia, 1965.

Catesby, Mark. *The Natural History of Carolina, Florida, and the Bahama Islands.* 2 vols. London: Printed for C. Marsh, T. Wilcox, and B. Stichall, 1754.

Chamberlain, Bernard Peyton. "Farmington: A History." *Magazine of Albemarle History* 29 (1971): 13.

Christian, W. Asbury. *Lynchburg and Its People.* Lynchburg, VA: J. P. Bell, 1900.

Clinton, Dewitt. "Extracts from *American Agriculture and Botany.*" *AF*, July 2, 1819, 108–9.

Cobbett, William. *The American Gardener.* London: C. Clements, 1821.

———. "Fruit Tree Cultivation." *AF*, February 21, 1823, 399.

Cocke, John Hartwell. Diary. Papers of John Hartwell Cocke, 1758–1879. Accession #5680, UVA.

Cocke, Louisa B. Diary. Papers of John Hartwell Cocke, 1758–1809. Accession #5680, UVA.

Collins, Minton. Seed catalog. *Virginia Gazette and Richmond Daily Advertiser,* January 24, 1793.

Cornett, Peggy L. "Seeds at Monticello: Saving, Storing, Sharing." *Twinleaf* 19 (2007): 10–17.

Crevecoeur, Hector St. John. *Letters from an American Farmer.* 1782. Reprint, Garden City, NY: Dolphin, 1963.

Crosby, Alfred W. *Ecological Imperialism: The Biological Expansion of Europe, 900–1900.* Cambridge: Cambridge University Press, 1986.

Crouwells, Peter. Peter Crouwells and Co. seed offerings. *Virginia Journal and Alexandria Advertiser,* April 13, 1786.

Cutright, Paul R. *Lewis and Clark, Pioneering Naturalists.* Lincoln: University of Nebraska Press, 1969.

Dankaerts, Jasper. *Journal of Jasper Dankaerts, 1679–1680.* Edited by Bartlett Burleigh James. Translated by J. Franklin Jameson. Henry C. Murphy: Project Gutenberg eBook, http://www.gutenberg.org/ebooks/23258.

Darlington, William, ed. *Memorials of John Bartram and Humphrey Marshall.* Philadelphia: Lindsay and Blakiston, 1849.

de la Vega, Garcilaso. *Cometarios Reales*. 1609. Reprint, translated by Sir Clements Robert Markham. London: Hakluyt Society, 1876.

Faris, William. *The Diary of William Faris: The Daily Life of an Annapolis Silversmith*. Edited by Mark Letzer and Jean B. Russo. Baltimore: Maryland Historical Society, 2002.

Favretti, Rudy J. "Landscape 'Mythtakes' in Historic Preservation." *Magnolia* (Spring 1988): 3–4.

Fernandez de Oveido, Gonzalo. *La Historia General de las Indias*. Book VII. 1535. Reprint, Madrid: Imprenta de la Real Academia de la Historia, 1851. http://www.cervantesvirtual.com.

Fithian, Philip. *Journal and Letters of Philip Fithian, 1773–1774*. Edited by Hunter Dickinson. Charlottesville, VA: Dominion, 1957.

Fitz, James. *Southern Apple and Peach Culturist*. Richmond, VA: J. W. Randolph and English, 1872.

Fitzpatrick, John C., ed. *The Writings of George Washington from the Original Manuscript Sources, 1745–1799*. 39 vols. Washington, DC: Government Printing Office, 1931–44. Reprint, New York: Greenwood, 1970.

Ford, Paul Leicester, ed. *The Writings of Thomas Jefferson*. Letterpress Edition. 10 vols. New York: G. P. Putnam's Sons, 1892–99.

Ford, Worthington Chauncy, ed. *Letters of Jonathan Boucher to George Washington*. Brooklyn, NY: Historical Printing Club, 1899.

———. *Thomas Jefferson Correspondence*. Printed from the originals in the collections of William K. Bixby. Boston: By the author, 1916.

Fowler, Damon L., ed. *Dining at Monticello: In Good Taste and Abundance*. Charlottesville, VA: Thomas Jefferson Foundation, 2005.

French, George. Seed list. *Virginia Herald* (Fredericksburg), January 21, 1800.

Fuchs, Leonhart. *De Historia Stirpium . . . .* Basel, 1542.

Gardiner, John, and David Hepburn. *The American Gardener*. Washington, DC: Joseph Milligan, 1804.

Gerard, John. *The Herball; or, Generall Historie of Plantes*. 1633. Reprint, New York: Dover, 1975.

Gill, Harold B. "Doctoring the Diseases of Virginia." *Colonial Williamsburg Journal* (Autumn 1992): 45–47.

Graff, Henry. "Monticello Seeds Sprout at White House." *NBC*, October 21, 2010. http://www.nbc29.com/story/13364372/monticello-seeds-sprout-at-white-house.

Greene, Wesley. "Papers." Landscape Department, Colonial Williamsburg, Williamsburg, VA.

Griswold, Mac. *Washington's Gardens at Mount Vernon: Landscape of the Inner Man*. Boston: Houghton Mifflin, 1999.

Grove, William Hugh. "Virginia in 1732: The Travel Journal of William Hugh Grove." Edited by Gregory A. Stiverson and Patrick H. Butler. *VMHB* 85 (January 1977): 18–44.

Hamilton, William. "Some Letters from William Hamilton of the Woodlands, to His Private Secretary." *Pennsylvania Magazine of History and Biography* 29 (January 1905).

Harbury, Katherine E. *Colonial Virginia's Cooking Dynasty*. Columbia: University of South Carolina Press, 2004.

Hatch, Peter J. *The Fruits and Fruit Trees of Monticello*. Charlottesville: University Press of Virginia, 1998.

———. "Fruits and Vegetables at Monticello: A Study of Varieties and Culture." Thomas Jefferson Foundation, JL.

———. "'Public Treasures': Thomas Jefferson and the Garden Plants of Lewis and Clark." *Twinleaf* 5 (2003): 8–15.

Heath, Barbara, and Amber Bennett. "'The Little Spots allow'd them': The Archaeological Study of African-American Yards." *Historical Archaeology* 34 (2000): 38–56.

Hedrick, Ulysses P. *A History of Horticulture in America to 1860*. New York: Oxford University Press, 1950.

———. *Beans of New York*. Albany, NY: J. B. Lyon, 1931.

———. *Peas of New York*. Albany, NY: J. B. Lyon, 1928.

Henrey, Blanche. *British Botanical and Horticultural Literature*. London: Oxford University Press, 1975.

Hess, Karen, ed. *Martha Washington's Booke of Cookery*. New York: Columbia University Press, 1981.

———. "Mr. Jefferson's Table: The Culinary Legacy of Monticello." Manuscript, September 9, 1999, Thomas Jefferson Foundation, JL.

———. "Thomas Jefferson's Table: Evidence and Influences." In *Dining at Monticello: In Good Taste and Abundance*, edited by Damon L. Fowler. Charlottesville VA: Thomas Jefferson Foundation, 2005.

Hill, John. *The Gardener's New Kalendar*. London: T. Osborne, 1758.

Holmes, John M. *Thomas Jefferson Treats Himself: Herbs, Physicke and Nutrition in Early America*. Fort Valley, VA: Lofi Press, 1997.

Holt, Theophilus. A catalogue of garden seeds, &c. for sale by Theophilus Holt, at his nursery garden, City of Washington . . . January 1, 1808. Printed Ephemera Collection, portfolio 190, folder 14. Rare Book and Special Collections, LOC.

Hornsby, Joseph. "Joseph Hornsby's Diary." American Memory online series, LOC.

Hulton, Paul. *America 1585: The Complete Drawings of John White*. Chapel Hill: University of North Carolina Press, 1984.

Jefferson, Thomas. "Garden Book, 1766–1824" [electronic edition]. *Thomas Jefferson Papers: An Electronic Archive*. Boston: MHS, 2003.

———. "A General Gardening Calendar." *AF*, May 21, 1824, 72.

———. *Notes on the State of Virginia*. Edited by William Harwood Peden. Chapel Hill: University of North Carolina Press, 1954.

———. "A statement of the vegetable market of Washington during a period of 8. years wherein the earliest & latest appearance of each article within the whole 8. years is noted." In Randall, *Life of Thomas Jefferson,* 1: pl. following p. 44.

———. Thomas Jefferson Weather Memorandum Book. The Thomas Jefferson Papers. Series 7. Misc. Bound Volumes. Vol. 2. Weather Record, 1776–1818, LOC.

Jeffreys, George W. "Papers for the Farmer." *AF,* March 31, 1820, 15.

Josslyn, John. *New England Rarities Discovered*. London: G. Widdowes, 1672.

Kalm, Peter. *Travels in North America*. 1770. Reprint, New York: Dover, 1966.

Kelso, William M. *Archaeology at Monticello*. Charlottesville, VA: Thomas Jefferson Memorial Foundation, 1997.

———. "Summary Report of the Archaeological Investigation of the Garden at Monticello." Research report for Thomas Jefferson Memorial Foundation, April 1981.

Kiple, Kenneth F., and Kriemhild C. Ornelas, eds. *The Cambridge World History of Food*. http://histories.cambridge.org/collection?id=set_cambridge_world_history_food.

Kohan, Eddie Gehman. "Obama Foodorama." http://obamafoodorama.blogspot.com/.

Lawson, John. *The History of Carolina*. 1714. Reprint, edited by Francis Latham Harris. Richmond, VA: Garrett and Massie, 1937.

Lee, Richard Henry. Memorandum Book, 1776–1794. Garden notes transcribed by C. Allan Brown. HL.

Lehman, Karl. *Thomas Jefferson, American Humanist*. Charlottesville: University Press of Virginia, 1985.

Leighton, Ann. *Early American Gardens: "For Meate or Medicine."* Boston: Houghton Mifflin, 1970.

Lemaire, Etienne. "The Market Accounts of Etienne Lemaire." Prepared by Amy Rider, Colonial Williamsburg Foundation, August 19, 1996.

Letter to editor. *AF,* February 4, 1820, 360.

Lithen, John. John Lithen Nursery broadside, 1800. Pennsylvania Horticultural Society, Philadelphia.

Looney, J. Jefferson, et al., eds. *The Papers of Thomas Jefferson: Retirement Series*. 7 vols. to date. Princeton, NJ: Princeton University Press, 2004–.

Loudon, John C. *Encyclopaedia of Gardening*. 3rd ed. London: Longman, Hurst, Rees, Orme, Brown, and Green, 1825.

Lucas, Ann. "The Philosophy of Making Beer." Thomas Jefferson Foundation "Keepsake," April 12, 1995, JL.

Malone, Dumas. *Jefferson and the Rights of Man*. Boston: Little, Brown, 1951.

———. *Jefferson the President*. Boston: Little, Brown, 1970.

———. *Jefferson the Virginian*. Boston: Little, Brown, 1948.

Marchione, Margherita, ed. *Philip Mazzei: Selected Writings and Correspondence*. Vol. 3. Cassa di Risparmi e Despositi di Prato, Italy, 1983.

Marshall, Thomas. "Destruction or Prevention of the Cutworm." *AF,* July 13, 1821, 125.

Martin, Peter. *The Pleasure Gardens of Virginia, from Jamestown to Jefferson*. Princeton, NJ: Princeton University Press, 1991.

McEwan, Barbara. *Thomas Jefferson, Farmer*. Jefferson, NC: McFarland, 1991.

McGee, Harold. *On Food and Cooking: The Science and Lore of the Kitchen*. New York: Scribner, 2004.

McMahon, Bernard. *The American Gardener's Calendar*. Philadelphia: B. Graves, 1806.

———. McMahon broadside seed list, c. 1804. Pennsylvania Horticultural Society, Philadelphia.

"Melons, How to Protect Them from the Depredations of the Bugs." *AF,* August 9, 1822, 157.

Miller, Philip. *The Gardener's Dictionary*. 1754. Reprint, Lehre, Germany: Verlag Von J. Cramer, 1969.

———. *The Gardener's Dictionary*. 8th ed. London: Printed for the author, 1768.

———. *The Gardener's Kalendar*. 4th ed. London: Printed for the author, 1765.

Milton, John. *Paradise Lost*. New York: John B. Alden, 1889.

Monardes, Nicholas. *Historia medicinal de las cosas que se traen de neustras Indias Occidentales*. 1574. Translated by John Frampton. London: Paules Churchyard the figne of the Quenes, 1582. http://eebo.chadwyck.com.

Moore, Stacy. "'Established and Well Cultivated:' Afro-American Foodways in Early Virginia." *Virginia Cavalcade* 39 (1989): 70–83.

Morgan, Philip D. *Slave Counterpoint: Black Culture in the Eighteenth-Century Chesapeake and Lowcountry*. Chapel Hill, NC: Published for the Omohundro Institute of Early American History and Culture by the University of North Carolina Press, 1998.

Noël Hume, Audrey. *Archaeology and the Colonial Gardener*. Williamsburg, VA: Colonial Williamsburg Foundation, 1974.

Norton, J. D., and Susanne A. Schrage-Norton. "The Upper Garden at Mount Vernon Estate, Its Past, Present and Future: A Reflection of 18th Century Gardening." Research report. Mount Vernon, VA: Mount Vernon Ladies Association, September 25, 1985.

O'Malley, Theresa, and Marc Trieb, eds. *Regional Garden Design in the United States*. Washington, DC: Dumbarton Oaks, 1995.

"Orchards." *AF,* September 7, 1821, 191.

Ovington, John. *A Voyage to Suratt in the Year 1689*. London: Jacob Tonson, 1696.

Owens and Leckie. "Garden and Flower Seeds." *Virginian* (Lynchburg), March 27, 1826.

Parkinson, John. *Paradisi in Sole Paradisus Terrestris*. London: Humphrey Lownes and Robert Young, 1629. Reprint, New York: Dover, 1976.

———. *Theatrum Botanicum*. London: Thomas Cotes, 1640.

Parkinson, Richard. *The Experienced Farmer's Tour in America*. London: John Stockdale, 1805.

———. *A Tour in America, 1798, 1799, and 1800*. London: J. Harding and J. Murray, 1805.

Penningroth, Dylan C. *The Claims of Kinfolk: African American Property and Community in the Nineteenth-Century South*. Chapel Hill: University of North Carolina Press, 2003.

Peterson, Arthur G. "Commerce of Virginia, 1789–1792." *William and Mary Quarterly*, 3rd ser. 10 (1930): 302–9.

Peterson, Merrill D. *Thomas Jefferson: Writings*. New York: Library of America, 1984.

———. *Visitors to Monticello.* Charlottesville: University Press of Virginia, 1989.

Phillips, Ulrich B. *American Negro Slavery*. Baton Rouge: Louisiana State University Press, 1966.

Prentis, Joseph. *Williamsburg Joseph Prentis: His Monthly Kalendar and Garden Book*. Introduction by Rollin Woolley. Chillicothe, IL: American Botanist, 1992.

Randall, Henry S. *The Life of Thomas Jefferson*. 3 vols. New York: Derby and Jackson, 1858.

Randolph, Anne Cary. Account Book, 1805–1808. LCC. Transcribed by Gerard W. Gawalt as "Jefferson's Slaves: Crop Accounts at Monticello, 1805–1808." *Journal of the Afro-American Historical and Genealogical Society* 13, nos. 1 and 2 (1994): 19–38.

Randolph, John. *A Treatise on Gardening*. 1793. Reprint, Richmond, VA: Colonial Williamsburg Foundation, n.d.

Randolph, Mary. *The Virginia House-wife*. Edited by Karen Hess. Columbia: University of South Carolina Press, 1984.

Randolph, Sarah Nicholas. *The Domestic Life of Thomas Jefferson*. 1871. Reprint, Charlottesville, VA: Thomas Jefferson Memorial Foundation, 1978.

Randolph, Thomas Mann. "Speech before Albemarle Agricultural Society." *AF*, June 18, 1824.

Randolph Household Account Book, 1827–1828. Private collection. On loan to the Thomas Jefferson Foundation, Charlottesville, VA.

Rayner, B. L. *Sketches of the Life, Writings, and Opinions of Thomas Jefferson*. New York: Francis and Boardman, 1832.

Rives, Judith Walker. "The Autobiography of Mrs. William Cabell Rives." Typescript, Rives Family Papers, compiled by Elizabeth Langhorne #10596-d. Special Collections, University of Virginia Library.

Sarudy, Barbara Wells. *Gardens and Gardening in the Chesapeake, 1700–1805*. Baltimore: Johns Hopkins University Press, 1998.

Schoepf, Johann David. *Travels in the Confederation* [1783–84]. Translated and edited by Alfred J. Morrison. 1911. Reprint, New York: Burt Franklin, 1968.

Seed Savers Exchange. *Harvest Edition and Yearbook*. Decorah, IA: Seed Savers Exchange, 1986–present.

Sewall, Thomas. *A Lecture Delivered at the Opening of the Medical Department of the Columbian College*. Washington, DC, March 30, 1825.

Simmons, Amelia. *The First American Cookbook: A Facsimile of "American Cookery" 1796*. Edited by Mary Wilson Tolford. New York: Dover, 1984.

Simple, Jeremiah. Letter to editor. *AF*, July 7, 1820, 117.

Sloane, Hans. *A Voyage to the Islands Madera, Barbados, Nieves, S. Christophers and Jamaica*. London: B. M., 1705–25.

Smith, Andrew F. *Peanuts: The Illustrious History of the Goober Pea*. Urbana: University of Illinois Press, 2007.

———. *The Tomato in America*. Columbia: University of South Carolina Press, 1994.

———, ed. *The Oxford Encyclopedia of Food and Drink in America*. 2 vols. New York: Oxford University Press, 2004

Smith, Margaret Bayard. *The First Forty Years of Washington Society*. Edited by Gaillard Hunt. New York: Charles Scribner's Sons, 1906.

——— [Mrs. Harrison Smith]. "The President's House Forty Years Ago." *Godey's Lady's Book*, November 1843, 212–19.

———. "Recollections of a Visit to Monticello." *Richmond Enquirer*, January 18, 1823.

Sowerby, E. Millicent, ed. *Catalogue of the Library of Thomas Jefferson*. 3 vols. Washington, DC: LOC, 1955–59.

Spurrier, John. *The Practical Farmer*. Wilmington, DE: Brynberg and Andrews, 1797.

Squibb, Robert. *The Gardener's Calendar for South-Carolina, Georgia and North-Carolina*. 1787. Reprint, Athens: University of Georgia Press, 1980.

Stampp, Kenneth. *The Peculiar Institution: Slavery in the Ante-Bellum South*. New York: Vintage, 1989.

Stanton, Lucia C. "Cultivating Missionaries." Thomas Jefferson Foundation "Keepsake," April 12, 1990, JL.

———. *Free Some Day: The African American Families of Monticello*. Charlottesville, VA: Thomas Jefferson Foundation, 2000.

———. "Nourishing the Congress: Hospitality in the President's House." In *Dining at Monticello: In Good Taste and Abundance*, edited by Damon L. Fowler. Charlottesville, VA: Thomas Jefferson Foundation, 2005.

———. *Slavery at Monticello*. Charlottesville, VA: Thomas Jefferson Foundation, 1996.

Stanton, Lucia S., and Dianne Swann-Wright. "Getting Word: Monticello's African-American History Project." Charlottesville, VA: Thomas Jefferson Foundation, 2006.

Stetson, Sarah Pattee. "American Garden Books Transplanted and Native, before 1807." *William and Mary Quarterly*, 3rd ser., 3 (1946): 343–82.

Strzemien, Anya. "Michelle Obama's Condé Nast Traveler Cover: Date Night, Camp Obama and DC Hot Spots." *Huffington Post*, April 8, 2010. http://www.huffingtonpost.com/2010/04/08/michelle-obamas-cond-nast_n_529840.html.

Sturtevant, Edward Lewis. *Sturtevant's Edible Plants of the World*. Edited by U. P. Hedrick. 1919. Reprint, New York: Dover, 1972.

Swem, Earl G., ed. *Brothers of the Spade: Correspondence of Peter Collinson of London, and of John Custis, of Williamsburg, 1734–1746*. Barre, MA: Barre Gazette, 1957.

Tapley, William T., Walter D. Enzie, and Glen P. Van Eseltine. *Vegetables of New York: The Cucurbits*. Report of the New York State Agricultural Experiment Station. Albany, NY: J. B. Lyon, 1937.

Tayloe, John. "Gardener's Work." In "Minute Book of John Tayloe, 1805," VHS.

Taylor, Col. Francis. "Diary, 1786–1799." Transcribed by Barbara A. Farner, Library of Virginia. Mason Neck, VA: Gunston Hall Plantation, 1996.

Thweatt, Rev. Henry C. "Visit to Monticello in 1825." In "Descriptions of Monticello, 1780–1826." JL.

"To Kill Blue Thistle." *AF*, January 7, 1825, 323.

Tucker, Arthur O. "The Myth of the Colonial Herb Garden." *Magnolia* 20, no. 2 (2005): 14–19.

Tucker, George. *The Life of Thomas Jefferson*. London: Charles Knight, 1837.

Vilmorin-Andrieux, M. M. *The Vegetable Garden*. 1885. Reprint, Berkeley, CA: Ten Speed Press, n.d.

Virginia Jefferson Randolph Trist Cookbook. Trist Family Papers, 1818–1916. Accession #5385-f, UVA.

Watson, William. "Some Account of an Oil, Transmitted by Mr. George Brownrigg, of North Carolina." *Philosophical Transactions of the Royal Society* 59 (1769).

"W. D." "Notices of Pernicious and Improfitable Plants Which Infest the farms of Chester Co., Pennsylvania." *AF,* March 2, 9, 16, 1827, 403, 411–12, 597–98.

Weaver, William Woys. *Heirloom Vegetable Gardening.* New York: Henry Holt, 1997.

"Weeds." *AF,* January 23, 1824, 347.

"Weekly Reports of George Washington's Gardener, January 7, 1797–January 26, 1799." Mount Vernon, VA: Mount Vernon Ladies Association, 1991.

Whealy, Kent, and Arlys Adelman, eds. *Seed Savers Exchange: The First Ten Years.* Decorah, IA: Seed Savers, 1986.

White, William. *Gardening for the South.* Athens, GA: A. O. Moore, 1859.

Whiting, K. Brooke. "Gen. J. H. Cocke's Vanishing Legacy: The Gardens and Landscape of Bremo." Richmond, VA: Garden Club of Virginia, 2000.

Wilkes, Garrison. "Current Status of Crop Plant Germplasm." *CRC Critical Review in Plant Science* 2 (1983): 33–81.

———. "The World's Crop Plant Germplasm—An Endangered Resource." *Bulletin of Atomic Scientists* 33, no. 2 (1977): 6–16.

Willich, Anthony, and Thomas Cooper. *Domestic Encyclopedia.* 2 vols. Philadelphia: Abraham Small, 1821.

Wilson, Gilbert L. *Buffalo Bird Woman's Garden.* St. Paul: Minnesota Historical Society Press, 1987.

Wilson, Mary Tolford. "Peaceful Integration: The Owner's Adoption of His Slaves' Food." *Journal of Negro History* 49, no. 2 (1964): 116–27.

Wiltse, Charles M., and Harold D. Moser, eds. *The Papers of Daniel Webster.* Hanover, NH: University Press of New England, 1974.

Worth, James. "An Account of the Insect So Destructive to the Peach Tree." *AF,* December 31, 1824, 335.

———. "Observations on Insects, with a View to Arrest Their Destructive Ravages." *AF,* March 7, 1823, 394–95.

INDEX

Note: Page numbers in *italic* indicate photographs.

ILLUSTRATION CREDITS

Archives of the Moravian Church in America, Southern Province, Winston-Salem, NC: 9.14; Daniel Arnardet, photo: 3.11; Philip Beaurline, photo: 3.8; Joyce N. Boghosian: 5.10; Sonia Brenner, photo: 3.5; Rick Britton, mapmaker: pp. 52, 98–99; Cherokee Garden Library, Kenan Research Center at the Atlanta History Center: 1.6; Patricia Clark, photo: 2.14; Colonial Williamsburg Foundation: 3.5, 3.21, 4.4; Collection of Cranbrook Academy of Art/Museum: 5.12; Coolidge Collection of Thomas Jefferson Manuscripts, Massachusetts Historical Society: 1.8, 1.9, 2.2, 2.4, 2.5, 2.9, 2.19; Mrs. John Page Elliott: 3.12; Garden Club of Virginia: 4.6; Lara Call Gastinger: 5.16; Belinda Gordon, photo: 2.3, 2.21, 3.2, 3.13. 7.10–7.12, 7.15, 8.2, 8.13, 9.10; Betty Carter Fort Greig: 4.5; Peter J. Hatch, photo: 2.10, 3.3, 3.17, 3.18, 3.19, 4.4, 4.17, 4.19, 4.21, 4.23, 5.15, 7.4, 7.9, 7.13, 7.16, 7.18, 8.6, 8.7, 9.4, 9.8, 9.16, 9.17, 9.19, 9.22; Garry Henderson, photo: 5.12; Skip Johns, photo: 1.10, 3.16, 5.17, 7.7, 9.3; H. Andrew Johnson, photo: 2.8, 3.14; William Kelso, photo: 3.20; Library of Congress: 2.18, 3.23; Library of Virginia: 3.7; Robert Llewellyn, photo: pp. ii, vi, viii, x, xii, xiv, 1.1, 1.3, 1.4, 1.5, 2.1, 2.13, 2.22, 2.23, 3.1, 3.6, 3.9, 3.10, 3.24, 4.1, 4.7, 4.8, 4.10, 4.11, 4.13– 4.15, 4.18, 4.20, 5.1, 5.2, 5.7–5.9, 5.14, 5.18, pp. 120, 122, 123, 6.1, 6.3, 6.4, 6.6–6.8, 6.10, 6.12–6.20, 6.21, 6.23–6.27, 6.29–6.31, 7.1–7.3, 7.5, 7.6, 7.8, 7.14, 7.17, 8.1, 8.3–8.5, 8.9–8.12, 8.14, 8.15, 8.17, 8.18, 9.1, 9.2, 9.5, 9.6, 9.9, 9.11–9.13, 9.15, 9.17, 9.18, 9.20, 9.23–9.26, pp. 234, 236, 255, 256, 264; Richard MacDonald/New Media Systems, photo: 4.6; Halsey Minor: 3.3; Mount Vernon Ladies Association: 1.7, 3.17; Rare and Special Collections, National Agricultural Library: 6.5. 6.1, 6.22; The New York Public Library, Astor, Lenox and Tilden Foundations: 4.24; Laura Foster Nicholson: 5.12; National Portrait Gallery, Smithsonian Institution: 1.2; Mr. and Mrs. Peter O'Hara and Mr. and Mrs. R. Carter Wellford IV, 3.4; Edward Owen, photo: 2.17; Réunion des Musées Nationaux/Art Resource. NY: 3.11; Mollie Ridout, photo: 3.4; Anne Bell Robb: 5.11; Smithsonian American Art Museum Washington, DC/Art Resource, NY: 2.12; Special Collections, University of Virginia Library: 2.15, 2.16, 3.5, 4.16, 4.22, 6.9, 6.28, 8.8, 8.16, 9.21; Carolyn and David S. Thaler, Baltimore 2.14; Thomas Jefferson Foundation/Monticello: pp. ii, vi, viii, x, xii, xiv, 1.1–1.3, 1.10, 2.1, 2.3, 2.6–2.8, 2.10, 2.11, 2.13, 2.17, 2.20–2.23, 3.1, 3.2, 3.6, 3.8–3.11, 3.13, 3.14, 3.16, 3.18–3.20, 3.22, 3.24, 4.1, 4.2, 4.7, 4.8, 4.10–4.15, 4.17–4.21, 4.23, 5.1–5.9, 5.14, 5.15, 5.17, 5.18, pp. 120, 122, 123, 6.1, 6.3, 6.4, 6.6–6.8, 6.10. 6.12–6.20, 6.23–6.27, 6.29–6.31, 7.1–7.18, 8.1–8.7, 8.9–8.15, 8.17, 8.18, 9.1–9.13, 9.15–9.20, 9.22–9.26, pp. 234, 236, 255, 256, 264; University of Virginia Library: 2.7, 2.21, 4.2; Katherine Wetzel, photo: 3.22; The White House: 5.10; University of Erlangen-Nuremberg Library: 6.2; Wadsworth Atheneum Museum of Art/Art Resource, NY: 6.32